RENEWALS 458-4

DATE DUE

D0787634

THE
FOLKSTORIES
OF CHILDREN

WITHDRAWN
UTSA Libraries

Publications of

the American Folklore Society

New Series

General Editor, Marta Weigle

Volume 3

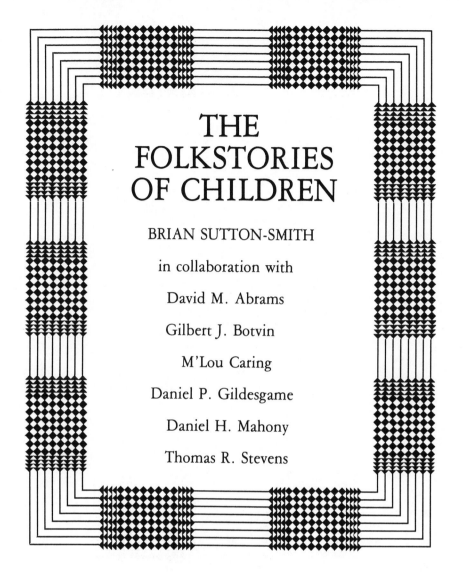

THE
FOLKSTORIES
OF CHILDREN

BRIAN SUTTON-SMITH

in collaboration with

David M. Abrams

Gilbert J. Botvin

M'Lou Caring

Daniel P. Gildesgame

Daniel H. Mahony

Thomas R. Stevens

University of Pennsylvania Press
Philadelphia, 1981

Copyright © 1981 by Brian Sutton-Smith
All rights reserved
Printed in the United States of America

Library of Congress Cataloging in Publication Data
Sutton-Smith, Brian.
  The folkstories of children.
  (Publications of the American Folklore Society: New Series; v. 3)
  Bibliography: p. 38
  1. Folk-lore and children. 2. Children as authors. 3. Fantasy in children. 4. Folk-lore and
children—New York (City) I. Title. II. Series: American Folklore Society. Publications of
the American Folklore Society: New series; v. 3.
GR475.S9   398'.09747'1   80-20246
ISBN 0-8122-7781-3
ISBN 0-8122-1108-1 (pbk.)

LIBRARY
The University of Texas
At San Antonio

To Allen Schwartz

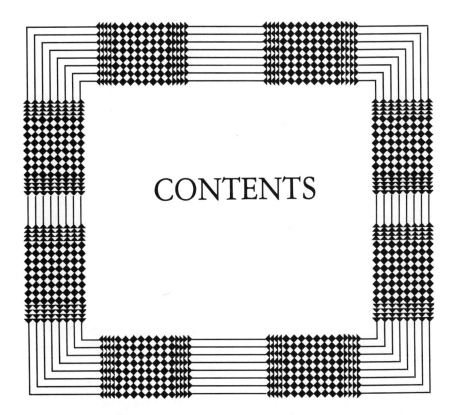

CONTENTS

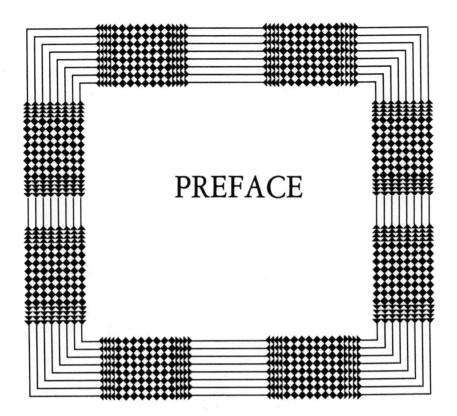

PREFACE

The present work was part of a larger project supported by the National Institute of Education (Project number 3–4015, Grant number NE–G–00–3–0133). The results of that project on "the enculturation of the imaginative processes between the ages of five and seven years and their effects upon classroom activity" are to be found in the Educational Resources Information Center, Early Childhood Education, University of Illinois (Bureau number BR–3–4015, published September 1976, 326 pages).

The present work is composed of stories collected from children between the ages of two and ten years. The location of the fieldwork for Part 1 of this work was the Soho Center for the Arts and Education on Prince Street in the Soho section of New York. We are indebted to Jeanna Gollobin for her support of this work. Her interest in the children's artwork and creativity made it possible for our collector Dan Mahony to gain more complete material than is usually possible from children of such a young age. He collected stories from two- to four-year-old children. Many thanks are due to him for his enthusiasm and his initiative in compiling this collection.

The location of the fieldwork for Part 2 was Public School 3 on Hudson and Grove on the Lower West Side of New York. Here again we are indebted to the special interests and skills of the principal, John Melser, an expert on the aesthetic education of children (see, for example, his introduction to *In the Early World* by Elywyn S. Richardson [New York: Random House, 1972]). We are indebted also to the classroom teachers, Leila Steinberg, Sheila Rothgart, Isabel Hanelin, and Dan Zulawsky, who were most encouraging and supportive of our work. We continued to work in their classrooms in the second year, and also followed up their original group of 119 children in the classrooms to which they moved in their second year. Most of the older nine- and ten-year-olds moved on to other schools, and so we have only one year's record of their stories. The new teachers who allowed us into their rooms and to whom we are also grateful were Barbara Bowers, Ellen Wook, Laura Schwartzburg, Diane Mullins, Mendy Samstein, Frelyn Edelstein, Pat Laltrella, Len Cohen, and Jori Schwartzman.

The storytakers in the first year were the author together with the chief research assistant, David M. Abrams, and Gil J. Botvin, M'Lou Caring, Daniel P. Gildesgame, and Thomas R. Stevens. In 1977 David Abrams presented a dissertation based on these stories entitled "Conflict Resolution in Children's Storytelling: An Application of Erikson's Theory and the Conflict-Enculturation Model" (Columbia University, 1977). Gil Botvin had presented a dissertation on the same material the year before: "The Development of Narrative Competence: A Syntagmatic Analysis of Children's Fantasy Narrative" (Columbia University, 1976). Another student, Leland Peterson, working with another sample of stories, tested some of the methodology in story collecting. His dissertation was entitled "Constraining the Storytelling Situation: Does It Make a Difference?" (Columbia University, 1976). The various articles that have arisen from these theses and are either published or in press are listed at the end of this preface.

In the second year many new storytakers became involved. Daniel Mahony developed a novel method of scoring children's stories (1977). Other collectors in the second year were Joy Dryer, Elaine Sturtevant, Catherine Cattell, Katholeen Kampfe, April Cibelli, Susan Speilberg, Mary Chaffee, Anthony Russo, Maria Weiner, Julia Rowland, Jamie Sunderland, Adjepong Afrifah, John Barell, and Rosalyn Kauftheil. Many other students went on to study and collect stories in other places and with other children at P.S. 3, and their enthusiasm was also important to us, but they will not be listed here. At the University of Pennsylvania our deliberations on the stories were greatly assisted by discussions with Professors D. Ben-Amos, C. Ferguson, S. Heath, B.

Kirshenblatt-Gimblett, W. Labov, and G. Prince. In addition, I received valuable help from my students Linda Hughes, Diane Kelly, and MaryAnn Magee, as well as John McGuigan and Terri Ezekiel of the University of Pennsylvania Press.

In all, we took one or more stories from 350 children. When we began our work we did not fully appreciate the importance of children's stories in their lives. On scholarly grounds we supposed that the caricatural creatures of their stories must have something to do with the children's sense of their personal fate. During the three-year course of our study, however, I experienced a professional crisis and came to realize that most human beings in stress, when forced to come to a conclusion with insufficient information at hand, will do so in caricatural ways. The caricature of children's stories, as of adult soap operas, is not unlike the behavior of otherwise sophisticated persons caught in situations of stress and ambiguity. For children as for adults, there is early wonderment as to how one can possibly deal with villainy and deprivation, and whether these can be overcome by one's own skill or with the help of benign strangers. In my own predicament, the students that I have listed here were benign friends, and I thank them once again for their help. I would thank also such good colleagues as Lois Bloom, Roger Myers, Gary Bridge, and Rosalie Schonbar for their help throughout this time, and give particular thanks to my legal counsel, Allen Schwartz, who, like the proverbial cowboy on the white horse, finally made it all make sense. Even so, before that—largely because of my wife, Shirley, and my children, Katherine, Mark, Leslie, Mary, and Emily—there was always more sense than there was absurdity, though, like the children in these stories, we often achieved it inversely, through joyous communal nonsense. We give a thank you at this point to our foster grandparents, Abe and Helen Borut.

Apart from all that, however, it has been most gratifying to work with these kinds of data. Not since my earlier studies of children's games (*The Folkgames of Children* [Austin: University of Texas Press, 1972]) have I found children so enjoyable. I have long had the belief that we understand children better and assess them more correctly when we study their spontaneous behavior than when we study them as captive beings in our laboratories, in classrooms, and in front of the television set. Even more important, their stories beggar and will long outlast our meager attempts at theoretical interpretation.

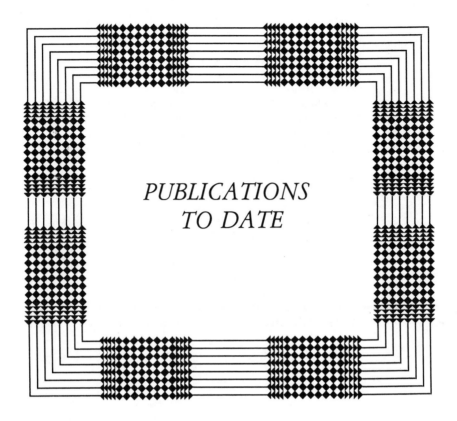

PUBLICATIONS
TO DATE

Abrams, D. M.
  1977   A developmental analysis of the trickster. In *Studies in the anthropology of play,* ed. P. Stevens, pp. 145–54. Cornwall, New York: Leisure Press.
Abrams, D. M., and Sutton-Smith, B.
  1977   The development of the trickster in children's narratives. *Journal of American Folklore* 90: 29–47.
Botvin, G. J.
  1977   A Proppian analysis of children's fantasy narratives. In *Studies in the anthropology of play,* pp. 122–32.
Botvin, G. J., and Sutton-Smith, B.
  1977   The development of structural complexity in children's fantasy narratives. *Developmental Psychology* 13: 377–88.
Caring, M. L.
  1977   Structural parallels between dreams and narratives. In *Studies in the anthropology of play,* pp. 155–74.
Mahony, D. H.
  1977   The society and geography of the story world. In *Studies in the anthropology of play,* pp. 133–44.

Sutton-Smith, B.

1977 Ein soziolinguistischer Ansatz zum Verstandis von Spielhandlungen. In *Handlungen theorie interdisziplinar*, ed. Hans Lenk, vol. 4: 239–50. Munich: Wilhelm Fink Verlag.

1978a Initial education as caricature. *Keystone Folklore* 22: 37–52.

1978b Listening to little stories. In "The Mind of the Child," a special issue of *Harpers Magazine* (April), ed. M. Witty, pp. 53–55.

1979a Epilogue. In *Play and learning*, ed. B. Sutton-Smith, pp. 295–322. New York: Gardner Press.

1979b Presentation and representation in children's narratives. *New directions in child development.* 6:53–65.

Sutton-Smith, B., and Abrams, D. M.

1978 Psychosexual material in the stories told by children: the fucker. *Archives of Sexual Behavior* 7: 521–43.

Sutton-Smith, B.; Abrams, D. M.; Botvin, G. J.; Caring, M. L.; Gildesgame, D.; and Stevens, T. R.

1975 The importance of the storytaker: an investigation of the imaginative life. *Urban Review* 8: 82–95.

Sutton-Smith, B.; Mahony, D. H.; and Botvin, G. J.

1976 Developmental structures in fantasy narratives. *Human Development* 19: 1–13.

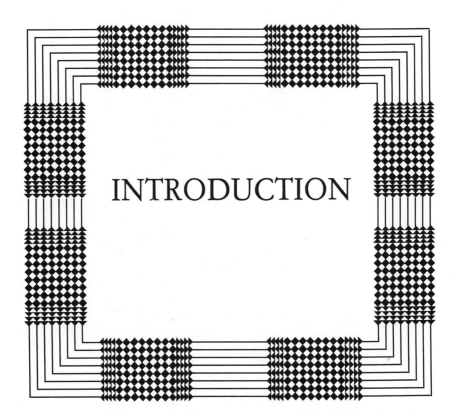

INTRODUCTION

The major purpose of this work is to make a collection of children's stories available to a larger public. Such a collection, systematically taken, has not been available since *Children Tell Stories,* by Pitcher and Prelinger (1963). The present collection extends the range from two-year-olds to ten-year-olds, whereas the earlier work ended with five-year-olds.

The title of this work, *The Folkstories of Children,* presents something of an anomaly. The stories that are dealt with in this book were made up by the children and so do not, on the surface, seem to be of a folk character—not if folklore is defined as "traditional items of knowledge that arise in recurring performances" (Abrahams 1976, p. 195). They might easily have been termed fantasy narratives and in some earlier articles we have done just that (Sutton-Smith, Botvin, and Mahony 1976). But part of the function of this book is to show that when given the opportunity, children are inveterate tale tellers, and the tales they tell have considerable similarity to traditional folktales. They are not the same as folktales, but they share major common elements with them. It follows from the fact that we have been able to make use of analytic

1

systems first applied to folktales and myths that there must be some important parallels between these different genres. The children's stories may be less well structured than fairy tales, folktales, legends, and myths, and they may be replete with modern content, but they nevertheless have the same basic plot structures and the same general concerns with fate, fate overwhelming, and fate nullified as do those other genres. Furthermore, the repetitive nature of the stories that most of the children tell indicates that if the children were given the audience they desire, and if children came to tell each other's stories, the stories might indeed become folktales. But at present they are not folktales; they are more like tales in some embryonic stage. For this reason we have chosen to call them folkstories.

In the following sections we deal, first, with our efforts at analyzing these stories, second, with our speculations on their origins, and third, with our methods of collection. We conclude with some speculation on the character of narrative as a kind of mental activity.

The collection that follows is divided into the verse stories of the two- to four-year-olds and the plot stories of the five- to ten-year-olds. Whereas the second set of stories represents the accommodation of the older children to the hero norms of western civilization, the first set represents the younger children's assimilation of those hero norms into their own characteristic forms of organization. As with many developmental phenomena, playful assimilation precedes realistic accommodation even within the domain of fantasy itself.

Analyses of the Stories

VERSE STORIES OF THE TWO- TO FOUR-YEAR-OLD GROUP

Children's stories usually have been analyzed in terms of their underlying symbolism of psychosexual development (Gardner 1971; Pitcher and Prelinger 1963), or in terms of their plot structure. Currently there are a number of kinds of plot analysis of children's stories available in the psychological and folkloristic literature (for example, Leondar 1977; Mandler and Johnson 1977; Maranda and Maranda 1970; Menig-Peterson and McCabe, 1977; Propp 1958; Stein 1978). Our approach has also been primarily concerned with types of plot analysis. The stories of the youngest group, the two- to four-year-olds, however, did not seem to lend themselves very readily to this kind of analysis. Gilbert Botvin modified the analysis that Vladimir Propp made of Russian folktales in order to make it suitable for use with our children's stories (1976). His analysis yielded ninety-one elements that he felt could describe these stories, and those elements are listed in table 1. He found that when the elements were in turn subcategorized into beginning (introduction, preparation, complication), middle (development), and ending (resolution and ending), then the very youngest children told stories that were mainly beginnings and endings, whereas the oldest children in the sample more proportionately distributed the ninety-one elements over the subcategories (see table 2).

Table 1. *Narrative Elements in Children's Folktales (after Botvin)*

Initial Situation

I: Preparation

Elements preceding disequilibrium
    Threatening situation
    Threat
    Interdiction
    Compliance
    Violation
    Warning of impending danger
    Deception
    Deception discovered
    Self-defeat

II: Complication

Disequilibrium: lack
    State of insufficiency
    Excess
    Misfortune
    Task
    Test

Disequilibrium: villainy
    Prepare for (physical) attack
    (Physical) attack
    Prepare for (nonphysical) attack
    (Nonphysical) attack
    Chase
    Stalk

III: Development

Counteraction
    Prepare for (physical) counterattack
    (Physical) counterattack
    Chase
    Stalk
    Struggle

3

Table 1. continued

Translocation
    Departure
    Natural translocation
    Magical translocation
    Return

Transformation
    Natural transformation
    Magical transformation

Chance
    Fortuitous discovery
    Fortuitous circumstance
    Unfortunate circumstance
    Receipt of unexpected gift

Reward and punishment
    Reward
    Punishment

Reconnaissance
    Observation
    Interrogation
    Acquisition of information
    Failure to acquire information
    Search
    Find object of search
    Failure to find object of search

Notification
    State of insufficiency made known
    Excess made known
    Misfortune made known
    Attack made known
    Counterattack made known
    Escape made known
    Rescue made known
    Villainy made known
    Notification of intended departure
    Notification of intended escape

Alliance
    Offer of assistance
    Refusal to provide assistance
    Refusal to accept assistance
    Breaking of an alliance

Defense
    Prepare to defend
    Defend

Table 1. continued

Markers
    Introductory marker
    Terminal marker
    Parallel action marker
    Flashback marker
    Convergence marker
    Character shift marker
    Perspective shift marker

Without a middle or development section there is very little sense of plot in the stories of the youngest children. Consider the following two stories, both from children under three. The first is from Bill and the second from Alice (see collection below):

The monkeys
they went up sky
they fall down
choo choo train in the sky
the train fall down in the sky
I fell down in the sky in the water
I got on my boat and my legs hurt
daddy fall down in the sky

The cat went on the cakies
the cat went on the car
the cookie was in my nose
the cookie went on the fireman's hat
the fireman's hat went on the bucket
the cookie went on the carousel
the cookie went on the puzzle
the cookie went on the doggie

Clearly, plot analysis might not be the most useful way to approach the stories of these youngest children, but such an approach is not useless. Certain features indicated by plot analysis are present in these examples and the other early stories. They are usually couched in the past tense; they are usually (but not always) about impersonal characters; and these characters usually experience a disequilibrating event. The last is regarded by some as an essential element in plot analysis (Leondar 1977; Todorov

6

Table 2. Percentage of story elements in each story segment for three- and twelve-year-olds

	Beginning	Middle	Ending
Three-year-olds	80%	3%	18%
Twelve-year-olds	34%	41%	25%

1975). In proper stories, however, equilibration is supposed to be re-established, whereas in these examples it is not.

If plot analysis makes a contribution, but is not sufficient to explain these stories, we must also look elsewhere. We notice that there is not only no development in the above stories, but also very little sense of time. The first story by Bill is four little stories, one about a monkey, another about a choo choo train, a third about himself, and a final one about daddy. More typically, our two-year-olds sequenced their events throughout the story, and it is this sequencing, in which each event is tied to the one before it, that we will here call "chronicity" (after Labov 1972). The following story by Cathy has such chronicity:

> Batman went away from his mommy
> mommy said "come back, come back"
> he was lost and his mommy can't find him
> he ran like that to home [she illustrates with arm movements]
> he eat muffins
> and he sat on his mommy's lap
> he fell to sleep
> and then him wake up
> and it was still nighttime
> and his mommy said "go back to bed"
> and him did
> and then he wake up again
> and then the mommy told him to go back to bed
> and he did all night
> and then it morning time
> and his mommy picked him up
> and then him have a rest
> he ran very hard away from his mommy like that
> I finished

Although there is little systematic published evidence, our ongoing inquiries are showing us that children can maintain such a line of chronicity in their personal narratives before they can tell fictional stories. So, our second major conclusion (the first being that some minimal plot-like features are borrowed), is that children may borrow chronicity from their narratives of personal experience. They have already demonstrated this competence there, so why not use it here?

There are other directions we can take in looking for the nature of the specific competencies that are being displayed in these stories. For example, the reader will note that the stories of Part 1 have a permutational quality. The storytellers seem to focus on a particular vector such as falling down, or crashing, and keep it going through many of the stories, each time varying it in different ways, until finally giving it up for some other motif after a year or so. We can find analogous kinds of behaviors in children's play, in their language, and in their drawings. We may then conclude that perhaps the children are relying on some kind of cognitive organization of their responses with which they are already familiar in other domains. However we, as adults, do not readily perceive it because of our attempts to find the logic of plot in what they are doing.

Theme and variation as a cognitive "grammar"
It can be argued that children have a particular kind of cognitive organization or internal "grammar" that is central to the way in which they put their stories together. This grammar parallels Piaget's description of infants' sensory-motor circular reactions, in which there is an endless repetition and variation of centrally focused behaviors (1963). Again in their second year, children at play will repeat actions with objects, often for long periods of time. A baby doll is first fed, then washed, then changed, then put to bed—and the series is repeated again and again. Sometimes it is the toy that provides the pivot for the series of actions; at other times it is an action (dropping or throwing) that is the pivot for a series of objects. But in either case there is some central focus or theme, some figure that is separated out from the background and then repeatedly recontextualized within a series of other contingent backgrounds. When an action is the centration it is typically exaggerated; and when an object is, it usually has the built-in hyperbolic features of toys or has some salient perceptual features that can act as signifiers. I have argued elsewhere that this perceptual segregation of figure exaggeratedly exercised against changing grounds is a primary feature of young children's voluntary action, as well as a way to get children's attention for educational purposes (Sutton-Smith 1978b). Other evidences of expressive behavior that might be regarded as exemplifying this kind of voluntary action are the ways in which at the two-word stage of language children often will use one word as the kingpin for others (baby go, mom-

8

my go, daddy go, etc.) (Bloom 1972), just as after the scribble stage in drawing children develop a central pattern that they repeat in slightly changing contexts (Arnheim's "primordial circles," 1954). In clay this pattern is the "snake" (Golomb 1974); in music it is the repetition of one note against slightly different contrasts (Werner 1948); and at later ages in central person games it is the use of one player as the central focus through whom all the action flows (Sutton-Smith 1972). One might argue that the apparent egocentricity of childhood and its apparent centrations are used in the expressive world as a preliminary kind of objectification, but instead of the centration being egocentrically in the subject, it is located in the object that is now a word, a toy, a scribble, a player, etc. The argument is that theme and variation may be a primordial principle of expression of subject-object relations. What we see in these activities is not simply repetition to some point of redundancy, but a systematic kind of relating of the major theme and the central figure to a sequence of changing backgrounds.

In order to transcend a solely perceptual approach or a learning approach to this analysis, and to hint at its historical reverberations, we have preferred to call this kind of action "theme and variation." Our aim is to give scope to the idea that the child is involved in the manipulation of forces or modes of action in a systematic and patterned way. From a structural point of view the forces are themes; from a motivational point of view they might be called vectors.

The stories of Part 1 illustrate the tendency for children in this sample to focus over 50 percent of the time on a particular vector to which they keep returning across their stories and into which they introduce variations. However these phenomena are interpreted, they clearly provide evidence of young children's capacity for thematic abstraction (Scollon and Scollon 1979). At two years of age, vectors and characters are about equally often used as constants across the stories. As the children get beyond the ages of three or four, the constant within the stories becomes the central character, not the central vector.

It is apparent from the few samples given above that many more things are happening in these stories than the repetition of a particular vector or particular character, although reference to those elements explains much of what is important in the story variance. Furthermore, the vectors suggest that a powerful struggle is going on, as children attempt to come to narrative terms with fateful, perhaps conflictful matters.

Still, if we are to see this variation around a constant as some elementary form of cognitive structure, it needs a more systematic description than we have yet given of it. To this end, analogies from music might be useful. Typically, themes are established early in the

9

piece and then are continually repeated, but varied in innumerable ways, constantly confirming and yet denying expectation in an emotionally arousing manner (Meyer 1956). The variations are not random but are made systematic by various kinds of relation to the central theme. The particular way in which the composer patterns the variations involving the constants can be considered his style.* Typically, the artist works within a remarkably narrow range, but with an infinity of nuances (Gombrich 1979).

Having suggested that the children in our sample characteristically persist in using certain themes over considerable periods of time (see the dated stories in the collection below), we can look more carefully at the examples given above to see how they organize these relationships of theme and variation, or order and disorder,or unity in diversity, as Gombrich (1979) might have it. In the first example, Adam at two years, eleven months gives a list of objects about equally divided between the animate and the inanimate. In so doing, he teaches us that listing or arranging temporally is an elementary way of establishing order, which also is characteristic of small children's early manipulative behavior (Applebee 1972). In his third story, which he told three days later, we see the possible introduction of a dynamic element when one item on his list is "a broke car," but this is the only whisper we have of what we are calling here a "vectorial interest."

The stories by Bill and Alice, above, appear to constitute a step up, because theme and variation are clearly manifested. There is an episodic chronicity in their stories. The major feature of Bill's style in his story is a concentration on the "up and down" vector, and the rotation of that vector through several characters who are important to him. Everything else seems constrained to that end. He keeps his location constant (in the sky). He uses various syntactic devices to heighten constancy, namely, the repetition of the article "the" and a noun, and the use of the pronoun "they" to refer to the monkeys. Six months later we can observe that some of his characters do not just fall down, but begin either to fall and get up again or not to fall at all. The first character thus liberated is Cookie Monster.

A Cookie Monster hurt his foot
and Cookie Monster stay up
and fall down again
he get up again
that's all

*I am indebted to my son, Mark Sutton-Smith, for this clarification.

Some time later the monkey is similarly liberated, and two months later, the boy does not fall down. Thereafter, it seems that we move to the more characteristic kinds of symbols usually associated with phallic concerns in the psychoanalytic literature. In a sense, the apparently random line ("I got on my boat and my legs hurt") in his first story, above, is a symbolic forecast of what will come nine months later when there is much more evidence in his stories of being bitten, bumped, burned, broken down, eaten, or killed, than of the earlier going up and falling down vector. Apparently, and speaking symbolically, when one has the courage not to fall down, one can then deal with the afflictions of Erikson's stage of initiative (or castration).

In his progress through his stories, Bill continues to use the article "the" or "a" and a noun as repeated elements, and, like most children, he increasingly makes use of the conjunctions "and" and "then" as constants. The biggest change in ensuring constancy after the first six months for Bill, however, is his use of chronicity throughout the stories, not just across a couple of lines. All the other two-year-old children, except Alice, also use chronicity throughout each story. We believe that articles and conjunctions are for Bill tactics that are subordinated, as is his scene of action, to permit an almost frontal focus, first, on his falling down vector and, later, on his killing vector. If we had to name his style, we would say he is a kind of centralist who bores in on his vector with a certain relentlessness. This style is hinted at in the first story, by the way he heightens the power of the vector through his excellent metaphor of the "choo choo train in the sky," thus elevating the most powerful thing he can think of, and then having it fall down.

Perhaps we can get a better grasp of Bill's style by contrasting it with Alice's, which is so radically different. As in Bill's stories, the vectorial action is the most constant theme. But Alice's objects of action change from line to line and her characters change every line or so, though there is some constancy. Alice uses the article "the" throughout like a conjunction. Knowledge of the context, and the way Alice relates to it, is important to an understanding of her style. While the objects of her sentences in the story appear to be randomly chosen, in fact they were all picked up from the toys in the room where she was telling this story. So, where Bill takes his radical vector (the fear of falling down) and permutes it through a variety of symbolic and real creatures, including himself, with considerable consistency over time, Alice has a more "scanning" kind of technique for dealing with her central theme (being bumped, stepped on, etc.), which because of the scattered nature of the objects she uses takes on a more distanced or peripheral quality. She leads us away from the central vector, not toward it. But note that her apparent randomness

11

is always achieved by exactly the same variational design of a radar-like sweeping of her environment for cues; her technique of variation is constant even if the content in which it results is not. We might sum up by saying that in stylistic terms, Bill is a kind of centralist and Alice a kind of peripheralist in their manipulation of vectors. Although Alice's story content seems less consistent from time to time than does Bill's, her technique of telling a story is consistent.

Six months later, Alice is still pursuing the same kind of peripheral style. Thus:

> The slide hits the swing
> and the bench bumped the ceiling
> the bag bumped the fence
> the watergun bumped the cigarette
> the swing bumped the water fountain
> and the slide bumped the puddle

She told this story in the park, where all the objects were about her and caught her wandering attention. The effect, it seems to us, is to draw attention away from her central vector in order to make it more light-hearted and less dangerous. In such a crazy world, what can "bumping" really matter? She has used a fictional propensity to make light of the matter. Where Bill, over time, shows in his stories some progress from a more passive to a more active attitude about his fate, as do most children, according to Abrams (1977), there does not seem to be any comparable vectorial progress in Alice's stories.

Only the early half dozen or so stories by Bill and Alice were characterized by their line-by-line disjunctive chronicity. Thereafter, the rest of their stories, like all of the stories by the other two-year-olds, were characterized by a line of chronological development throughout. This element makes the examples of two-year-old Clarence, Beatrice, and Cathy more coherent. They have the same characters throughout, and a line of action is pursued wherein each piece can be seen to have followed the piece before, rather than to be only a repetition of it with new characters and objects. This is not to say, however, that there is plot development and a logical coherence between one set of actions and the next—that development will come later.

Enough has been said at this point to illustrate, we believe, the relevance of the analysis of vectorial constants and to show that one can indeed consider the various story elements (semantic, linguistic, etc.) in terms of patterns of themes and variations. Moreover, it seems that this kind of analysis can yield some insight into the different kinds of styles employed by children in their storytelling. Clarence, in story 4, uses a centralist technique like Bill's. The stories by Beatrice and Cathy are much more complex and their styles involve an interplay of several themes at once. Both have a going away and coming home vector, but where in Beatrice's story it is related to a direct female oedipal kind of expression (having babies), in Cathy's story it is more typically masculine and phallic (Batman runs away). Both make a heavy use of conjunction-like expressions ("now," "and") as well as pronouns to give continuity across lines. Clearly, there is much more to the matter of styles of theme and variation than we have been able to suggest here.

We wish to turn to another implication from the musical notion of theme and variation. In music, these kinds of structures are mediated through sounds. We now raise the possibility that in stories also theme and variation may be mediated by prosodic elements, such as meter and rhyme; that is, on one level the stories might be held together by the way they sound, not just by what they mean or by their syntax.

The stories as verse
We have been seeking to establish that the very earliest of children's stories have a distinctive kind of cognitive structure that displays parallels with other modes of early expression by children. This structure also parallels major modes in the arts, in particular those of music and decoration. Much of what we have had to say is similar to Gombrich's analysis of the psychology of decorative art (1979). Further, we have illustrated, though certainly not yet established, that when these stories are thought of in terms of theme and variation, a useful step may be taken toward establishing the nature of differences in story style in early childhood.

Nevertheless, up to this point, all theme and variation considerations have had to do with the prose of the stories rather than their prosody. We were so locked into formal prose and into the formalities of plot analysis that only after four years of analysis of these stories did their most obvious characteristic as verse present itself to us. Our attempt to think of them as music finally liberated us to the extent that we could see them as poems.

The two samples by Bill and Alice are most pertinent. The collection reveals that verse in alliance with narrative loses importance after age three. The following characteristics identify these very early stories, however, as a kind of verse, though these are infant versifiers and their devices are not fully under control. First, all the stories tend toward a line-by-line size regularity. They are told as lines, not as continuing sentences. Second, they are generally told with a strong and regular beat in the manner of most nursery rhymes: for example, "Old King Cole was a Merry

Old Soul.'' The beat in ''Old King Cole'' is trochaic (long—short) and the four beats make it a trochaic tetrameter. There is much more variety here, but the strong beat and the regularity of its use are verse-like. In addition to these metric and rhythmic elements, however, there are repeated sounds (rhyme-like), as well as alliteration, assonance, and consonance. Many of the same words are repeated (''sky, went on''). Alliteration is most noticeable in Alice's verse (cat—cakies, cat—car, cookie—carousel). The consonance occurs in the beginnings of lines with the use of the same or similar articles (in Bill's verse) and the assonance at the end of lines (in Alice's verse) with hat—bucket, carousel—puzzle, etc.

Although elements of this kind are not so noticeable in other young storytellers who have a better chronological line, the regularity of line length and stress is still retained. Interestingly, even after Alice gains in her sixth story the same kind of chronicity within a story, she occasionally relapses. Thus, in her ninth story, she tells us:

There was a little bird named Bluejay
and he said ''caw caw''
a chair jumped over the truck
and a shoe stepped on a truck
and a mouse went on a train track
and that's the end

Here she has regressed to the earlier, more episodic story, and has reintroduced repeated sounds, alliteration, and consonance. Even Cathy (who began telling stories at age two years, nine months), after a year of telling fairly coherent stories, becomes sufficiently familiar with the storytaker (Dan Mahony) that she lapses into rhyme in a manner reminiscent of Ruth Weir's classic recordings of Anthony, her two-year-old son, in *Language in the Crib* (1962). Thus, in her twelfth story Cathy produces the following kind of seminarrative verse story:

Now there was a pa ka
boon, goo
there was a dog doo doo
and he didn't like dog doo doo
then there was a man named Snowball
and he didn't like snow
cha cha
doo choo
cha cha

doo choo
I named dog doo doo
Christopher say
dog doo doo
then there were a boy named Taw taw
o
too too
then there was a Captain Blooper he had a book and he were very
    bad and it hurt him
then there was a blooper pa pa
pa pa
there was Superman coming and he hurt both of him knees
then they were flying and they went right in the ocean and he got
    bite from a shark
and he didn't like when he got bite from a shark
then kla kla toe toe
tee tah
caw caw caw caw caw caw caw caw caw caw caw caw caw caw caw caw
    caw caw caw caw caw caw caw caw
now say pah pah kla klee
sa see
too tee
tah tah too tee
chee chaw
ta klu
kli klu
kla kla
klu fu
klee kla
koo koo
say say
klee klee
klip kla
klee klee
klip kla
she she
fik ahh
tungoo nah
ka pa
popeye the sailor man
bad guy him be very bad to him
and I spit out a words

Although, in general, after the age of three and one-half years, the stories
of the children could not well be characterized as verse, the vectorial
character of the stories and the regularity of line and other verse effects do
not entirely disappear. Our most gifted four-year-old, Ingbert, told the
following story, which is both a remarkable narrative and a kind of continuing poem on eating. The sequence follows the chronology of a picnic,
but almost every normal picnic expectation is defied or reversed. We get
an unexpected picnic, unexpected members, unexpected eating habits,
and unexpected consequences that are repeated and repeated. Nothing
goes right, but there is an elegiac quality to the whole piece.

> Once upon a time there was a family of tigers, bears, and lions
> and they went out for a wild animal picnic
> the wild animal picnic was made of baby rabbits
> that's what they ate
> they took the rabbits alive and they killed the rabbits at the picnic
> and when they ate the rabbits the blood washed out all the meat
>   where they were chewing so they missed all the parts where they
>   were chewing
> when they missed it they only got a tiny bit of their tooth left
> they kept chipping their teeth cause they forgot to take out the
>   bones
> they kept chipping their teeth so much they only had one tooth on
>   the top and one on the bottom
> then they swallowed the rabbit
> after they chipped their teeth and had dinner they went home and
>   had roasted beef rabbit
> then after they swallowed the rabbit and after they had dinner they
>   went to sleep and they all dreamt the same thing
> and that's all

Lest there be any doubt of this boy's tendency to conjoin story and verse,
as well as to parody both, at five years, one month, he tells the following:

> Once upon a time the once upon a time ate the once upon a time
>   which ate the once upon a time
> and then the once upon a time which ate the once upon a time ate
>   the princess once upon a time with the king
> and then the once upon a times died
> then the end ate the end
> the end
> the end

then the end died
then the end died
then the end died
then the end died
and then the end the end the end died
the end with a the end
the end
the end

Given that we are dealing here with one small sample from New York City, our discovery of a verse-like quality in young children's stories must be regarded as tentative at best. Still our work is apparently not exceptional. Shirley Heath, in her work with storytelling among working-class black children in a Southeastern community (in press), also found similar stories among the two- and three-year-olds. With her permission I cite the following stories:

Story 1
    Way
    Far
    Now
    It a church bell
    ringing
    dey singing

    you hear it?
    I hear it

Story 2
    UP
    Way up dere
    All time up
    Earnie
    Petey got it [potato chips]
    All up dere

Story 3
    Tessie Mae come
    Come 'round here
    Come -dum
    Da-dum, Da-dum
      Da-dum

17

Story 4
    Teegie got a bike
        a new bike
        a bike to ride
    See Teegie bike?

Story 5
    Track
    Can't go to the track
        dat track
        to dat train track
    Big train on the track
    Petey down by de track
    Moma git 'm
        track
        train track
    He come back

Again we see strong beat, rhyme, alliteration, assonance, and consonance. Heath, in a personal communication, explains the collection of these stories as follows:

The stories were collected over a period of seven years in a small Black rural-oriented community in the Piedmont Carolinas. Approximately twenty children were members of the community during this period, and stories were collected in interactions across all ages. All households contained one or more members, ages 21–45, who worked in jobs providing salaries equal to or above that of beginning public school teachers in the region; jobs were, however, seasonal in local contracting work or textile mills, and work was not always steady. The children between the ages of two and four spontaneously told stories about things in their lives, things they saw and heard. They were almost never read to from books, except by an occasional older sibling who tried to "play school" and take the younger child on his/her lap for reading (Heath 1980). They heard fanciful stories told by adults and older siblings; these stories were based on exaggeration of real-life events, ironic juxtaposition of happenings, individuals with reputations for "cutting the fool," and highly exaggerated accounts of what might befall a "bad" child. Males were considered the best story-tellers, and young adult males frequently engaged pre-school boys in cooperative stories. In these, the older adult would start a story, and the child would protest, deny, or build on to the story begun by the older male. These cooperative stories sometimes went on for days, picking up where they had left off when interrupted by a household activity or departure for work.

In sum, we have termed the stories of our youngest children "verse stories" because of the predominant role of prosodic effects and because of the theme and variation structure. Others might prefer to call this part of our collection simply "narratives" rather than "stories." Yet we are reminded by Prince (1973) that all the great Western epics and many non-Western ones are in verse. Lord's analysis (1973) of the way young folksingers come to learn the body of the folksong tradition through mastering various formulas for line length, meter, accent, boundary, or alliteration, and then learn to put these at the service of major themes, seems to provide the most fitting paradigm for the material presented here. Our young verse storytellers, like Lord's learning folksingers, appear to be adopting formulas from various sources—stories, narratives, and the prosodic character of language—in order to generate their own first themes and variations. As we shall see below, however, many of the prosodic elements quickly give way to a literate, not a poetic, orientation (Scollon and Scollon 1979).

PLOT STORIES OF THE FIVE- TO TEN-YEAR OLD GROUP

Although the stories of the older group do not, in general, have the verse-like characteristics of the younger group, the desire to versify was present constantly. Some children were unwilling to begin telling stories until they had first regaled us with parodies of commercials or obscene rhymes. So it appears to us that the undercurrent of rhyme and rhythm persists, though usually it is differentiated into other kinds of playful discourse. Still, the specialization is not complete, and some of the children in this older collection occasionally burst into verse in the midst of their stories, as, for example, six-year-old Deirdre (story 5), seven-year-old Elizabeth (story 4), six-year-old Carl (story 6), and seven-year-old Felix (story 5). The collection does not reflect the frequency of such behavior.

For the most part, however, our analyses of the older stories were in plot terms, using two major techniques. The first is the Maranda system, which analyzes the stories in terms of what happens to the characters. The second technique, developed by Botvin, focuses on the way the ninety-one elements listed in table 1 above are organized into sequences. In addition, we paid some attention to story content and story symbolism, and reference is made to those elements below.

19

The Maranda technique

The system borrowed from Maranda and Maranda (1970) postulates four levels of development through which children proceed in their development of story plots. In the first level (i), there are tales in which one power overwhelms another and there is no attempt at response; in level ii, there are tales in which the minor power attempts a response but fails; in level iii, there are tales in which the minor power nullifies the original threat; in level iv, there are tales in which not only is the threat nullified, but the original circumstances are substantially transformed. Tales of the last sort are like hero tales in which, having destroyed the monster, the Prince returns, marries the Princess, and takes over the Kingdom. These steps of the Marandas may be regarded as stages in the development of the hero tale. Examples of the stories at each level are as follows.

Level i. The most common response at this level is that the subject is threatened or overcome by a monster or there is a lack or deprivation to which no response is made. In a few cases, we are only told of the presence of the monster with some implied threat, or someone else is hurt, or we are scared, or the monster is described. One thinks of paralysis in the face of fear when seeking the biological counterparts to this response. Examples:

(a) This is a story about a jungle. Once upon a time there was a jungle. There were lots of animals, but they weren't very nice. A little girl came into the store. She was scared. Then a crocodile came in. The end. [Girl, age five]

(b) The boxing world. In the middle of the morning everybody gets up, puts on boxing gloves and fights. One of the guys gets socked in the face and he starts bleeding. A duck comes along and says, ''Give up.'' [Boy, age five]

Level ii. The predominant responses here are those of escaping or being rescued. The monster may be attacked, but the attack is not successful. This is what the Marandas term ''failed mediation.'' In this subject group, some children convert the monster into a benevolent creature. One may join with him in attacking others, or simply make him a non-dangerous entity. On occasion, the benevolent monster has to persuade the mother (now the negative force) that he may be taken into the home quite safely. Unlike most fairy tales and folktales, there is little reference amongst this group to the interference of magic or luck, an indication perhaps of the inner rather than the outer directedness of this particular population. In most cases, those who rescue us do not succeed in getting rid of the original threat either, so that these are level ii responses.

Henry Tick

Chapter 1: A few years ago Henry Tick lived in a hippy's hair, but he got a crew cut so Henry had to move. He went to the dog pound but it was closed. He went to the pet shop but it was closed too. Finally he found a nice basset hound. So he moved in. He got a good job at the circus jumping two inches in mid-air into a glass of water. One day he jumped but there was no water. He was rushed to the hospital. They put twelve stitches in his leg. Well, he never went there again. The end.

Chapter 2: One day Henry Tick was walking down the street when he almost was stepped on. He was so startled he jumped in the shoe! He was in the shoe for about fifteen minutes when the person took off the shoes and put them in the closet. Henry jumped out and ran into the next room, which happened to be the bathroom. He jumped into the toilet, by mistake of course. He was trying to get out when some nut flushed the toilet. Henry almost went down the drain.

Chapter 3: Henry got out of the toilet. The first thing he did was wash. He found a damp washcloth in the sink. He wiped himself thoroughly and then dried off. He went into the next room and watched the football game. The end. [Olive, age ten]

It should be noted that in the Henry Tick story, Henry escapes his various dangers, but in no way nullifies them. They still exist and may well return.

Level iii At this level, the story's central character is successful in rendering the threat powerless in some way or in supplying what is lacking. The enemy may withdraw. The nullification of the threat may be accomplished by the good services of others, as in the following story of a pussy cat who gets separated from his loved ones but is finally, after many travails, once again absorbed into a loving family.

A Story about a Pussycat

There was this old cat. It was wandering around the streets and had nowhere to live. It was pregnant and it has nowhere to stay to have its babies and then it ran into another cat. The other cat said,

"There's a burnt-out house where you can go and have your babies." And she said, "Where?" "Down the road and turn left." Two months passed and she had her babies. She died, it was wintertime. All the other babies got took by someone else except one little baby. This baby was frozen. She hardly could move. She got into the warmest spot. Someone dropped something out the window and she took it and it made her warm. She got very sick. Someone took her in and made her better. She was a playful kitten. She knocked over so much stuff and they were too poor and no one to give it to so they let it go in the street. It was springtime. She was able to eat again. And she was wandering around looking for a home to stay in. Once in a while she would see another cat and play with it. And sometimes people would hold the little kitten. The kids would ask their mothers if they could keep it but their mothers would say no—it's too hard to keep a little kitten. One day this little girl came over. She had one older sister and one baby sister. She was ten years old. She asked her mother if she could keep it. Her mother said no. The girl's name was Lisa. Lisa was gonna be eleven in two days. Her mother did not know what to get her for her birthday. She put it in the box and cleaned it and gave it food, went to the pet store and got a cat box and wrapped it. It was Lisa's birthday. Lisa thought it was an empty cat box and was starting to cry but when she opened it she was glad and the little girl took care of it and fed it milk and food and the little kitten lived with Lisa happily ever after. [Girl, age nine]

Level iv. At this level not only is the danger removed, but there is a complete transformation, so that there is clearly no possibility of this threat or this lack returning again.

In the following example, the writer has a story in three chapters. The first chapter has a level ii ending, the second chapter has a level iii ending, and the final chapter has a level iv ending.

Mr. Hoot and the Married Lady [level ii]

One night Mr. Hoot was sitting in his house thinking why he never had any fun. He said to himself, "Maybe I'm too shy." So he said to himself again that he was going to go out and get into mischief. He got on his coat and put on his contact lenses and he was off. There he was strolling from bar to bar. At his fifth bar, he decided to have a drink. He pounded on the table and said, "Two martinis on the rocks." While he was waiting for his two drinks he took off his shoes and socks and picked his feet. Then he got his drinks and chug-a-lugged them down the hatch. After his drinks, he saw a beautiful lady in the corner of the bar. So he went over to her and said, "Can I buy a drink?" She replied "No thank you. I'm not finished with this one." Then she said, "Anyway please sit down and we will talk."

A big guy walking out the men's room came over to Mr. Hoot and said, "Are you fooling with my wife? How dare you," and picked Mr. Hoot up and threw him on the ground. The moral of the story is—you can't tell a married lady from a single lady.

Mr. Hoot and the Stewardess [*level iii*]

Once Mr. Hoot was sitting in the bar with his friend Bobby the Baboon. They were discussing going to Hollywood. Mr. Hoot said to Bobby, "Let's go next week." So they made all the arrangements and before they knew it they were on the airplane going to Hollywood. While they were on the airplane, Mr. Hoot saw this very attractive stewardess. So Mr. Hoot called her over and said, "Hi, what's your name?" she said, "Laura Since, what's yours?" "Harold Hoot," he said. Then he said, "How long have you been working for the airlines?" She replied, "Two years and seven months." Then they started talking about where they lived and other things like that. Then a little baboon said, "Hey would you stop it with the lady and let her do what she's supposed to be doing." Then Harold got mad and said, "Shut up, you little baboon." Then Bobby said, "Hey, are you sounding off on my kind? How dare you." "Oh, Bobby, butt out of this," Harold replied. Then the little baboon said, "Shut up, you overgrown owl." Then they really started going at it. They were throwing pillows and suitcases at each other and cursing at each other. Then Harold gave him a good sock in the face and that was the end of the adventure.

Mr. Hoot Gets Married [*level iv*]

Once Harold was sitting in a restaurant at a table all by himself. Then he noticed there was a female owl sitting down by herself. Mischievously he walked over and asked her what her name was. She said, "Mary Gline." Then Harold thought for a moment and said, "Are you the girl that broke her wing when you were nine years old?" Then she said, "What's your name and how did you know about my wing?" "Well," said Harold, "I knew about your wing because your name sounded very familiar, so I thought back to my childhood and remembered a girl named Mary broke her wing, and my name is Harold Hoot." Then she said, "you were the kid they called Hoot the toot." "Oh yeah," Harold replied. "I forgot about

that." Then they started to talk about their childhood and ate dinner together.

After that night they went out to dinner, to movies and did lots
of other things like that. After about a year, they told their parents
they were going to get married. Their parents agreed and they had a
wedding. They had the most beautiful wedding you can imagine.
For their honeymoon they went to Niagara Falls. Then after that
they settled down in a nice house in Poughkeepsie and had boys
named Bobby and Peter. Last and not least, they lived happily ever
after. [Boy, age ten]

When the stories were classified in these terms there was a significant age
trend. Older children in this sample tend to tell the higher-level stories.
We have now made the same analysis several times and such a chronological age shift is always forthcoming. There is no sex difference across
the four levels, though there is a difference in style of solution. That is,
the boys more often reach level iii or iv by having their hero overcome the
villain; the girls more often reach that level through an alliance. From the
cross-cultural evidence presented by the Marandas, it is clear that there
are many societies where no such belief in one's ability to overcome fate
exists, and in those cultures the stories often do not rise above the first or
second levels. Again we find that some of our younger children, even
five-year-olds, occasionally tell fourth level stories.

The Botvin technique
As we relied upon the Marandas (and they on Lévi-Strauss) for one
system, we used another famous source for another system: the Russian
folktale analyst Vladimir Propp. In his *Morphology of the Folk Tale*
(1958), he set out the fundamental elements of action that constitute a
story's basic components. He suggested that the number of these components is limited and that they always appear in the same order.

There are two levels of action that occur in stories, according to
Propp: primary and secondary. At the primary level there are two basic
types: villainy versus villainy nullified, and lack versus lack liquidated.
They might be thought of as basic systems of disequilibrium and
equilibrium restored. Other primary elements include material that is
preparatory, intermediate, or consequential to the establishment of these
major boundaries.

The secondary functions are the somewhat more concrete ways in
which these primary functions are mediated. Thus villainy can be mediated by threat, attack, chase, violence, torture, etc. It can be nullified by

defense, escape, release, and defeat. When we scored the number of these elements occurring at each age level we found an average length of about three such elements for the five- and six- year-olds, four elements for the seven- or eight-year-olds, and about six for the nine- and ten-year-olds. There were no sex differences in these units of length. What tended to occur at ages five and six was that the dyadic units of attack and defense, or chase and escape, tended simply to get repeated, implying perhaps a primitive reversibility. It may be that chase and escape, and attack and defense, are culturally occurring reciprocal systems that the child first models and that become for him prototypes of true reversibility. We know that they occur in games at about the same time they enter into narrative, and the evidence from games is that they are first simply mimicked without any cognitive control of the reversibility involved. The finding that tales at first lengthen by repetition is similar to Garvey's finding with the turn-taking rounds of early childhood (1977). The next step is a stringing together of these secondary dyads; thus, trap-escape, attack-escape, or scared-successful, must go together, or loses-finds, flooded-swims, loses-finds, to quote some actual examples.

In his study, done with a sample of sixty stories from five- to ten-year-olds, Botvin developed a seven-step structural system based on a combination of Propp's primary and secondary characteristics (Botvin and Sutton-Smith 1977). In brief, the steps plotted out and tested are:

1. a fragmentary step
2. the appearance of the primary dyads of villainy and lack, just one in each story, with several other secondary elements
3. the increasingly systematic arrangement of the secondary elements in an intermediate position between the dyads
4. increasing the number of primary dyads
5. expanding each of these dyads with appropriate secondary elements
6. the development of embedded primary subplots within the major dyad
7. multiple subplots.

An analysis of variance (for fixed effects) yielded a significant age shift across these categories. However, this effect for ages five to ten was produced mainly by a shift up from step three at ages five and six to step four at ages seven and eight to step five at ages nine and ten. Which means that at five and six years we have in this sample a basic dyad with intermediate secondary functions. By seven and eight years we have an expansion of these multiple dyads by intervening elements.

INTRODUCTION

Figure 1

Botvin's Seven Steps of Narrative Complexity

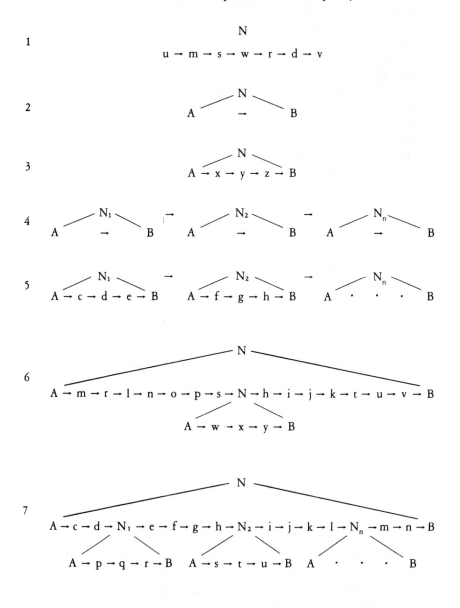

What is interesting in this system is that there seem to be only two qualitatively novel steps. When the dyad first appears at step two as a way of organizing the story, this is a major move forward. All subsequent steps until six, which has subplots, seem more to be extensions and enlargements using these basic principles. One might argue that the structural system has two components, an addition of new principles and an increase in the carrying capacity of those principles.

This is an important point because Applebee (1972) in his analysis of the complexity of the Pitcher and Prelinger tales (1963), found that simple measures of complexity (such as number of words, characters, incidents, etc.) did not covary with his structural measure of complexity, which was based on Vygotsky's analysis of the development of concepts from heaps, through complexes, to chains. With age held constant, each form of complexity analysis moved along a separate path.

This brief presentation cannot do justice to Botvin's analytic system. It does not even mention the semantic grammar he developed for further analysis of the sequential predictability of the plot elements described (1976).

In concluding this section on plot analysis, we reiterate our statement that these are just a few of the many ways in which the narrative structure or text can be approached. All we wish to illustrate here is the complexity of the child's acquisition of this competence. Telling stories is a remarkable mental feat.

Story content and story symbols
The present group of stories allows for many kinds of content analysis. Some of the more obvious elements that have been noted by Abrams (1977) are that the younger children, from the ages of three to eight years, significantly more often told tales about wild and domestic animals and monsters. Older children (eight to fourteen in his study) more often told tales that were human dramas, about romance or science fiction. Still, all kinds of stories were to be found at all age levels. Other kinds of content that did not differentiate between these age groups were fantasy, numbskull, detective, sea adventure, creation myth, romance, ghost, nonsense, true hero, trickster, eternal return, separation, explanatory, disaster, cowboy, and magic.

Not surprisingly, the sexes differed on some of these contents: the boys told significantly more tales of villainy, and the girls more of deprivation; the boys told more of contest, and the girls more about domestic animals. But they did not differ significantly on any of the other categories listed above.

The symbolic analysis of children's stories usually has proceeded along Freudian grounds (Pitcher and Prelinger 1963; Gardner 1971). The present stories show many elements that would be interpretable in these terms. We have, for example, picked out those stories in which the psychosexual elements were obvious and have examined them to see if there is any systematic change with age (Sutton-Smith and Abrams 1978). What we found among those children who were prepared openly to tell such stories was that in this sample the stories simply became more explicit, with more reference to sex organs and sexual processes, as the children grew older. The stories increased in complexity with age, but they did not increase in indirectness of expression. Our findings here match the approach of Legman (1968) rather than that of Wolfenstein (1954), whose thesis was that "obscenities" would become more indirectly expressed with age because, following Freud, she supposed that as humor rises in society it must assume a veil of increasing politeness. While that thesis may have been true in Vienna at the turn of the century, and is still true in many sections of upper-status modern society, there are many parts of society where expression has become increasingly direct, not indirect, with age. Still, we hasten to add that this kind of story was obtained only from boys, and from boys who were rated as unusually aggressive and rebellious by their principal.

Another kind of symbolic analysis carried out by Abrams (1977) was based on the work of Erikson (1951). Erikson theorizes that across the age groups with which we have dealt here, children are preoccupied with a series of major life crises. From about three years onward, they are concerned with being able to express initiative or with being overwhelmed by feelings of guilt at so doing. When they reach school age, a new conflict between feeling industrious and feeling inferior arises. By the time they move into junior high school, the predominant issue is that of establishing a personal identity versus feeling only a general role diffusion. Abrams found that when the stories were analyzed in these terms, they showed a chronological shift in these concerns corresponding to the Eriksonian predictions.

More importantly, Abrams was able to show that within each of Erikson's stages, children show increasing competence and activity in their storytelling. The earliest-told stories within each age level were generally resolved with passive Maranda i and ii endings; the older children within that same crisis era told Maranda tales more often with the active iii and iv endings. This is a particularly exciting finding because it shows the way in which the original conflicts faced by the child (at least as described by Erikson) are responded to in terms of a developmental system of plot resolutions that the child adopts from the larger culture. That is, the culture not only puts him into these conflicts in a developmental order (the Eriksonian thesis), but also provides him with the means of managing those conflicts by providing him with models of their solution. This finding parallels what we have earlier established as the case in games (Roberts and Sutton-Smith 1962). In another study, we have shown that when the stories were analyzed in terms of Freudian primary and secondary process elements, the boys showed the expected shifts in the direction of secondary process, but the girls did not (West, Martindale and Sutton-Smith 1980). This finding was somewhat like that of Caring, who showed that although there were no Maranda-level sex differences in the stories of boys and girls in this sample, when their dreams were compared and scored in Maranda terms, the boys showed development and the girls did not (1977). All we can comment at this time is that these differences are puzzling and perhaps might parallel some of the differences that have been noted in the games of girls and boys, in which boys generally have access to higher levels of game organization (Sutton-Smith 1979a).

While there is much more of a general symbolic nature that could be discussed (see for example, Bettelheim 1975), we have taken the position that such symbolic analyses are more appropriate as a part of a thorough case study of the individuals who are telling the stories, as in the work of Gardner (1971). We were here concerned with normative or typical, rather than idiographic, considerations.

Origins of the Stories

Up to this point, we have briefly outlined various kinds of analyses that we have used with children's fictional stories. In addition, however, we have speculated on the origins of these stories, supposing that children living in certain kinds of environments become story generators. Their first stories seemed to us to be the product of the unique kind of theme and variational grammar through which they organize all of their expressive behaviors. In their attempt to tell stories, they have taken also into their grammar many of the sounding aspects of the language they hear about them, as well as some features of plot stories and the chronicity of their other personal narratives.

But there are, in addition, many other potential causative factors that we have not in any way assessed. It is not likely that we can at this point in narrative research comprehend what all of these factors might be, but still, there is something to be said about them. First, our emphasis on the importance of disequilibrium in children's stories parallels what is known about their dreams and nightmares, which at an early age are also disequilibrial.

Nightmares are said to be the prototype of human terror and helplessness. It is, therefore, reasonable to think that, arising out of human conflict, they add their own motive to the desire of children to narrate a dramatic event to their parents. Although these nightmares and dreams as they are told tend to have a disjointed or dramatic character, they do exist in their own right as an independent instigation to the storytelling habit. Naturally a child could not use this vehicle unless language was available, and the child might be less inclined to use language if the regular telling of fantasy was not possible. But it is reasonable to believe that the telling of nightmares or dreams could emerge regardless of the learning of the storytelling frame, and by itself provide a prototype for storytelling.

At this point again, however, the reaction of the listeners is all-important. A culture may make a great deal of the dreams of its people (Noone and Holman 1972), or, as has been more typical in western civilization, it may react with embarrassment. These eruptions of internal life are a leakage that usually has not been warmly accepted, even if from kindly parents there has been support and consolation for the dreamer. This means that the reporting or nonreporting of nightmares does not necessarily lead to the telling of stories. But, in practice, there seems to be a tendency for parents who will listen to such nightmares, and who will tolerate the accounts of dreams that children increasingly bring to breakfast between the ages of four and seven years, also to be supportive of the stories that their children tell. That is, we suspect that the parent's willingness as a listener, when the child has urgent matters to report from his own inner world, may be a critical element in the development of the child as a ready storyteller. At this time we cannot differentiate between the contribution made by the parents or older siblings as model tale- or story-tellers, and the contribution made by them as willing listeners, but we suspect that either or both may be important constituents in the development of the readiness for "storytelling events" either at home or in the school. The further question of why the dreams that are told when the child is roused in the night are mainly the fragments of daily processes, while the dreams that are recollected or told in the day have more of the drama and unity of stories, is a puzzle that is probably of some importance in understanding storytaking, but not one to which there is an easy answer. If some dreams are a first formulation of an integrative response to conflict, however, they would provide a model of synthesis that a storyteller also could use. In this case, then, the occasionally dramatic dream may be a model for storytelling. At this point we do not know whether they are separate internal and external sources for the storytelling event, or whether the dreams as told have already suffered some transformation from the usually fragmented daily-process dreams as experienced. Perhaps the dream as told is already a synthesis of night elements and daytime learned frames. Whatever the case, we clearly must take into account this parallel between the disequilibrial and conflict-laden nature of early dreams and the similarly disequilibrial character of early stories.

In our analyses, the children's dreams that we collected (but that are not reported here) could be analyzed in the same way as the children's stories, by Maranda and Botvin techniques, the difference being that they were more disjointed and often fragmentary (Caring 1977; L. T. Mack 1974; R. D. Mack 1974).

In summary, we have described a child's built-in theme and variational cognitive mechanism, as well as dreams, to provide both formulae and content for the generation of their own stories. But even if dreams are not made use of in this way, the most direct and internal source that children have available for a model is their own play. Although play is very different from stories (Scarlett and Wolf 1979), Garvey's data show that the contents of both are similar. Her three- to five-year-old children go through sequences in active play that are very similar to the Maranda-like sequences observed in stories between the ages of five and ten (Garvey 1977). In sociodramatic kinds of play it is not always easy to tell what is play and what is story. A child's ability to make up stories while playing is the basis for most play diagnosis and therapy, as well as a bridge between child and adult (Saltz et al. 1977). It would not be surprising if when first asked to tell their own stories, children borrowed from dramas that they have acted out in sociodramatic play.

Still, even if children provide their own cognitive grammar of theme and variation and borrow contents from their dreams and play, it is improbable that they would tell stories without the example of those around them. In the first place, it seems that they hear language as a kind of sounding phenomenon. Thus, we know that they can imitate its intonations before they can grasp its meaning (Menyuk 1971). Furthermore, they tend to be spoken to in a way that emphasizes the musical aspects of the language. The registers for children make much of prosody (Ferguson 1978), rhythm, and stress. When adults are playing with children or telling them stories, the prosodic and paralinguistic characteristics are heightened even further. Perhaps it is not surprising, therefore, that when children tell their first stories, they incorporate prosodic features. In a reanalysis of Ruth Weir's *Language and the Crib*, Abrams found an earlier mastery of prosodic than of prose elements (Abrams and Sutton-

Smith 1977b). Work with older children at play also indicates earlier mastery of prosody. McDowell has shown that children master the intonation and stress of riddles before they comprehend their logic (1979). There are other examples in Kirshenblatt-Gimblett (1976).

In one of our current studies we have discovered evidence that some parents coach children in how to tell stories. They provide them with the kind of scaffold of questions and omissions ("What comes next" "What happened then?") that Bruner and his associates have found in the child's learning to recount experiences or to label pictures (Bruner 1978; Ninio and Bruner 1978; Ratner and Bruner 1979). But there are ethnic differences in whether coaching occurs or how it occurs. Heath describes the quite different "leading" and responsiveness of her two groups of Southeastern black and white parents to older children. The white group of parents did not encourage storytelling, something they regarded much the same as lying. The black parents and older siblings were much more encouraging—with teasing, etc.—and supported their children in exaggerating and dramatizing their tales.

In addition to direct coaching by adults, another kind of environmental support undoubtedly is hearing stories and folktales from parents (Pellowski 1977; Lüthi 1976). In the one study of this kind of transmission Goldstein found that about a third of the parents questioned said they made up stories for their children, and about two-thirds said they read from standard collections, but only a handful told traditional tales (1975). Most of the stories told were fantasies, and they were told at bedtime or meal time, in the living room or the car. It was usually the mother who told the story to one child at a time and in a tone and style appropriate for tale telling to the young (or "motherese").

Other children do not often seem to be a source of fictional storytelling, except in adolescent summer camps (Knapp and Knapp 1976), at least among the kind of middle-class children with whom we are dealing, although in other cultures and subcultures (Heath 1980) they can be such a source (McDowell 1975). However, other children are a source of games, humor, and rhymes. Other sources may be the mass media, particularly television. In our analysis we found that the boys' stories showed a much higher proportion of television elements than did the girls' stories. If television is an influence on fictional narrative, it seems to affect the boys more (Botvin 1976).

In summary, we see the particular register that parents use for talking to children, especially for playing with them or telling stories to them, as affecting the character of their early stories. While there are some data about the stories parents tell to children, as well as about their attitude to storytelling as such, we know much less about how they specifically encourage children to tell stories and whether they assist them as much as they assist them in recounting their everyday experiences when young. When children go to elementary school, of course, they do begin to get assistance in writing stories and sometimes in making them up orally.

Setting the Stage

We have discussed the meaning of the stories in abstraction from the actual telling of them. That is, we have discussed our analyses and our speculation on the meaning of the stories as texts, as if these could be abstracted from the contexts in which they occurred, as if they were monologues instead of dialogues (Levitt 1978). We move now to remedy this imbalance. We seek to describe just how these stories were communicated to us and to examine how this process of transmission may have affected the texts that we have been examining. Here we are concerned to understand how the character of the story is generated by the nature of the performance in which it occurs.

The stories were collected from children in two places. The first was a preschool for children aged two through five in Greenwich Village, New York. The second was a public school in the same area for children of ages five to eleven. The stories were collected in the public school from the fall of 1973 to the spring of 1975. The stories in the preschool were collected from the fall of 1974 through the fall of 1975. As it was not possible for all of the children's stories to be printed in this collection, two principles of selection were used. First, those children were chosen who had volunteered stories throughout the two-year period of the inquiry. Second, those children were included who had told the most stories. The present sample documents approximately two-fifths of the children in the intensively sampled classrooms of each school; 16 out of 22 in the preschool, and 36 out of 119 in the public school. The children in the preschool were in two age groups (1–2 and 3–4 years), and the children in the public school were in four classes, each with overlapping age groups (5–6, 6–8, 7–10, 8–10 years). The samples recorded here include half of the stories collected in these two locations: that is, approximately five hundred out of a thousand stories.

The preschool students tended to be children of young and ambitious parents who paid to have their children attend the school. The public school was an alternative school first established by the agitation of the parents against the original school, which they regarded as too formal for their interests. This meant that these parents had chosen to send their children to this public school. The school itself, within the limits of the provisions and staffing of the New York educational system, attempted to make greater than usual use of parent volunteers and of the arts in the curriculum. The intelligence scores of the children were predominantly superior (115–130).

The storytakers, who were graduate students in psychology, male and female, were introduced as "people who like to collect stories from children, and someone to whom you may tell a story at any time you wish." Some weeks were spent in each classroom playing with or helping the children in their work before an explicit general request was made for stories. Although most children came voluntarily to tell their stories when the storytaker arrived, before the first year elapsed each child in the class was asked at least once for a story. Stories were taken with the storytaker sitting on the floor or at a desk and always being approving. As the story collection was accumulated by this largely voluntary method, and as the present selection was of those who told stories the most frequently, it follows that the sampling within this school group is from among the most verbal children. In short, the pupils of both schools are the offspring of highly intelligent parents (working in the arts, advertising, and the professions), and the present selection of stories tends to be from the most verbal children. In the public school, however, the four classrooms used were typical of the school as a whole. No claims are made for the representativeness of the sample. In fact, we know from some of our own work elsewhere that the stories told in other middle-socioeconomic-range schools are typically two years below the present sample in structural level (Petersen 1976). Part of the value of the present "bright" sample is what it might tell us about the more sophisticated children of today, and perhaps foretell about the leaders of tomorrow. The following collection includes six children at each of the preschool age levels (three boys, three girls), except year four, and six children at each of the public school age levels (three boys, three girls). At four the sample was lopsided because of a lack of girls at this age level.

For the most part, the stories were written down by the collector. When they were written by the children, that fact is indicated at the beginning of the story. Although it is preferable to use video tapes or audio tape recorders for precision of collection and linguistic reanalysis, that was not generally possible in the conditions under which we worked. Open classrooms in alternative schools tend to be very noisy places. Most of our collecting activity took place in the midst of busy parallel classroom activities, with much bustle and banging of blocks. We sought not to attract special attention to ourselves, but to be available for those who had a story to tell. Special apparatuses tend to attract attention, not dispel it. Moreover, as we will show, children are particularly sensitive, and the stories they tell can be shown to be related to the method by which they are collected. The present method has, if anything, slowed these children down. The reader is asked to imagine that there are conditions under which these children would be even more verbally skilled than the productions presented in this work lead one to believe. The collection speaks well for the brightness and imaginativeness of some modern children.

Still, having made a choice to emphasize the voluntarism of the children rather than the efficiency of recording, we have necessarily sacrificed much situational material that might otherwise have been available to us, as well as much of the expressive data of storytelling. We hasten to add, however, that while this stricture applies to this collection, it does not apply to all of our other work, where some of these more subtle matters have been investigated and will be subsequently reported. What we have clearly shown in this work is that those who define themselves as "storytakers" and take on an approving role—only asking for clarifications of what they have not heard properly, and only asking, "But did you ever make up a story yourself?" after receiving something other than a fictional narrative—receive a great abundance of wonderful fantasies. Why these are not generally told to schoolteachers and others raises an interesting empirical question for future inquiry.

What then do we know about how the conditions of our own storytaking activity affected the stories that we collected? First, even though our conditions were voluntary, 10 percent of the children never did tell us a story of their own accord. There were no age differences in failing to report a story; several children at each age level did not. Over the two years of our collecting activity, half of the children told no more than five stories, another quarter told as many as ten, and the rest told from ten to twenty stories.

While there are probably a number of reasons why certain children preferred not to tell stories, teachers rating these children on a 1 to 5 scale of adjustment rated those who told few stories or none significantly less well adjusted (Sutton-Smith et al. 1975). However, although the teachers did not particularly follow who was or was not telling us stories, it is possible that they noticed some of those who were not and that their ratings were biased by that knowledge. From the literature on play therapy, we may perhaps extrapolate that children who are less well adjusted find play of any sort, including narrative "play," more difficult. However, we are driven to the caution that, as Wolf and Gardner (1979) have shown, some children are less interested in this kind of expressive medium, being more interested in spatial-constructive kinds. It is also quite possible that some introverted children do not like this kind of social experience.

About two-fifths of the children told their first stories in the first month of storytaking, another two-fifths in the second month, and the remainder in the third month. Boys of ages five through seven years told significantly more stories ($p < .01$) than boys of eight through ten years, but there were no significant differences by age for the girls. Boys told longer stories to male storytakers, and girls told longer stories to female storytakers (Botvin 1977). Both sexes told more imaginative stories to male storytakers and more realistic tales to female storytakers (Petersen 1976). The differences between "real" and "imaginative" were defined after the manner of Pitcher and Prelinger (1963).

When we first asked children to tell us a story that they had made up it became clear that this was not an entirely intelligible request. Only 66 percent actually gave us what we asked for. The rest gave us a mixture of personal narratives (17 percent) and poetry, riddles, jokes, rhymes, etc. (17 percent). It is perhaps surprising that in a school in as sophisticated an area as this one was, only two-thirds of the children knew what we wanted, at least at the first request. Thereafter, we had few exceptional responses.

Beyond this kind of information we have very little way of knowing how our conditions of collecting affected the stories that we include in this volume. That some children were able to take us into their confidence and proceed without fear or care is indicated by the obscenities that are included and that we have discussed elsewhere (Sutton-Smith and Abrams 1978). Yet from our other research we note that when the storytaker meets constantly with the child, the stories become even more complexly symbolic than those that are to be found in this collection. All we can add is that under voluntary conditions of this kind, the children's stories certainly exceed the levels to be found in that other tradition of psychological research where stories are used primarily for the purposes of assessing child memory (Mandler and Johnson 1977; Stein 1978)

Conclusion: Narrative as Mind

Finally, we must address ourselves to the potential significance of the present kind of research. One of the most exciting developments of the past twenty years has been the attempt by social scientists to guess at the nature of mental structure. While the search for the nature of mind is as old as philosophy, recent advances in neurological and computer sciences have suddenly appeared to put us nearer to a grasp of how the mind may work. We can say, ''The mind is like a computer,'' and from the way we organize computer programs, test what our minds do against what we know computers do. There is reason to believe that in some respects we do organize our mental operations in a hierarchical fashion, just as computer programs are organized. Prior to the advent of the computer, however, it was sometimes argued that the mind works like a player playing a game of strategy (making decisions, deceptions, etc.), or like a player playing a game of chance (taking a bet on the best probabilities). Each of these comparisons also tells us about some aspects of the human mind. Perhaps the mind is all of these things and many others. Still, as neither computers nor games of strategy and chance existed at the advent of civilization (Roberts and Sutton-Smith1962), perhaps they are not the most basic sources for a model of the human mind. Instead, it can be argued that since storytelling is as old as human history in every group about which there is knowledge (Prince 1973), narrative is a fair candidate for being such a basic model. From this point of view, the most basic human mind is a storytelling one. It envasiges its life as episodes of excitement and drama, as villainy and deprivation and their nullification. It dreams of the rise and fall of heroes, ideologies, marriage, war, mortality, and biography. Onto this more basic mind stuff, the increasingly rational calculations of probabilism, strategy, and planning are subsequently grafted.

If this point of view is taken, then it becomes of value to examine how storytelling competence develops in children in order to learn how they make this basic kind of mind stuff. How are narrative minds created? How are the pieces of the mental program called ''storytelling'' put together? Later it can be asked what difference it makes if one has more or less facility with this basic equipment. Let me say at this point that I suppose that a mind is sometimes a story, and sometimes a game of strategy or a game of chance, and sometimes many other things. All I wish to do at the moment is indicate that it is reasonable to consider the mind as narrative, and therefore to consider our analysis of narrative as an analysis of mind. This work, as it happens, deals only with one kind of narrative, the story kind. There is another kind that has to do with reporting one's personal experiences, and this kind seems to occur earlier in children's lives than do fictional narratives (ages two to three years). For all we know, the personal narrative may be more basic than the story kind. Or it may not: no one has clarified to what extent life is guided by veridical versus fantastic narrative. But since it is generally concluded that our myths are as native to us as is water to fish, it is not surprising that we do not have too much understanding of these matters. Our lives may be multiple stories, or they may not. The present work may be a story that is being told about stories, or it may be a "scientific" description of stories. It is true that it takes place within the scholarly realm that has the latter name. But science is a story about man's conquest over nature and over himself, and it is seldom seen as anything but a kind of victory, or a kind of monster. So if science is in the first place a story, then this work is one story among many. It is time to raise the curtain and see how well stories can be told by young children.

Bibliography

Abrahams, R. D.
  1976 The complex relations of simple forms. In *Folklore Genres*, ed. D. Ben-Amos. Austin: University of Texas Press.
Abrams, D. M.
  1977 Conflict resolution in children's storytelling: an application of Erikson's theory and the conflict enculturation model. Ph.D. dissertation, Columbia University.
Abrams, D. M., and Sutton-Smith, B.
  1977a The development of the trickster in children's narratives. *Journal of American Folklore* 90: 29–47.
  1977b Re-analysis of Ruth Weir's *Language in the Crib*. Paper presented to the Society for Research in Child Development, New Orleans, Louisiana.
Ames, L. B.
  1966 Children's stories. *Genetic Psychological Monograph*, 73: 337–96.
Applebee, A. N.
  1972 The spectator role. Ph.D. dissertation, University of London.
Arnheim, R.
  1954 *Art and visual perception*. Berkeley: University of California Press.
Avedon, E., and Sutton-Smith, B.
  1972 *The study of games*. New York: Wiley.
Bettelheim, B.
  1975 *The uses of enchantment*. New York: Knopf.
Bloom, L.
  1972 *One word at a time*. The Hague: Mouton.
Botvin, G. J.
  1976 The development of narrative competence: a syntagmatic analysis of children's fantasy narratives. Ph.D. dissertation, Columbia University.
Botvin, G. J., and Sutton-Smith, B.
  1977 The development of structural complexity in children's fantasy narratives. *Developmental Psychology* 13: 377–88.
Bruner, J. S.
  1978 The role of dialogue in language acquisition. In *The child's concep-*

tion of language, ed. A. Sinclair, R. J. Jarrella, and W. J. M. Levelt, pp. 241–256. Berlin: Springer-Verlag.

Bruner, J. S., and Sherwood, V.
1976 Early rule structure: the case of "Peekaboo." In *Life Sentences,* ed. R. Harré, pp. 55–62. New York: Wiley.

Caring, M.L.
1977 Structural parallels between dreams and narratives. In *Studies in the anthropology of play,* ed. P. Stevens, pp. 155–74. New York: Leisure Press.

Erikson, E.
1951 *Childhood and society.* New York: Norton.

Ferguson, C. A.
1978 Talking to children: a search for universals. In *Universals of human language,* ed. J. H. Greenberg. Palo Alto: Stanford University Press.

Gardner, R. A.
1971 *Therapeutic communication with children: the mutual storytelling technique.* New York: Science House.

Garvey, C.
1977 *Play.* Cambridge: Harvard University Press.

Gelman, R.
1978 Cognitive development. *The Annual Review of Psychology.* Palo Alto: Annual Reviews.

Georges, R. A.
1969 Toward an understanding of storytelling events. *Journal of American Folklore* 82: 313–28.

Goldstein, K. S.
1975 The telling of non-traditional tales to children: an ethnographic report from a Northwest Philadelphia neighborhood. *Keystone Folklore* 20: 5–17.

Golomb, C.
1974 *Young children's sculpture and drawing.* Cambridge: Harvard University Press.

Gombrich, E. H.
1979 *The sense of order.* Ithaca: Cornell University Press.

Gould, R.
1972 *Child studies through fantasy.* New York: Academic Press.

Heath, S. B.
in press Questioning at home and at school: a comparative study. In *The ethnography of schooling: educational anthropology in action,* ed. George Spindler.

Isaacs, S.
1935 *Social development in young children.* New York: Harcourt Brace.

Kirshenblatt-Gimblett, B.
1976 *Speech play.* Philadelphia: University of Pennsylvania Press.

Knapp, M., and Knapp, H.
1976 *One potato, two potato.* New York: Norton.
Labov, W.
1972 *Language in the inner city.* Philadelphia: University of Pennyslvania Press.
Legman, G.
1968 *Rationale of the dirty joke.* New York: Grove Press.
Leondar, B.
1977 Hatching plots: genesis of storymaking. In *The arts and cognition,* ed. D. Perkins and B. Leondar. Baltimore: Johns Hopkins University Press.
Levitt, A.
1978 Storytelling among school children: a folkloristic interpretation. Ph.D. dissertation, University of Pennsylvania.
Lord, A. B.
1973 *The singer of tales.* New York: Atheneum.
Lüthi, M.
1976 *Once upon a time: on the nature of fairy tales.* Bloomington: Indiana University Press.
Mack, L. T.
1974 Developmental differences in the manifest content of the dreams of normal and disturbed children. Ph.D. dissertation, Columbia University.
Mack, R. D.
1974 A comparison of developmental differences in the manifest content of Tunisian and American dreams. Ph.D. dissertation, Columbia University.
Mandler, J. M., and Johnson, N. S.
1977 A structural analysis of stories and their recall: "once upon a time" to "happily ever after." *Cognitive Psychology* 9: 111–51.
Maranda, E. K., and Maranda, P.
1970 *Structural models in folklore and transformational essays.* The Hague: Mouton.
McDowell, J. H.
1975 The speech play and verbal art of Chicano children. Ph.D. dissertation, University of Texas.
1979 *Children's riddling.* Bloomington: Indiana University Press.
Menig-Peterson, C. L.
1977 Structure of children's narratives. Paper presented to the Society for Research in Child Development, New Orleans, Louisiana.
Menig-Peterson, C. L., and McCabe, A.
1978 Children's orientation of a listener to the context of their narratives. *Developmental Psychology* 14: 582–92.
Menyuk, P.
1971 *The acquisition and development of language.* Englewood Cliffs, New Jersey: Prentice Hall.

Meyer, L. B.
1956 *Emotion and meaning in music.* Chicago: University of Chicago Press.
Ninio, A., and Bruner, J. S.
1978 The achievement and antecedents of labelling. *Journal of Child Language* 5: 1–15.
Noone, R., and Holman, D.
1972 *In search of the dream people.* New York: W. Morrow.
Pellowski, A.
1977 *The world of storytelling.* New York: Bowker.
Petersen, L. W.
1976 Constraining the child's storytelling situation: does it make a difference? Ph.D. dissertation, Columbia University.
Piaget, J.
1963 *The origins of intelligence in children.* New York: Norton.
Pitcher, E. G., and Prelinger, E.
1963 *Children tell stories: an analysis of fantasy.* New York: International University Press.
Prince, G.
1973 *A grammar of stories.* The Hague: Mouton.
Propp, V.
1958 The morphology of the folktale. *International Journal of American Linguistics* 4, No. 24: 1–134.
Ratner, N., and Bruner, J. S.
1979 Games, social exchange and the acquisition of language. *Journal of Child Language* 5: 391–401.
Roberts, J. M., and Sutton-Smith, B.
1962 Child training and game involvement. *Ethnology* 1: 166–85.
Saltz, E., Dixon, D., and Johnson, J.
1977 Training disadvantaged preschoolers in various fantasy activities: effects on cognitive functioning and impulse control. *Child Development* 48: 367–80.
Scarlett, W. G., and Wolf, D.
1979 When it's only make-believe: the construction of a boundary between fantasy and reality in storytelling. *New Directions for Child Development* 6: 29–40.
Scollon, R., and Scollon, S. B. K.
1979 *Linguistic convergence: an ethnography of speaking at Fort Chipewyan, Alberta.* New York: Academic Press.
Stein, N.
1978 The comprehension and appreciation of stories: a developmental analysis. In *The arts, cognition and basic skills,* ed. S. Madeja, pp. 231–49. St. Louis: Cemrel.
Stewart, S. A.
1979 *Nonsense: aspects of intertextuality in folklore and literature.* Baltimore: Johns Hopkins University Press.

Sutton-Smith, B.
1972 *The folkgames of children*. Austin: University of Texas Press.
1975 Play as adaptive potentiation. *Sportswissenschaft* 5: 103–18.
1976a Current research in children's play, games and sports. In *The humanistic and mental aspects of sports, exercise and recreation*, ed. T. T. Craig, pp. 1–4. Chicago: A.M.A.
1976b A structural grammar of games and sports. *International Journal of Sports Sociology* 2, No. 11: 117–38.
1977 Ein soziolinguistischer Ansatz zum Verstandis von Spielhandlungen. In *Handlungen theorie interdisziplinar*, ed. H. Lenk, vol. 4: 239–50. Munich: Wilhelm Fink Verlag.
1978a *Dialektik des spiels*. Schorndorf: Verlag Karl Hoffman.
1978b Initial education as caricature. *Keystone Folklore* 22: 37–52.
1978c Listening to little stories. In ''The mind of the child,'' a special issue of *Harpers Magazine* (April), ed. M. Witty, pp. 53–55.
1979a Toys for object and role mastery. In *Educational toys in America: 1800 to the present*, ed. K. Hewitt and L. Roomet, pp. 11–24. Burlington, Vermont: Robert Hull Museum.
1979b The play of girls. In *Becoming female: perpectives on development*, ed. C. B. Koop and M. Kirkpatrick. New York: Plenum.
1979c *Play and learning*. New York: Gardner Press.
Sutton-Smith, B. and Abrams, D. M.
1978 Psychosexual material in the stories told by children. *Archives of Sexual Behavior* 7: 521–43.
Sutton-Smith, B; Abrams, D. M.; Botvin, G. J.; Caring, M. L.; Gildesgame, D.; and Stevens, T. R.
1975 The importance of the storytaker: an investigation of the imaginative life. *Urban Review* 8: 82–95.
Sutton-Smith, B., Botvin, G. J., and Mahony, D. H.
1976 Developmental structures in fantasy narratives. *Human Development* 19: 1–3.
Todorov, T.
1975 *The fantastic*. Ithaca: Cornell University Press.
von Sydow, C. W.
1965 Folktale studies and philology: some points of view. In *The study of folklore*, ed. A. Dundes, pp. 219–42. New York: Prentice-Hall.
Vygotsky, L. S.
1962 *Thought and language*. Cambridge: M.I.T. Press.
Weir, R.
1960 *Language in the crib*. The Hague: Mouton.
Werner, H.
1948 *The comparative psychology of mental development*. New York: International University Press.
West, A., Martindale, C., and Sutton-Smith, B.
1980 Age trends in content and lexical characteristics of children's fantasy

narrative productions. Paper presented at the Annual Meeting of the Eastern Psychological Association, Hartford, Connecticut.

Wolf, D., and Gardner, H.

1979 Style and sequence in early symbolic play. In *Play and learning,* ed. B. Sutton-Smith. New York: Gardner Press.

Wolfenstein, M.

1954 *Children's humor.* Glencoe, Ill.: The Free Press.

PART ONE:
VERSE STORIES

*Ages Two through
Four Years*

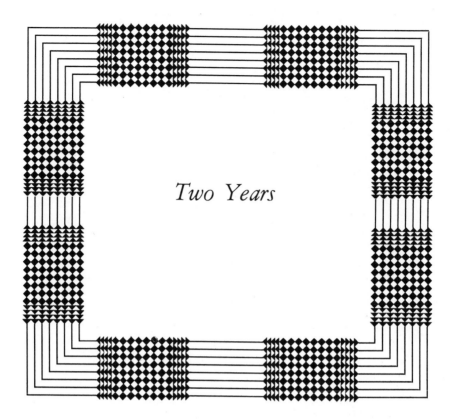

Two Years

Adam
(b.9/24/72)

1. 8/5/75

    A monkey
    a dog
    a book
    a fish

The verse stories in this section were collected over a period of slightly more than one year. This means that the children were at the age level mentioned when the earliest stories were collected, but they were older when they told the later stories. Birthdates are given after each name, and these along with the story dates allow precise calculation of a child's age. The names of children have been changed throughout to preserve both the privacy and the innocence of their expression.

2. *8/8/75*

> monkey
> fish
> my daddy
> a boat
> a man in the boat

3. *8/8/75*

> truck
> a broke car
> a dog
> a car
> a mommy
> a daddy
> a house
> a book

Alice
(b.5./10/72)

1. *2/17/75*

> The cat went on the cakies
> the cat went on the car
> the cookie was in my nose
> the cookie went on the fireman's hat
> the fireman's hat went on the bucket
> the cookie went on the carousel
> the cookie went on the puzzle
> the cookie went on the doggie

2. *2/17/75*

> The dog went on the puppet
> the puppet went on the house
> the house went on the pigeon

3. *5/13/75*

> The dog jumped over the fence
> [and then repeats the last story]

48

4. *6/3/75*

     Peter
     went over the castle

5. *7/15/75*

     The slide hits the swing
     and the bench bumped the ceiling
     the bag bumped the fence
     the watergun bumped the cigarette
     the swing bumped the water-fountain
     and the slide bumped the puddle

     [story told in park with all the objects present]

6. *7/25/75*

     I saw a worm jumped over the fence
     and a fly got on the worm
     and the dirt got in the worm's mouth
     the worm went ''ow'' [demonstrates]
     that's the end

7. *7/29/75*

     [Alice is reading a book to Dan: *All About You,* by Gail Mahan,
     Hallmark books.]

     One day there was a girl named Nammy and a boy named Tommy
     [picture shows a boy and girl]
     then there was a fire in the house
     she had trees in the house
     a kitty came in the house
     and a doggie bit the kitty
     and the man hit the kitty

8. *7/29/75*

     The worm jumped over the tray and a people stepped on it
     people stepped on the worm

and somebody lied on it and swimmed on it in the water
and somebody stepped on the worm
and somebody lied on a people
a shoe lied on the worm and floated

9.   7/30/75

There was a little bird named Bluejay
and he said "caw, caw"
a chair jumped over the truck
and a shoe stepped on a truck
and a mouse went on a train track
and that's the end

10.   8/13/75

One day there was a monster creeping at the people
and stopped itself
and shoe stepped on it
and the end

11.   8/13/75

Cat in the hat
he climbed everywhere
and the cat ate him all up

12.   10/4/75

[Dan: Tell me a story about a little girl.]

Little girl got lost
and she found a rocketship 'cause that one was almost taking off
that's the end

13.   10/20/75

Cat jumped over the fence and the fence jumped the cat
and the cat jumped under the fence and fence went under the cat's
   stomach

and that's the end
and the robber killed the cat and that's the end.

14. *1/12/76*

A little girl was sitting in the morning on the chair
and she was eating breakfast
and she was sitting on a chair eating her breakfast and her mother
    said "time for her bath"
and then that's the end

15. *4/11/76*

Once upon a time there lived a horse and that's the end

16. *4/11/76*

Once upon a time there lived a zebra and the zebra he went to the
    park
and he got lost
and he didn't know his way home
so he had to try both ways
and he had to tell the police which way to go
that's the end
he had to tell him what house was like
the zebra telled the police
and that's the end

17. *4/11/76*

Once upon a time there lived a little girl and she went in her bath
and she did the alphabet
and that's the end

18. *4/11/76*

Once upon a time there was a boy
and he watched TV
and that's the end

Beatrice

(b.4/22/72)

1. *1/24/75*

    She makes pee on the floor
    then she goes with her mom to the ferris wheel
    now she went home and saw her dada
    and now the daddy went away
    now her grandpa is dead
    now she crept into her bed
    now she had a new baby
    the mother said "no babies allowed"
    now all the people were stuffy and and had medicine
    the end

2. *2/22/75*

    The man stayed home
    the children went out
    then a Cookie Monster came
    then the Cookie Monster went away
    and the mommy was angry
    and then the father was angry
    and then the children went out again
    then the father went out
    then the mother went out
    they went to the park
    then they went home
    and then the father was doing work
    and then it was getting late
    the children went to sleep
    and the mommy and the father went to sleep

3. *8/8/75*

    The mother went out
    father
    child
    then the Cookie Monster came
    then the policeman came and take the monster away
    then the father had to do some work

then the mother had to do some work
then all of them went to sleep
then the father had to go out to a meeting and then to work
then he takes a little walk
and then the window opened
then the mother went out to a meeting
then she came back home
then the daddy and mother and children stayed home and go to
    sleep
then the mother had to read some books
and then the daddy had to read some books

[Dan: Who's it about? Beatrice: I don't know.]

4. *8/13/75*

The mother went out
then the father went out
then the mother went out again
and then the father went out
then the children went out
then policeman came
the mother came back from the meeting
then the father came back from the meeting
then a Cookie Monster came
and the policeman came again
then the Cookie Monster went away

Bill
(b.9/27/72)

1. *1/15/75*

Monkeys
they went up sky
Cookie Monster
he flew down in the sky
fall down in the sky

2. *2/17/75*

The monkeys
they went up sky

they fall down
choo choo train in the sky
the train fall down in the sky
I fell down in the sky in the water
I got on my boat and my legs hurts
daddy fall down in the sky

3. *7/7/75*

A monkey fall down
man fall off
a man get up
and man fall down
I fall down on my umped
I finished

4. *7/7/75*

A monkey fall off
my mommy fell off
mommy got sick and had to go to the doctor
and my mommy came home
my daddy fall off
and my boy fall off
and now I fall off
and daddy fall off
and my daddy fall off again
and I hurt my knee
and I fall down again
and Nancy cried [another child present]
and Nancy had a toy
that's all

5. *7/11/75*

Monkey fall off
man fall off

6. *7/15/75*

Monkey broke his sheet
the monkey fell down

his get wet
his get dry

7. *7/16/75*

A Cookie Monster hurt his foot
and Cookie Monster stay up
and fall down again
he get up again
that's all

8. *7/17/75*

The monkey fell off a painting
the Cookie Monster came up

9. *7/18/75*

Boy fall down
that's all

10. *7/22/75*

Monkey didn't fall
monkey stayed here
monkey didn't fall down

11. *7/25/75*

The hat didn't fall down

[Bill sees hat nearby]

12. *7/29/75*

Big boy walk
a big Cookie Monster have big arms
that's all

13. *7/31/75*

A train came on a train track

and the other Cookie Monster came
that's all

14.   *8/5/75*

A boy
a other boy came
Cookie Monster went away
that's all

15.   *8/8/75*

A boy didn't fall down
and the Cookie Monster fall down
and that's all

16.   *8/13/75*

A king
and a Cookie Monster
it get bit
[Dan: What got bit? Bill: Cookie Monster.]
that's all

17.   *8/13/75*

A Cookie Monster on the stairs
another Cookie Monster bumped his lip
that's all

18.   *8/13/75*

A burn house fall down
a fire burnt the house
that's it

19.   *9/11/75*

The big Cookie Monster up in the sky fall down
the monkeys had hats
blue hats and white hats
then a big old Cookie Monster eat the cookies

the big Cookie Monster jumped up in the sky
and the big Cookie Monster again jump in the sky
then the big flower went boom
the fire engine broke down
the fireman fixed it
and the airplane go in the street [Bill acts out airplane landing]
that's all

20. *2/20/76*

A big giant monkey story . . . how can I tell it?
a monkey was after the tiger
he was afraid
he eat him up
[Dan: Who? Bill: The tiger eat the monkey.]
a big giant gorilla killed the tiger
he was Bill
then he killed the tiger
and then he was all dead
a big wolf came
a hunter killed the wolf
and then another wolf came and another and another and another
and another and another and another and another and another and
another and another
a lot of wolfeses came out
and that's the end

Cathy
(b.6/2/72)

1. *2/14/75*

Cat in the hat
cow jumped over the moon
the dog laughed

2. *6/10/75*

Batman
Batman crashed in a car
Batman walked home

he see his mommy
Batman had toys

3. *6/17/75*

The cat and the dog
they crashed in a car
then they walked home with their mommy and daddy
it was a kitty cat daddy and a kitty mommy and a dog mommy and
        daddy
that's all

4. *7/15/75*

Batman got crashed in the fence
him fall down
him walk home
and then he went to bed
him have a good sleep
I finished

5. *7/17/75*

Batman got crashed in a car
him went home
him went to bed
and then him have a bottle
and that is the end

6. *7/18/75*

Batman went away from his mommy
mommy said "come back come back"
he was lost and his mommy can't find him
he ran like that [Cathy demonstrates] to home
he eat muffins
and he sat on his mommy's lap
he fell to sleep
and then him wake up
and it was still nighttime
and his mommy said "go back to bed"
and him did

and then he wake up again
and then the mommy told him to go back to bed
and he did all night
and then it morning time
and his mommy picked him up
and then him have a rest
he ran very hard away from his mommy like that
I finished

7. *8/1/75*

Batman dig
he went to bed
him come right up
then him mommy said "go back to bed"
and Batman got woke up again
and him mommy said "go right to bed"
him mommy smack him bum
he went away
and then he went home
I finished

8. *8/8/75*

[holding teddy bear]
teddy bear
another teddy bear
another one
[repeats three times]
I finish

9. *10/20/75*

Batman
Batman went away
then him spank him
and then him went again
his mamma spank him
him didn't know
then him went away all the way
him fall in the water
someone bit him in the water

a whale bit him
and him said "no" to him
mamm
and him didn't go back to bed
I want to make a picture of it
and then him mamma spank him [Cathy demonstrates]
and him got hit
and then him mamma said "no"
and that is the end

10. *5/2/76*

Ki ki
ka ka
ku ku
Charley eat children now he eat dog food
Rufus eat dog food
he made hand prints with paint
I want to make a picture of it
[Dan gives Cathy a pen and paper]
and then a boy named Kockey
they didn't like his name
and then he change his name
and his name was Snow Mountain
he named Sharkey
though he didn't like every single name
then he say "I Superman"
but he is not he named Lip
he named dog doo doo
the people say dog doo doo

11. *5/2/76*

There once was a cat
and then he didn't want any
he ate dog doo but he didn't want any more
then he said "I don't like what I'm eating"
and he said "I don't like dog doo doo but I'm eating dog doo doo"
cha cha cha
choo choo choo
koo koo city I ooh, coon glong glong shi shah shah
Glin glong

tah tooo chit tee
caw caw
choo choo
la la
lingah
soo soo
ka ka
dong dong
fell ee
sardines
cookie
dis sa
fingally

12. *5/2/76*

Now there was a pa ka
boon, goo
there was a dog doo doo
and he didn't like dog doo doo
then there was a man named Snowball
and he didn't like snow
cha cha
doo choo
cha cha
doo choo
I named dog doo doo
Christopher say
dog doo doo
then there were a boy named Taw taw
o
too too
then there was a Captain Blooper he had a hook and he were very
    bad and it hurt him
then there was a blooper pa pa
pa pa
there was Superman coming and he hurt both of him knees
then they were flying and they went right in the ocean and he got
    bite from a shark
and he didn't like when he got bite from a shark
then kla kla toe toe
tee tah

caw caw caw caw caw caw caw caw caw caw caw caw caw caw caw caw
caw caw caw caw caw caw caw caw
now say pah pah kla klee
sa see
too tee
tah tah too tee
chee chaw
ta klu
kli klu
kla kla
klu fu
klee kla
koo koo
say say
klee klee
klip kla
klee klee
klip kla
she she
fik ahh
tungoo nah
ka pa
Popeye the sailor man
bad guy him be very bad to him
and I spit out a words

Clarence
(b.7/22/72)

1.   *1/15/75*

   Three ducks
   quack

2.   *2/14/75*

   Frogs
   they went in a house
   they went in a park
   they pushed on the people
   the people got hurt
   they got mad at the frogs

3. *5/13/75*
Batman
then he ran away
then he crashed into a car
he cried

4. *5/22/75*

Superman
he crashed into a truck
he boomed up in the water
and he boomed up in the air

5. *6/17/75*

Batman
Batman fight
he crashed in the robber
he got crashed in the big truck
supermarket
the supermarket flew away
and Batman flew away with his cape
that's the end

6. *6/26/75*

Robin
a monster came and Robin got scared
people
they crashed
they swallowed and pushed him up
down on the floor they got
roar
there was a tiger coming

7. *7/7/75*

Superman
Superman ate a fish
then the fish swimmed away
then Superman fell down
he crashed there [Clarence points across the room]

and the fish ate the Superman
Superman went down
he went on this [points to object on table]
he felled on Cathy [another child nearby]

8. 7/15/75

Batman
he got crashed
and he got hit on
he got bumped on then he hurts hisself
he climbed up here [Clarence climbs fence]
and he climbed up again [again]
he runs [Clarence runs]
and then that's the end

9. 7/19/75

A big Superman
he fell on you [points to Dan]
he felled on the floor
he fell on Bill [another child nearby]
he got killed
he boomed his car

10. 7/18/75

The little boy flew up in the air
he banged
he went to bed and his mother said "go back to bed"
[Clarence was present for Cathy's story of 7/18.]

11. 7/22/75

The robbers stole my daddy's bike
and he took a car and he hurt hisself
he went on your head [points to Dan]
he felled off [demonstrates]
he jumped off [Clarence jumps off chair]

12. 7/30/75

A robber came and stole the money and the bank

he couldn't get in so the bank was closed
then they give it to the other people
and a frog ate the money from the people
the frog ate some flies and the flies ate some people
he jumped out of the water
then he did
he had
he was thirsty so he drinked some water in his pond
then he jumped back in his pond
that's the end

13.   *8/1/75*

A robber came and stoled the money
and the bank
and he went on Bill's top
that's the end

14.   *9/11/75*

Batman
he flied
he fell down
and he did pop on the balloons

15.   *9/14/75*

Superman
Batman
Robin
Superman
Batman
Robin
he flied
that's the end

16.   *10/4/75*

Batman fell down
then he flew
then he flied
then he fell

then he fell on my knee
that's the end

17. *10/20/75*

It's called Superman
flew up and fell right into the tank
then he bumped into a girl
then he bumped into a boy
and another boy
then he bumped into a policeman
then he went under there [he points]
he walked very quietly 'cause it was dark
jumped onto the car
then Batman fell into the other one
then they went home
[Dan: Who's who? Clarence: Batman and Superman.]
the end
[Note: paper cutouts of policeman, girls, boys, were present.]

18. *10/20/75*

Car
bow car
man broke car
car got broke
broke
no more broke car

19. *10/29/75*

Batman
and Superman
and she bumped her head
[Dan: Who?]
Supergirl did

20. *10/29/75*

A boat
two boats
Fire Island

21. *11/5/75*

The Lone Ranger
ride his horse

22. *12/15/75*

Bad Bart
he killed a baddie
Tonto the Indian
then Bad Bart killed a woman with a baby
that's all

23. *12/15/75*

A book
a house
all broken
a fas . . .

[Clarence has a flashlight.]

24. *2/16/76*

There was a witch
and then the girl was in trouble
and then she locked the oven
and then the witch said stick your head in the oven and
    make sure now it's hot
and then she [the witch] locked it
and then there was a kid
and there was a cage
and her brother was in there
and then she unlocked it
and then she went home and saw her daddy
and their stepmother left
and lived happily together

25. *2/19/76*

Once upon a time there was a pstew
upon a time and a lion came and scare him
[Dan: Who?]

scare him
and then he went scuba diving [Clarence picks up stethoscope
    and uses it as an aqualung]
and then
and then he shot him and then he went phew
and then he lived happily together again

26. *4/11/76*

Once there was a man had troubles of his own
yellow bellow Jack and what not he was stone
he tried and he tried to get away

27. *4/11/76*

Cowboys fight
cowboys shoot the robbers
then the bad guy and then horsey came
then the cowboy came and fight
then big horsey

28. *5/2/76*

Horsey
and I go
and then my Daddy
and then I go and my Daddy
and then I go on an airplane
and I went on a horsey
and I get on a train
and go home
 and then go sleep
then go home

[Dan: Did this really happen? Clarence: Yeah.]

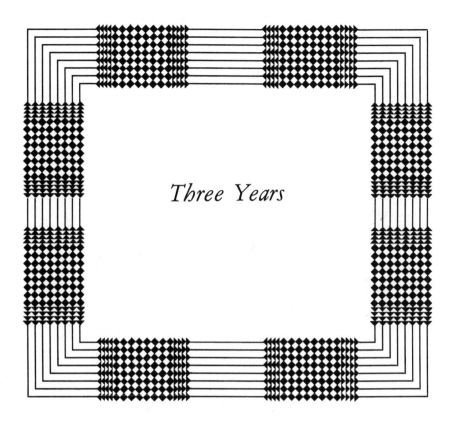

Three Years

Danielle
(b. 11/28/71)

1. *2/14/75*

> The cat and the dog
> the dog ate a flower
> the milk jumped over the cat
> the moon runned over the rocks
> the children go on top of the dog
> the clock ran over the cat
> and the whip went over the rip
> the paper went on the dog
> the glop went over the glop
> Kate jumped
> Ann jumped on a whoop

2. *2/17/75*

    The rat ran over the wup

3. *5/13/75*

    A cow jumped over the . . .
    Sleeping Beauty and the Prince
    there was Kermit the frog
    then he was making noise
    that's all
    then there was water in the playground
    and then what happened there was Sesame Street

4. *5/22/75*

    Batman went over Superman and Wonder Woman came
    and then Robin came
    mommys and daddys came
    Superman went over Robin

5. *10/20/75*

    The diddle fiddle jumped over the cow
    and then the cow and the chicken went over the mice
    the mailman went over the cat
    the water fountain
    then the teacher came and get the kids and go to school and
        pick up
    and then the birds jumped over the cat litter
    the little fiddle went over Cathy's head
    then and then the person squirted water fountain and them got
        hurt
    Jim and Paul
    the shoe went over the dish
    shoe went over Cathy
    little fiddle went over the dish
    and then Cathy kissed everybody
    [Dan: Who? Danielle: You, you kissed everybody.]
    Kim's head run over the dish bouncing like a ball
    and then everybody went home and then went to school and eat
        snack and have silent time
    the swing over the dish

and then the cat went over the dish and made the dish dead
then on my birthday everybody came on my birthday

6. *10/29/75*

The watch went over the water
the kangaroo went over the watch
and then it kissed the mother watch
the baby kissed the mother into the water
and then when the watch went over the dilly
the water went over the stroller.

7. *11/10/75*

The squirrel
the acorn
then the squirrel went over the acorn
the squirrel ate it all up
then the music came on and they just laughed at the music
no the squirrel laughed at it
and the dillow went over the dillow
[Dan: What is a dillow? Danielle: A dillow is like a kangaroo.]
and then it went over the painting that dried
that's all

8. *11/10/75*

The picture went over the rocket
then the painting went over the mouse
the tiger went over the books
then the story went over the sorry
then the picture went over yome
then the picture went over Peter's head
yoke went over yoke
then the Peter the Wold came
then finger went over to Peter
that's it

9. *11/10/75*

The diddle went over the fiddle
then the ankle went over the ankle

then the ankle went over the table
then the fiddle went over the fiddle
and then the picture ran over the painting
that's it

10. *12/8/75*

Once there was an apple
and then it got hit
and then there was a spoon and the apple walked with it
and they got a letter named apple
that's it

11. *12/8/75*

My mommy went to the circus
the diddle went over the cat
the mommy saw the cat quickly
but she missed the elephant and also she went to sleep with the
      elephant
and then she slept with the hippopotamus
and she slept with me

12. *12/8/75*

One day she saw a queen dress
and that's it

13. *12/8/75*
The diddle went over the fiddle
the father went over the cuckoo

14. *1/12/76*

Cookie Monster experiment
he walked up across the street and then it went up on Sesame
      Street
that's it

15. *1/16/76*

The first day of Christmas

then they came while they were all sleeping
he opened the door with the keys
Santa said to give all his toys to all the kids
the mother and daddys and the kids
that's it

16. *1/27/76*

Little Red Riding Hood
Little Red Riding Hood went into the forest
and then she got lost in a shark
that's it

17. *1/27/76*

Little Red Riding Hood
she was down by her mother
that's it

18. *2/20/76*

A ——— went to starn
then it was Valentine's Day and it was the last day of school
the duck went over the hurtz
then they ate the woks up and they got fatter and fatter like Fat
    Albert
the currants are work if you give them some soil
I forgot to give them some soil
answer the phone
it was the daddy
daddy's home
daddy, won't you give me a hug
won't you give me a hug, mother
Yeah hug hug hug
oh ho
"I can't find it" said daddy
we got to stay home with the babysitter
dog went over the cow
the cow said "make us"
is dumb for a cow

19.   *2/19/76*

> The dirtz
> the dirt went
> the cow went the dirt
> the dirt went over the redifz
> the thing went over the thing
> what a heavy cow
> and got
> no bread or the nothing
> don't make snack
> mommy and daddy go riding
> that's it

20.   *4/11/76*

> Once upon a time there was a dog
> the joker wanted to kill him but he ran away in the house's
>   hiding place
> and the balloon said "no more barking"
> then he went home and said "what a nice hiding place" to the man
> but man saved the dog's life and the seven dwarfs
> that's the end

21.   *4/11/76*

> Once upon a time the doctor said "nurse why not . . . just come
>   with me"
> the doctor said "come on nurse to the land"
> the end

David
(b. 6/23/71)

1.   *12/11/74*

> The three bears
> they flew up in the air
> then they came down and ate some honey
> then the tiger came
> then the tiger ate the fish

the fish was dead
and then a peacock came
it fly up in the tree and the tiger can't get it

2. *1/15/75*

The bears picnic
then the fish went up in the air
a real fish
then we ate the fish

3. *1/24/75*

The cat in the hat
went in a shell to a turtle
then a horse came
the turtle just runned away

4. *2/14/75*

The dog
and the cat ate the dog
then a fish came to eat the cat
then the fish find in
then a real dog ate the fish
it jumped up the sky in a rocket and see a moon and the sun
it runned up the stairs in a house and ran in the window
then it says "bink"
then that cat in a hat just popped out of the fish
then it get popped up the sky and take a ride in his car
then he was in his car
then his car was a Datsun
then his car bunked on the rocks

5. *2/17/75*

The cat in the hat
climbed out of water
and went in water and got fish
then a bear eat a hat
then cat lost his hat up the air

6. *3/20/75*

> A frog came and ate it
> then a kangaroo ate some meat

> [Titled: Pop Goes the Weasel]

7. *5/7/75*

> My cat went to the doctor
> the doctor was on vacation
> my cat jumped up onto a big airplane
> and after that the airplane went to the airport
> and after that the cat came out of the airport and went home

8. *5/13/75*

> The cat raced my daughter
> my tiger scratched my cat
> after that the tiger ran jump onto my car carrier
> after that it crashed
> and after that my tiger was sleeping
> then the truck was driving
> then the wheel got flat

9. *6/4/75*

> The duck ran after the cat
> after the cat jumped up on the ceiling
> the ceiling fell down on the school
> the ceiling went up again
> the wall fell down and we cut ourselves
> the wall went back up and we had to run to get a bandaid and
> put it on
> that's the end

10. *6/19/75*

> The cat in the hat
> the cat ran first
> then the tiger ate the egg
> the hat ran after the tiger
> then the cat got scared of the dog

11. 7/11/75

The bus catch a tiger
and after the tiger caught a cat and ate the cat
another cat ran very fast
then the tiger just looked at him and he just got scared of the cat
    'cause he was old he was gonna die
then my cat just got scared of the tiger a different cat
my cat's name is Alice

12. 7/18/75

The tiger catched the cat
then the cat ran away
he don't like the tiger
then the tiger just ran away to the cows
then the cows ran and ate the cat up

13. 7/25/75

Another tiger came
after there was a shell and a bird came out
and after he came out the tiger ran away to the cows
after the tiger wanted to live with the cows
and he said "could I live with all you cows?"
the cows said "yes"
and that's the end

14. 7/25/75

Another tiger came again
the tiger came and the tiger run out
ran after a cat a nice gentle cat
and after the tiger wanted to live with the cat
the tiger ran very fast and the cat
after they saw some cows
and the tiger and the cows ran and saw a bear
they saw some flies in the bear's house
because the bear wanted to live with some flies in a beehive
and some bees live in a beehive too

77

15. *9/12/75*

The cat and the hat chased the tiger
and the tiger chased the cat and the hat
and after they went to a farm to get some cows
after the cows came with us and go up to the country
we saw a country house
and we went into the house
and we went back to New York
and the cows went back to the farm
that's the end

16. *10/4/75*

Farm is here
and in the farm there was a cow and a horse
after that the horse ran to the farmer
farmer gave it some milk
and after the horse didn't like the milk
and the farmer said "what can I do?"
then cow comes
then the horse sucks the udders
and the horse says "I like that milk"
then they all went back in the barn
that's the end

17. *10/29/75*

The tiger catched the cat
and then the cat went to the barn
and then the cow ran up in the country with me on its back
the farmer put me on it
[Dan: Did this really happen? David: Yes.]
then the cat in the hat came and me and the cow ran and ran till
    we got to the country

18. *11/10/75*

Cat
cat in the hat
and then the cat wanted to live at a barn
cat ran after the vorn

78

[Dan: What is a vorn? David: A vorn is when a cow is running after
   a cat.]
then the cat sucks the cow's udders
and they're all back to the barn and they said "cat get out of there"
then the house said "stay here, stay here"
and the farmer said "stay here" also
then the cat got out of there and went for a walk with the cows
   that were with the horses
that's the end

19. *1/12/76*

I'll tell you a real story
once upon a time there was a tiger
and he ran to a farmer
the other tigers were
and the tiger said, the other, the tiger said "come in"
then he got dead
all the tigers got dead
outside in the earth
and all the horses came and saw
and all the rescue trucks came
and the firemen came but first they were on the street
and then Robin came and they didn't know what to do with that
   guy
the tigers
and then the tigers ran away to their home and that's the end

20. *1/27/76*

I tell you about any tiger and all the tigers and all the cows and all
   the cats and all the horses
one day was a tiger
and then he found a guy
and his name was David and it was his friend
and everyone went boom boom boom on the drums
and everyone welled for joy
then my tiger went whee ran over to the tiger, horses, cows
and then they saw a big giant shark
and then a big giant crocodile
and then they ran away
and came to my tiger's house
that's the end

21. *2/20/76*

The car carrier
it was bigger
it was longer than the car carrier
the back part was long but the trunk was very short but the back
    part was long
and it can go fast
faster than a bike
faster than a motorcycle
and a tiger came along and bite the car carrier
then a shark ate the whale up
and the car carrier
the end

22. *4/11/76*

Dream
dreamt about a movie
story
once there was a dragon
dragon is a long word
and he went over to the cow
then he went over to the horses
and then they went to all the dragons' house
and they ran ran ran and ran
until they came to a place and a shark just jumped out of the water
and they ran away quickly
and the shark died
and they took it to the farmer
the farmer cut off his head and the animals ate the shark up
the shark was a he
the end

23. *5/2/76*

Once there was a cat
and there was a dog chasing the cat and there was a tiger chasing
    the dog
and there was a lion chasing the tiger
they're all chasing each other
and a crocodile was chasing the lion
the end

Ephra
(b. 4/9/71)

1. *1/24/75*

One day daddy woke up and said "where's mommy?"
she's outside
she went to Grand Union
and then he went in the garden and he saw one flower missing
somebody came last night and took one
somebody called up and said "where's our plants and where's
    daddy's plants?"
all your plants are missing
and then one day somebody came up and looked on daddy's roof
    and said "where's our plants?"
and we all went home
I want to go home and get some plants and some seeds and grow
    them
that's it

2. *1/6/75*

One day a robber came and took some things off the roof
and took some plants outside
and the next morning daddy looked for the plants and there
    wasn't any
and everybody said "where's the plants?"
and everybody went home
everybody came back on the roof to look for the plants
and somebody else took the plants
and then the sheep came over and looked for the plants
"where's my plants?" said the bird
and everybody looked for the next morning and the next morning
and then everyone went home and lied down
"where's the plants" said everybody
all the animals came and said "where's Ephra's plants?"
the end

3. *2/17/75*

One day came a robber to the big plant
he took a plant

and he put it on the roof on the top of the house
a hippopotamus took a plant
and then came a giraffe
and them were friends
and they went outside to elevator
and then another animal came
it was the baby giraffe
and then he took a plant
and the next morning came another giraffe
and then another hippopotamus came
the end

4. *5/21/75*

Once there was a squirrel
and one day his mother squirrel came along
and then mother and father squirrel came along
and then his sister squirrel came along
and then a elephant came along
and then came a giraffe
and then they walked together
and then came a giraffe daddy
and then a mother giraffe came
and then all the friends walked to the pond to have a swim
and then a ladybug came along
and then a flower came
then a kid came along
and that's it

5. *5/29/75*

Once was an owl
and he lived in a tree
and his friends came
then his brother owl went upstairs
then a giraffe mother came
and that was his mother
and then his father pig came along
and then his sister pig came along
one went on a train
all them came along to the train too
then all the people went back into the houses

and then all the friends went to the circus
and then a lady came along
and then a friend came along
and that was his cousin
and then all the friends went to Brooklyn
and then went to a train
and then they got off the train
then went to the house
and went upstairs
and then have a river
and then them went fishing
and then somebody came along and said "this is me
I'm fishing too"
that's it

6. *6/4/75*

Once was a monkey
he swinged to a branch
and the monkey swinged to another branch
a squirrel went up on the tree
and once in a while a scarecrow came
and a giraffe came out of the mother giraffe
they all singed together
and sing a song about scarecrows
and them went home
then the monkey came back to swing on the monkey bars

7. *6/10/75*

Once a man went to the post office and mailed a letter
and it said "dear granny I wish you can come here"
and he always loved her
and it said "airmail"
and it came in the mail box
a mailman came and put it in the mailbox for granny
and that's it

8. *6/26/75*

Once lived three little pigs
and a wolf came along

and said "knock knock on my chinny chin chin"
and the wolf blowed the house down
and he ran to another house
and the wolf chases them there
and said "knock knock on my chinny chin chin"
and the wolf went to another house made out of bricks
then the wolf went on the chimney
and he went in it and fell in the fire
that's it

9. 8/5/75

Once was a horse
and a little farm
and some pigs were there
and once there was a apple tree
and there was a banana tree there
there was a little farmer who gave hay to the horse
and there was a little pond with little fish in it
and a little house
that's it

10. 8/8/75

Once was a tree
and there was a little doggie named
I don't really want to tell a story . . . okay?

[Dan: Okay.]

11. 8/13/75

Once was a horse
it lived with a pony
and in a little barnyard
and then a little baby pig
a little boy every single day were feeding them
that's it

12. 9/11/75

Once was a monkey
and lived by a tree

and every time he played on it he said "oooooh"
and there was a long mother chipmunk

13.   10/20/75

   I was from the country and when I was about to leave there was a
      big flood
   the bottom of the flood was mud
   and when I was leaving the roads were coming with water
   some water coming up to the roads and the roads got flooded
   and the cars had to turn into a boat
   that's it

   [Dan: This really happened? Ephra: Yes.]

14.   2/23/76

   Once upon a time there was a elephant and he lived happily
   and the monkey lived right next door
   and then a mountain lion scared them
   and frightened them away
   and so somebody else came
   and that's it

15.   5/2/76

   Once upon a time there was a giraffe whose name was bbbbb
   and he had another friend whose name was bbbbb
   and they went to the circus called gagagagagaga
   and
   and
   the circus had a clown named kukukuku
   and there was a monster called kukubird
   and there was a clown bird who was named kukukuku
   and then a monkey came to the circus and said "what is going on"
   "what is all this juju and bubu going on"
   that's it

16.   6/3/76

   Once upon a time there was a circus in England and the circus
      didn't like England anymore so they moved on over to Basil
      and something happened in Basil that they didn't like

a earthquake
and when they were acting the earthquake started
and when they were acting the earthquake was starting and the
    children went out of their mind
and that's it

Ezra
(b. 2/11/72)

1.   [no date]

Peter and the wolf
Peter and the wolf and Grandfather but the bassoons
Peter but the strings and once upon a time there was you
[points to himself]
the end

2.   7/22/75

Last night there was a monster
and then a scooter came and runned me over
and then the train came and picked me up
and then I was dead
then a record came and spinned me off
then a kitty cat came and said "wake up wake up"
then I waked up
and then Patty came and picked me up
and then I was sick
and then Kelly came
and then the bell
and the house
and then a umping came and picked me up and throwed me
and then a fat man came and picked me up
and then he put me in his shoe
and then he had a sweeper and sweeped me
and then he blowed the wind
and then he went like that [he demonstrates by opening and closing
    his mouth a number of times]
and then he took a funny story
and that was all

3. *7/30/75*

It's gonna be about a long snake and my mamma
The snake ate me and a baby
and my mamma came and picked me up
a dog came hide me
and it was a duck
and then what happened was a boat came and a guy picked me up
    into the boat
and the boat sailed for hours and hours
and then the monster bite me
and the guy put me on the airplane
and the boat towed behind the airplane
and a motor boat picked me up and they killed me and I was dead
and then it scared me and Patty
and it scared everybody
and that's the end

4. *7/31/75*

It's gonna be a shark
once a shark came
and then it bite me
and I was hiding behind its tail
that's all
then a friendly dolphin came
that's all
then mamma came
and then there was a train track
and the train runned me over
the train was on this track
and then it stopped
then a ''O'' came and it made me around and around
then a sharp thing cut me off
then that's all
and then there was a monster and a building
and wrecking machine knocked my building down and tored it up
then there was a large large large bulldozer
and it picked me up
and it dumped me into a nest
and then the birdies came
then there was a monster

and another monster
and another monster
then that's all now you know
then it was time to go to my mamma
and then that's all

5. *8/5/75*

It's gonna be about a ceiling
once upon a time there was my momma
and then once upon a time there was a shark
and I was hiding behind the tail
[Dan: Is this a dream? Ezra: Yes.]
and that's all

6. *8/12/75*

Once upon a time there was a ferris wheel
turn around and around and around
that's all
the end
it's just a short story

7. *8/15/75*

It's gonna be long
once upon a time there was a big big monster
bite my finger off
then I saw a long long book
and I read
and then there was tree bulldozed
and then my mamma and I went home
and a monster
another monster
another monster
another monster
another monster
another monster
another monster
another monster
another monster

another monster
another monster
another monster
another monster
another monster
another monster
another monster
another monster
that's all

8. *9/11/75*

A big big monster
and a big big crocodile came with fire in his mouth
and poison in his fire
and he killed me
and then he took a bite of me and he swallowed me

9. *9/11/75*

Um
alligator came and he belongs to the crocodile
and then a tiger came
a lion came
a elephant came
and a big apple came down from a tree
I thought it was a peach
(It's a dream again.)
a truck came
and a car came and runned me over
a racing car came
and that's the end

10. *10/2/75*

Once upon a time there was a monster
it scared me away from the cat
and then the cat went up in the sky
and he went up in the tree
and he ate the cat up
the end

11. *10/4/75*

Once upon a time there was a monster
scared the cat away
then the monster went away
then he ate the spider
the end

Frank
(b. 4/4/71)

1. *1/15/75*

The cat and the hat
they ate egg and ham
the cat didn't like eggs and ham
and then Sam liked eggs and ham

2. *1/15/75*

Pinocchio swam on the water
he picked him up
the crab on the water eat Pinocchio up

3. *1/24/75*

The monster and Spiderman
the girl cried
he named Hook
he hurt the girls
he go way
the end

4. *5/7/75*

The little white duck went swimming
then the crab came
a lobster came
then a ice-cream came
and a popsicle was playing by itself

5. *5/13/75*

The sign said "No Parking Lot"
the snake crashed the sign
it ran away
and the orange came
then the peanuts came too
the end

6. *6/10/75*

A bear went up to the air
it go in the book
he went to the office
then he went to school
he wanted to be home
and he went in the cage
glasses
bird

7. *9/11/75*

We went to the ship
and the ship was rockin' around and around
and we saw a dragon so we asked for a big Batman
and we had a rest
and we asked for fire
and the dragon came by
broke his head
and he got up and looked at his leg
and it broke
that was a short one

8. *10/1/75*

A story about the dragon
and the little girl said "there's a dragon in my room"
and the mother said "there is no such thing as a dragon"
and the dragon got bigger and bigger and bigger
and the dragon had no feet
and the dragon moved the house
and the dragon got skwak

squished
they sing songs that the story about the church
and the boy pet the dragon on the head
and it went longer and longer and longer
then it went up the air and came down
then it went up and down and up and down and up and down
the dragon
it's a play
I saw it
[Dan: The story about the church? The dragon was in it?
    Frank: Yeah.]
They paint the dragon

9. *10/2/75*

I got two stories to tell ya
about your body
you have a skeleton in your body
and you have bones
and the body keeps you going and going and going
when you fill up your body food comes out
then you go to the bathroom

10. *10/2/75*

It's about dinosaurs
It goes sak
all the dinosaurs disappeared
then fires and volcanoes came
went to the rocket ship
[Dan: What?]
somebody with one eye
they hide in the secret den
then a big giant monster ate the dinosaurs all up
and the end

11. *10/4/75*

Rock and roll
somebody went
a rock was moving and he was rolling
then the cow was moving

and the wind blowed the house
and it was stuck in the ground
the rain
the big rocket came and punched the rock and roll out
it's a rock that can talk
and it said "don't do that"
and little words came and they said
he came from the rain and they hit the rock and roll out
it's a long story you know
can you stop it?
I can't tell the long story

12. *10/17/75*

The ship went in the whale's tummy and captain was in the ship
and the whale tummy again
and then they had to get off
and Sam do the harpoon
and they got another story
I'm gonna tell you
Abiyoyo
He's a monster
a got nearest nearer and he's
I can't tell
the end

13. *10/20/75*

Tell you a story about the three button dragon
once upon a time there was a mountain
and
the clouds have to climb all over it
and there was a dragon
he didn't let somebody next to it
and a little lady came in and she would sit next to the dragon's
    mountain
and the dragon came and shoot fire at her
and she was scared and she didn't know what to do
the dragon and the old guys
and new good guys came and his name was old stick stoke
and he whacked his tail and the three button dragon started to run
the end

14. *10/29/75*

I don't know
[Dan: Tell one about a monster.]
a long long time ago there was a monster
and he ate people up
but he can't eat monster up
and that monster ate his tail
a egg came and crack his head off
he was gonna die and the motorcycle came and cracked
and then came a shell
the shell scratched him but it didn't hurt
he . . . and she came was nice to him

[Dan: Who? Frank: The monster.]

15. *10/29/75*

Long long time ago there was a knight
and he was a knight but not a real knight
he was an old knight
but he was sucking a lemon
and he was sucking and he found a buzzer [eats] and it was a plastic
      leaf
and know what happened?
he rolled a magazine
and he saw a scarecrow and he died again
[Dan: Who? Frank: The knight.]
the end

16. *11/10/75*

Okay
know what?
my daddy had a working house and he let me work there
and once upon a time a long time ago there was a cat
and then monster came and frightened the boy away
then there was a spider walking up the web
then a shell came and the robber came and sat on the log
a tack came and find another cat and the end

17. *11/10/75*

I got another story for you

once upon a time there a long time ago there was a peg
and the peg was going to ride on a horse
the end

18.   *12/8/75*

Once upon a time there was a shark and he was swimming in the
     water
and he found a whale
and the whale eat the shark up
and the razor cleaned everybody up
the end

19.   *12/8/75*

How about two dragons
once upon a time was a dragon
and he danced with the clouds
and nobody could be near his mountain
the end

20.   *12/15/75*

It's about a whaler
long long time ago there was a cat
and he met a whaler
and the whaler meeted a dog and the dog was meeted by a man
the man meeted a machine and the machine meeted another
     machine and another machine meeted a cow
and the cow meeted another cow
and the cow meeted the dog
and the dog meeted nobody
the end

21.   *12/15/75*

It's about a fish
and the fish's name is Fishey
and the fishey was getting into the water
and he swimmed and swimmed and a lobster came and he was a
     good lobster
and the fish came with him

95

and they both swimmed and swimmed and they met a frog
and the frog was good
and they swimmed and swimmed
and they saw a lamb
and lamb came
the end

22.   *1/27/76*

The rock
stayed there
and some people came and pick up the rock
and the acorn came
and arrow came
and stright came
and left came too
then there was a monster coming and ate the fish
the fish ate up the monster
and the monster came and he was a big monster
and he was a giant

23.   *1/27/76*

This one's called
it was about the loose
[Dan: What's that? Frank: It's a top.]
it's a african loose
a nail came and put the loose in the box
and box said
don't besturb him
and the box came and hit fox with his tail
don't disturb the baby loose
and the zebra came and hit him on the tail
[Dan: Who? Frank: The loose.]
the end

24.   *2/20/76*

One day there was a boy
boy found the cat
the cat round around and the boy too
and a dog came and chased the cat away

and the boy was sad
another dog came and a cat came and chased the dog away
and the boy went home
and he went to the store and buy some bread and buy some cookies
the end

25.   4/11/76

Once there was a bear
the bear said "moo"
and then the clam comes and bit his neck off
he put his neck back on
and then he put a class on his head
and then bing bang
and then he went up in the air and down
and everybody saw him up in the air
and then he put the belt on for the school
and then he puts the minds on
and that's the end

26.   5/2/76

A rabbit
and then a kangaroo came and fixed the rabbit up
then a pig came and washed him up but he couldn't wash him up
and then a tiger came
and washed his foot
[Dan: Whose? Frank: The rabbit's.]
and then a lion came and washed his neck off
and then he called the tiger up and said he had a swollen gland too
[Frank has swollen glands.]
that's the end

Gina
(b.4/12/72)

1.   9/12/75

The girl went out
the girl went away
and she went on the boat

she came back home
she drew herself
then the girl went down the thing [Dan: Eh?]
yeah
the thing you go down on a boat
the girl jump on the ceiling and she went on a car
she fell down
then she went out the boat
then she went out in a car so she could make up her mind

Four Years

Farrah
(b.11/18/70)

1. *1/21/75*

> Once there was a robber
> and then a girl was lost
> and the robber came and put her in jail
> and then the police came and got her out of jail
> and then the police put the robber in jail

2. *1/21/75*

> One day a robber stole some shoes
> and a kid wanted to go out and play with Julie
> and didn't know how to play with no jacket and shoes

when everybody was asleep a robber came and stoled all the shoes
   from moms and girls and childs
the end

3.   *1/6/75*

A robber came in the morning and stoled some jackets
and people wanted to go out and didn't know where their coats
and then the people asked the people "where their jackets been"
and the police came in the morning
and the people said "and who stole something?"
the end

4.   *2/17/75*

Once upon a time there was a little girl
she lived in a house with four kids and her mother and her dad
and she had one grandma and one father and one cat named Kitty
and she went outside to take a walk to the zoo
and the zoo was closed
and she recognized something
and there was no animals till Monday
and she came back home
and a dragon started to eat the girl
and then she finally got home
she knocked on the door and no one answered
and the dragon right eat her up
and the dragon told her to lie down and close her eyes
and ate her up
the end

5.   *5/21/75*

Once there was a cat who lived by the oak tree
and a person came to see him
and he said nothing
and the boy went home and gave him some food
the boy had a mother cat
and the boy gave the mother cat to the lonesome baby cat
then she put him to sleep
and they lived happy ever after

6. *8/8/75*

> A monster
> the monster ate the house
> the monster ate the kids
> the monster ate the dad
> the monster ate the cat and also the dog
> he ate the furniture
> and then he went home to the zoo
> the end

7. *9/11/75*

> Once there was a little girl who ate a green apple
> and she fell dead
> and then a prince came along and took the vase with a Cinderella in
>   it
> and he
> um
> took it away with his friends
> and then she sat up and the green apple fell out of her throat
> and then he turned to the new castle and they danced for a year or so
> and then they lived happily ever after

8. *9/11/75*

> This is about a zoo
> no
> Cinderella
> no Snow White
> once there was a little girl who went and found a green orange
> and she ate it
> and she fell dead
> and she fell dead in a gold vase
> and the prince took it away with his friends
> and they danced for a year or so
> and they danced
> and they danced
> and then they went to bed
> and they fell fast asleep
> and they lived happily ever after

9. *10/1/75*

Once upon a time there was a footprint in the house
the sister and brother the mother and the father was all sleeping
a stranger came to a house and he stoled some shoes
and he stoled some food
and then he went home
and then they got up
put their clothes on
put their shoes on
and saw a footprint that the stranger what he putted down last night
then the brother and the sister
and the sister was called Snow White
and the brother was called Brother
then there was two flashlights in the hall [objects present]
and they went and picked them up and went outside
and looked all over the town
they find the stranger
and they call the police
and the police put him in jail
that's all

10. *10/2/75*

Once upon a time there was farm
there was a little horse and a mother horse and a sister horse and a
    daddy horse
and then a brother horse
and then baby sister and the brother had a little walk
that's all

11. *10/4/75*

Once upon a time there was a apple tree
it lived by the house
and then it had apples
and they ate them all
[Dan: Who?]
the people in the house
a mother
a father
a sister and a brother

and a cat
and a baby
then they ate the apples
that's all

Garrett
(b. 10/3/70)

1. *7/16/75*

    Once there was this little mouse on a train track
    and the man came along and picked the mouse up
    and the mouse bit the man's finger
    ouch
    the end

2. *7/22/75*

    Once there was a mouse
    it was on a train track
    when the train came it ducked under the train track and he didn't
        get runned over
    so he got up
    and he went home
    and he get a train trap
    and he went over the train set
    he went down the stairs
    someone was about to step on him so he ran away
    and so he went down to the train
    and he set the trap on the train
    and then the train exploded
    and all the people got killed
    and Frankenstein came and got them up
    and the end

3. *7/25/75*

    Once there was a tiger
    he was in the zoo
    someone said "can I buy that tiger?"
    "no you can't, know why? because he's wild"
    and the end

4.   7/29/75

Once there was a tiger
but there were two King Kongs
and the tiger found a mouse on a leaf
and it was dead
but it really wasn't
and there was a duck on top of the house
and it was a yellow duck
and . . . um
a cat came along
and . . . um
there was another two cats
and those two cats thought that the mouse and duck were to eat
and so they ate the duck
and they ate the mouse
the end

[Dan: Who is the story about? Garrett: All those people.]

5.   7/31/75

Once there was a elephant
and once there was a tiger too
and the tiger bit a mouse
and the tiger bit the elephant
a wallabeast came along
and the wallabeast bit the tiger
and there was a bear too
[Garrett points out a picture of a bear and an elephant on the desk.]
the end

6.   8/1/76

Once there was a tiger
and there were two cats
they were friends
and there was a mouse too
and the mouse went over to a leaf
and he got on the leaf
and then a bird came and picked the mouse up and flew away with
    him

and he was for supper
the end

[Dan: Who's the story about? Garrett: I don't know.]

Howard
(b.4/9/71)

1. *5/29/75*

A ball of fire swang up and a tiger he jumped to the fire
and then a ball of fire came and jumped into the fire
a fire came up to the sky
and the baby got the fire and cried
and then the ball of fire came eat the fire
and then a ball of fire came and eat the baby
and a penguin came and eat the baby
there's two babies
and then fireman came and then telephone came
there's two telephones
three telephones
four telephones
six telephones
five telephones
monster came and then the peoples came to see the fire
to see what happened
and then they all got to the hospital
and then the airplanes came and crashed the fireman truck and got
    down the airplane
the airplane came and go down like this [he demonstrates]
and go boom to truck
then the car went fast and the airplane went fast
and then the airplane crashed over
he went to the sky
fell down to the truck
the car was there and the airplane went faster but the cars went up to
    the sky
a boat came and crashed the airplanes
and then airplane came and fire engine came and a policeman came
everyone came and they crashed over the airplane
and then the airplane got fired

and then no more airplanes
got five airplane
six airplane
then the other airplane came
then the small one came

[Toys present were two paper planes and a toy truck.]

2. *6/4/75*

Once upon a time there was a monster
and there was a parade
then the monster stopped the parade
and then the robot came and stopped the monster
and then Spiderman came and throwed a web at the monster and
    the robot
then Mr. Spock came and threw spots at Spiderman
and the spots make him sick
and measles came out
and he had to go to the doctor
that's all

3. *6/26/75*

One day was a bullfight
airplane came
monster
and then a blast-off came
and then airplane came again [two airplanes]
and then a racing car came and crashed the airplane
and then a baby came
monster came
everyone came
and then everyone stopped the fire
all the peoples came to see the fire
now it's finished

4. *7/7/75*

Someone got cut like this
[Howard imitates two fingers being cut off]
one day was a monster coming to get someone crying

it was green with a big nose
it was nighttime
and then a monster came and got her
her mommy was sleeping and her daddy was sleeping
and then the monster got her
and then a police came and got her and put her in her house
and then the police ran away.

[Dan: Who is this story about? Howard: Monster.]

5. *7/11/75*

One day was a monster
and then the monster came
and then he broke the whole world
and he broke the tree off by his-self
and he broke it with his hands

6. *7/16/75*

One day was a monster
all the monsters and the days they got all the people and put them in
    the fire
they were five King Kongs
and then it's finished

7. *7/19/75*

Monster over here
monster over here
over here . . .
[Howard points to various places on a blank page]
the monster came in here
[he points to lower left-hand corner]
he got all the peoples in the town
it's finished

8. *7/30/75*

One day monster came in a town
all the peoples in the town got scared
all the peoples in the town cried

107

and King Kongs and all the peoples got scared
and an airplane came and crashed
and he took all the peoples in the town's airplane

9. *7/31/75*

One day was a monster
a tiger came
a bowfly came
King Kong came
monster came
monster here
monster here
monster here
[he points to each of the corners of the page]
King Kong here
here
here

[he points as above]

10. *8/1/75*

One day was King Kong
Godzilla
um
and Godzilla and King Kong and fish
that's done

11. *8/8/75*

Pussy cat
over there
over here
over here
[Howard points to various spots on a page]
pussy cat go here
here
monster came over here
monster over here
here [different monsters]
finished

12. *8/13/75*

   [a dream]
   monsters
   my mommy came and scare the monsters away

13. *10/1/75*

   One day there was a King Kong
   and one day there was two monsters
   they were skinny and fat
   and then a monster came and watched the rain
   that's the end

14. *10/27/75*

   Once upon a time there was a man who was walking
   and the lobsters
   then the man was holding the lobster
   then he hold on the lobster
   and then he ate the lobster up and it was cooked
   and then the lobster ate the man up
   the end

15. *11/10/75*

   Peter and the wolf story
   Peter went out the groche and then the grandfather didn't want him
         to go
   then when Peter went the big wolf came out of the forest
   the end

16. *4/11/76*

   Once upon a time Batman came
   then Robin and Bat went in the Batmobile
   then they saw Joker
   then King Kong came and got Batman
   then King Kong fell right in the water
   then Batman and Robin went in the Batmobile
   the end

Ingbert
(b.6/27/70)

1. *4/30/75*

Once upon a time there was a family of tigers, bears, and lions
and they went out for a wild animal picnic
the wild animal picnic was made of baby rabbits
that's what they ate
they took the rabbits alive and they killed the rabbits at the picnic
and when they ate the rabbits the blood washed out all the meat
    where they were chewing so they missed all the parts where they
    were chewing
when they missed it they only got a tiny bit of their tooth left
they kept chipping their teeth 'cause they forgot to take out the
    bones
they kept chipping their teeth so much they only had one tooth on
    the top and one on the bottom
then they swallowed the rabbit
after they chipped their teeth and had dinner they went home and
    had roasted beef rabbit
then after they swallowed the rabbit and after they had dinner they
    went to sleep and they all dreamt the same thing
and that's all.

2. *4/30/75*

[A dream last night. Ingbert: I only had one but I'm still exhausted
'cause I couldn't get back to sleep.]

I dreamt that my Daddy was giving me a bike ride and I thought
    they were somewheres I didn't know
and then I went there there were some grownups that said "how
    cute" 'cause they saw I was crying

3. *6/17/75*

Once there was a dragon who went poo poo on a house and the
    house broke
then when the house broke the people died
and when the people died their bones came out and broke
    and got together and turned into a skeleton

and then the skeletons came along and scared the people out of the
town
and then when all the people got scared out of the town then the
skeleton babies were born
and then everyone called it Skeleton Town
and when they called it Skeleton Town the people came back
and then they got scared away again
and then when they all got scared away again the skeletons died
no one came to the town
so there was no people in that town ever again

4. 6/17/75

Once upon a time there was a ferocious monster King Kong
and he had two helpers and the helpers were named Frankenstein
and Godzilla
and then they all went out and scared the people
and when the people got out of the houses
and then they tore them up after they learned how to make camps
and then the monsters made a fire and then they ate the people
and then they got so fat that they popped
the end

5. 7/7/75

Once there was a ferocious dragon
the dragon was ferocious enough to jump on buildings and burn
them without burning them
and after he burned them without burning them he would step on
the building and the building would break in two
this is what would happen [he shows the bottom of his shoe]
yucky old yucky yucky candy
then after the yucky old yucky candy got on the buildings the
dragon went poop on the buildings
and then the poop splatted
and then the father that lived in the building went on to the roof
and he got his shoes all yucky
and then he came in and then he washed his shoes off in the bath
and after he washed his shoes off in the bath the poop went down
the toilet
the next time he took a bath he put his head under the faucet

little drips of dump went down little holes in his eyes
he took a shampoo and after all the dump splatted in his eyes
and after the dump went down his eyes he died
and that's the end

[Dan: What happened to the dragon? Did you forget it?
Ingbert: Yes. The dragon got so old that he died.]

6.   7/15/75

Once upon a time there was a big kingdom
and the son of the kingdom had a big watergun that was as big as a
    giant building
and after he tried shooting the squirt gun the water didn't go the
    way he wanted
and it was so powerful that it knocked him over when he squirted
    himself
and he tried it and he fell down so he didn't do it any more
the end

[Ingbert had a watergun in his hand.]

7.   7/16/75:   *The Gorilla Cat Fight*

Once upon a time there were two gorillas and three cats
and they all fought
and after they all fought the gorilla tore off one of the cats' heads
then the gorilla picked up a building and smashed the cat
and then all the cats died and then all the cats woke up
and then all the cats killed all the gorillas
the gorillas never woke up
the end

8.   7/22/75

Once upon a time there was a monster named King of Beasts
and King of Beasts went out for a walk
he walked for a hundred and two years and he died
his bones said "wake up, wake up"
and then his bones died and then his spirit said "wake up, wake
up"
        to his bones
the house became haunted

112

and then a person went in and the person got scared away and his
    brother bit the body part
his brother died
and then the other brother died in the same house
and then the same thing happened
and then often the same thing happened the same thing happened
    to both of them again and they were really dreaming that they
    died
after they woke up they really died
and then the skeleton said "wake up, wake up" and the spirit said
    "wake up, wake up" to the skeleton
the end

9.   *7/25/75*

Once upon a time there was a once upon a time
and there was a once upon a time
and then the once upon a times ate the once upon a time monsters
the end

10.   *7/25/75*

Once upon a time there was a Cookie Monster
and he fell in a big hole made of oatmeal cookies
and he ate them all
and the ghost came and ate all the cookies
and then the Cookie Monster came and ate all the cookies
and then they ate all the cookies
then the ice-cream cone came and ate all the cookies
and then Boy Wonder came and ate all the cookies
and then a thirtieth century museum came and ate all the cookies
and then the Cookie Monster came and ate all the Cookie
    Monsters
and then the Cookie Monsters came and the Cookie Monster ate all
    the Cookie Monster blood
and then the Cookie Monster blood ate all the Cookie Monster blood
the end

11.   *7/29/75*

Once upon a time there was a Cookie Monster
the Cookie Monster ate all the cookies

and a pit made of cookies
and then the pit eating the pit
and then the Cookie Monster died
and the pit died
and the second pit died and then the dead pit snapped its fingers
and then the live pit snapped its tongue like this
[he demonstrates to Dan]
the end

12.   7/29/75

Cookie Monster found a Cookie Monster
Boy fell cause he couldn't really see where he was going
[Ingbert was inside a costume of the Cookie Monster.]
the end

13.   7/31/75

Once upon a time the once upon a time ate the once upon a time
      which ate the once upon a time
and then the once upon a time which ate the once upon a time
      ate the princess once upon a time with the king
and then the once upon a times died
then the end ate the end
the end
the end
then the end died
then the end died
then the end died
then the end died
and then the end the end the end died
the end with a the end
the end
the end

14.   8/5/75

Once upon a time there was a big once upon a time town
and everyone was named once upon a time
and then the once upon a times ate the once upon a time which ate
      the once upon a times
and then all the once upon a times died and died

114

and then they laughed
and then everything died
and the whole world died
then the whole world whole world died
boy fell and got up
fell and went to dandyland
and then boy died
the end

15. *8/5/75*

(It's going to be a whole page.)
Once upon a time there was a once upon a time there and it died
and its parents cried
then a monster came and ate the parents
and the monster died
and then the monster came to life and the parents came to life and
    the world came to life
the end

16. *8/13/75*

Once upon a time there was a Cookie Monster
The Cookie Monster ate every Cookie Monster he could find
then they all died
and the panther ate them
the end

17. *8/13/75*

Once there was a biggest biggest in the biggest whole world
and then David came and killed David
and then he killed Goliath
the end

18. *8/13/75*

Once there was a skeleton town
the skeletons ate all the people they could find
and then all the King Kongs ate all King Kongs that ate the
    King Kongs that ate the whole world
the end

PART TWO:
PLOT STORIES
Ages Five through
Ten Years

Five Years

Abe

1. *10/24/73*

I'll tell you a story. He's going to be a pumpkin man. Once upon a time, there was a pumpkin man. And he lived in a little pumpkin house close by the city. And he wanted to go to the city, so he went to the pumpkin-mobile and he went faster than the speed bullet, more powerful than a locomotor. He could go down the highest hill in a single bound. And he went so fast that he past-ted the store that he wanted to go to. Then when he got back home, he went to bed. And that's the end.

Stories for this group were collected over a period of two years. Initially, all children are the age cited, but some children may be two years older when they tell later stories. Specific birthdates were not available for this older age group. Again, names have been changed to preserve privacy and, where relevant, innocence of expression.

2.   5/16/74:   *The Fat Dinosaur*

Once upon a time there was a great big dinosaur. He wanted a giant rabbit dinner. He found a tree. He never saw a tree before. He thought it was a rabbit. He tried to eat it but it was too hard. He looked and he found a real rabbit. He took it home, then he ate it. Someone knocked on the door then he opened it. He was still hungry. He saw an ant at the door and he ate it up. Then he ate a cow up. Then he found an elephant and he ate it up. Then when he was so fat he went to bed then he blew up. The end.

3.   10/1/74:   *The Elephant That Ate Too Much*

One day there was an elephant. He thought he couldn't catch anything. Then he started to look for a giant lion. He met a coconut tree. He didn't know what a coconut tree was. He thought a coconut tree was a lion because it had furry stuff all over it, so he ate it. What fun it was. He went home. He went to sleep. He blew up. The end

4.   11/12/74:   *The Walking Lunch Box*

One day this little boy was walking to school. Someone said something. He looked around and then he couldn't find anything who said that. Then he just walked on. He was at school. Well, then he started to play. It was lunch time. Then he opened his lunchbox and something said, "Ouch." Then he saw the lunchbox's mouth open. It said, "Ouch." It jumped down. It bit the leg and it ran away. And then it went home, destroyed the buildings. Then he went to the room. The end.

5.   1/24/75:   *The Wolf and the Three Rabbits*

Once upon a time there lived three rabbits. They all lived in a hole in the ground. They always went out for a walk in the night. One night they saw something. They wondered what it was. It was a wolf. The wolf started to chase them. The wolf started to run faster. He ran so fast, the rabbits stopped and the wolf skidded three miles. Then he bumped into a tree. He was very mad. He ran into the rabbits' hole. He was so mad that he crawled into the hole. The rabbits said, "What can we do?" One rabbit told the other two what to do. "Put a pot full of hot water near the door." While the wolf was sliding down the hole they opened the door and the wolf slid into the pot that was full of hot water. He was so hot that he ran up the hole and he ran to Africa, and no one ever saw him again.

6. *2/24/75: The Dinosaur Who Scared All the Cavemen*

Once upon a time there was a dinosaur. He was very hungry. So he set out to eat. He saw a village of cavemen. He went in the village and before you could say "Jack Robinson" the cavemen zoomed faster than lightning away from the village. One of the cavemen, while he was running away, said, "Boy, that dinosaur scared me." The dinosaur saw some meat and he ate it. He went back home. He went in his cave. He saw the cavemen and scared them half-a-mile. Then he went back to bed and he fell asleep. The end.

7. *3/21/75*

Once upon a time there was an ox and a tortoise. And they were fighting over to see who was the fastest. So they decided to have a race. So the rabbit ran as fast as he could when he saw the tortoise. So the ox laid down and took a nap. And when he woke up he saw the tortoise three miles away from him. And then he ran as fast as he could. Before he could reach the finish line the tortoise won. And he saw the tortoise taking home diamonds and diamonds and diamonds. And he was so mad that he went to the manager and the ox said, "I demand this money!" But the Mayor said, "But Ox, the tortoise won so he gets the money." And the rabbit ran as far as he could and nobody ever saw him again. And that was the end of the rabbit, and the tortoise stayed rich and rich. The end.

Agatha

1. *10/19/73*

There was a father that had a little girl that's name was Sally. They had a duck pond. Once the little girl went out to the duck pond to see the ducks and she saw one little duck that was lost. And she took it home and she lived happily ever after.

2. *10/19/73: The Halloween Night*

There were two children named Sally and Alice. They had a cat. It was reddish-orange. What shall we name this cat? Since it's reddish-orange, we'll call it "Pumpkin." They were very happy with Pumpkin. Pumpkin was a guy cat. He met up with a pretty girl cat. They had kittens. The girl cat was an old street cat. They called her Lisa. They called their old black kitten Blackie.

3. 11/7/73: *The Queen's Gift*

Once there was a princess and their father and mother. They lived in a castle up on a high hill. The king had a diamond ring they wanted to give to the queen. They had some guards to guard the ring, and the king sent it with the guards. The king said, "No, I want to guard it myself." But the guards didn't know that this was a villain who wanted to steal the ring. He stealed the princess, too. He took her off in a cart on a road that went through a *long* tunnel. The guards suddenly figured out. One of the guards said, "I think we've been tricked!" And the second guard said, "Where to look for her? A villain would take the tunnel under the hill—the *long* tunnel under the hill."

They all went. They caught up to them and brought him to the king. The princess was saved and the guards said, "One for all and all for one!" And they lived happily ever after.

4. 11/28/73

Once upon a time there lived a beautiful movie star. She lived in the old western days, but not far from her cabin where she lived there was these bandits and they had a plan; first to rob the stage coach and then get her. Then they began their plan. The girl not knowing about the robbery she sat and she just felt the warm fire in her log cabin fireplace. Not long after that the bandits soon finished robbing the stage coach and then they began to go to her house. They snuck in the window of the log cabin. They grabbed her inside a bag after they had snuck up on her. They brought her to their leader. Then they showed what they had got in the bag. Then they tied her up to a chair. There was a big fair for all the bandits and the movie star was tied up in the chair with the fair. Not long after the cops heard about it. They came scrambling to the fair as fast as they could. They saved the movie star and they arrested the bandits. And the chief of the cops had a wedding with the movie star and they lived happily ever after.

5. 5/16/74: *The Little Birds*

Once there were lots of birds. Each one was a different kind. One went to the sea to look for fish, for it was a seagull. Another liked to live in a dead tree, for it was an eagle. One lived in Japan. I don't know the name of this one, but it was pink. Another one had such blue eggs, for it was a bluebird. Now, the others, I forgot the names and the things that they did, but each one had a talent and beauty. Most of them were rare but the beautifullest one was a dove. It always went to a flower tree and brought a flower to decorate the bird's home. She was very nice, and her feathers were as white as very clean snow. She also lived with the forest animals. She made good friends with them. Once when she was going past a house in the woods someone caught her. They didn't put her in a cage and it was a nice home and sometimes she went flying outside. But she always came back. The end.

6. 11/26/74

Once there was a dog. She was a good old dog. She roamed the forest. Once somebody found her and she was only a puppy. They didn't know what to name her so they got a party of people and they were talking about what to name her. But they didn't know what to name her. Then they all started to get names for her. But none of them would do. Then the family's youngest daughter said, "I know what to name her—how about Little Ruff Ruff?" First she rolled under a chair, then she jumped onto the chair and Dad said that she was hungry. So they gave her some food. She was happy there. They treated her nicely. And she had a nice soft pillow to sleep on. But once they went on a vacation and they left her with a lady and she had two cats. It wasn't very nice there, because the cats always did mischief and blamed it on her. So she decided to run to her family. She sniffed her way there. Before she could get to the place they were already on their way home. Then she found them. Whenever they went on a vacation again they promised her they would bring her. The end.

7. 1/21/75

As soon as the toy man closed the door the tin soldiers started marching. All the dolls began to watch. It was the march of the tin soldiers. The Russian dolls began to dance. The jack-in-the-box began to pop. Everything was fine. The little lollipops began to dance. Everyone was happy. The parade went all through the night. The majorettes began to twirl their batons. Then came the tin machine man. Then everybody was very, very happy because the piñata was there. All kinds of clowns and play cars with people came from the piñata. Then the first rays of sunlight came in the window. They all went back to their places. The door was opened and the toy man came in. The end

8. 5/6/75

Once there were ten children. They were orphans and they couldn't go into an orphan company because they didn't have any money. So when they got older they decided to be tramps. And then hobos and sleeping on trains was fun but they thought they should earn money. So, they tried to find out what they did best. And they inherited something from each of their family. The first one inherited being a tailor from his grandfather; the second one an artist from his grandmother; the third a scientist from his father; the fourth he inherited being a grocery keeper from his mother; the fifth a stargazer from his great-grandfather; the sixth a doctor from his mother's friend; the seventh a postman from his great-great-grandfather; the eighth a creep from his great-great-uncle; the ninth a postwoman from his great-great-aunt; the tenth, well he didn't inherit anything from his great-great-grandmother or aunt, he inherited from the cavemen all of his ancestors. He became a great hunter. And they didn't earn very much money but the tenth never starved 'cause he could hunt pretty well. And even became rich. [she says—see the end of the story . . .]

Well, one day a very wealthy woodcutter saw him with a deer on a stick and he thought if he can hunt that well I'll give him a payment if he'll get me something for one week. And he did for twenty-five weeks and he became rich.

And that's the end of my little story—but it's a big story.

9. 6/24/75

Once there was this little girl and she always liked to do everything but she wasn't the least bit superstitious. She never read a story like *Pinocchio* that was fiction. Everything that she read had to be non-fiction. And she wouldn't believe anything anybody said. And one day they said that the ice-cream man was there and she didn't come and missed the ice cream. One day a person said that there was a birthday party and anybody could come. But she didn't come 'cause she didn't believe them.

Then it was her own birthday party and her Mother said, "Get up early, four more days 'til your birthday party. Better start planning." And she didn't do anything so she missed her own birthday party. (And if you think that's pretty bad you better hear the end first.)

Well, here it is, the end. . . .

There was a fire and she wouldn't believe anybody when they said that there was a fire. And she got all burned up.

10. 6/24/75

Once there was a little doggie and when he was three he ran away.

Well, he had to provide for himself. Then his mother and father discovered he was gone they couldn't find him. Then one day he found himself in a jungle Uka-buga and the address was 90002000Z. And the people heard about it. But they did not know the jungle Uka-buga and that was a jungle in Africa. And there's Dingoes in Africa. (Dingoes are wolves in the dog family.)

So, one day, when the pup was still a pup the Dingoes thought he was a baby Dingo and adopted him. And when he was let go he thought he was a Dingo himself. But he couldn't defend himself as well as the other Dingoes. And he was captured alive! And he was known to be the only Dingo caught alive and they sent him to California and painted him red.

And the red wolves mistaken him as one of them so he married one what was full grown and he was as big as a red wolf. He married and they had three pups. And one of the pups was a Dingo, the other of the pups was a red wolf and the other of the pups was a plain old ordinary dog like he was. And all of them were captured and they didn't know how in the world a red wolf could be part red wolf, part dog at the same time or fox either.

One day when they gave the red wolf a bath all the red paint washed off. And they thought it was a Dingo and sent it back to the forest. The Dingoes thought it was a dog. And once he returned to his home town he really was a dog and he shrunk back as small as a dog and went back to his owner. And that's the end.

Alan

1. 10/19/73

Sometimes I ask my friend, "Do you have your helmet and your Big Wheel?" And he says, "Yes, but I don't got my helmet." "But I've got it at home." And he said, "You watch my Big Wheel while I go home and get my helmet." And then he goes home and then he comes back outside, and then we can play a race. I win the race! I win the race!

2. 11/2/73

Once upon a time I and my friends went to the Park. We had Big Wheels and helmets. They had flags. Who was the winner? I almost won. We had some juice and lollypops and candies. We had a nice time. It was getting dark and we went home. Got up in the morning. School was closed. Then we went to Long Island to a nice beach. Went on the rides and had a lot of fun. Had a nice time and went home.

3. 11/28/73

One day Matthew came over to my house. My mother gave him some food. He's getting madder and I'm getting madder. People started to fight. I knocked him down. My mother said, "What happening 'round here?" Then I knocked him down on the bed. He kept fighting me. She gave him a whipping. Then both of us have something to eat. He throws food on my face. She spanks him again. We have the same food. He wants spaghetti, juice, tomato sandwiches. I go over to his house and his mother gave him a whipping. Three whippings. I came home.

4. 5/16/74: Me and My Teddy Bears

When I was at home I looked in the closet and I saw a big giant bear. I treated him like a nice little bear. We went to the park a lot. We slept together and also we ate together. Next morning we looked at a book together and then we helped our father paint the house. Next winter it was Christmas and I got a new jacket. My teddy bear got a baby teddy bear, and they lived happily together. The end.

5. 10/15/74

Once upon a time there was a little boy and his father and his mommy. And he went out in the woods to go hunting with his son. And the son heard an animal and he saw a little black feather coming up from the leaves. And he picked the leaf up and it was heavy. And then he looked down and saw a little baby kitten. And he told his father that, "Could I keep this baby kitten?" Then he took it home. And then he went out hunting again. And his father saw a mommy bear. And then he ate his lunch when he went back home. And then his father made a nest for the baby kitten. And they made a stuffed up ball. And the kitten liked to play with it very, very much.

Next Christmas he was in bed and then when he woke up the next morning he opened his box that had a baby teddy bear on the outside of the wrapper. And he opened it up and he saw a baby teddy bear. That's the end.

6. 11/12/74

Once in the woods there was a little baby kitten. And then a little baby came and the little baby liked the kitten. And he played with it and played with it and played with it. And then his mother called him. She said, "Baby . . . baby." The baby did not come. He liked the kitten very much. And then the baby's big brother came and got the baby brother. And his mother, father, sister said, "Why did you eat so fast?" And then the baby went to the bushes where he found the kitten. And then the . . . um . . . baby went playing with the kitten. And then the brother came and brung the kitten home. The end.

7. 1/24/75: The Little Boy and the Kitten

Once upon a time there was a little house, and people lived inside it. They were friendly. There was a little kid and he wanted a pet, but his mother and father didn't want to have a pet. The next morning he woke up. He was crying and he wanted a kitten so bad that he went to his mother and father's room to tell them that he wanted a kitten. He was begging so much for a kitten, so his mother and father got a kitten. Anywhere he goes, anything he does, he takes the kitten with him.

8. 2/10/75

Once upon a time there was a little boy in a big, big country. He lived in the woods with a lot of pets. He had lions and leopards for pets. He had so many pets that he had to find a pretty lot of food. He hunted and hunted for food. One day he woke up in the morning. He arrowed a coconut off a coconut tree. He had some breakfast. He was playing with his pets. He was going swimming. This little boy's name was Tommy. When he went swimming he saw a little baby dinosaur. He wanted his name to be Little Tommy. He wanted him for a baby pet. They ate with each other and played with each other, and then they went swimming with each other. For a couple of days they went to his cousin's house. It was his cousin's birthday, a matter of fact. They went boat riding with each other. They liked each other. Tommy and his baby dinosaur spent the night there. Next morning they were going hunting. They found a little cuffed bear, so they took home the baby cuffed bear. They feeded him a lot. They went swimming to the other side. They had a camping trip, and they had a lot of fun. And they ate, and they went to bed.

9. *4/25/75: Little John and the Baby Bear*

Once upon a time there was a boy. He lived with his mother and father. They lived in the woods. They hunted for food. When they went hunting one day they got their guns. Johnny got his toy pistol with a string that held on to the cork. And Johnny saw a little black fur from back of the rock. He went to the rock. He tried to pull that black feather. He pulled so hard that a little baby bear came out of back of the rock. Johnny was so surprised that he called his mother and father. They came running to Johnny. They saw that black bear. Johnny said, "Could I keep the black bear?" His mother said, "Yes." They went hunting some more. And they went back home. They had dinner. Johnny played in the back yard. Then it was time to go to bed.

Next morning they had breakfast and they watched TV. And Johnny's mother and father, they built a cage for the black bear. When they finished looking at TV, they played in the backyard. They played in the swimming pool, and played volley ball in the pool. And they ate a snack and they finished.

The black bear was hungry, so they gave the black bear some carrots. Then they watched TV, and after TV they ate dinner. Then they played some more. Then it was time to go to bed.

Next morning they ate breakfast and they went hunting again. Then when they got home they built a house for the bear. Then they ate a snack. Then they watched TV. Then they ate dinner. Then they played some more. Then they went to bed. The end.

Ann

1. *10/16/73*

Once upon a time there was a castle. The princess and the king were there. Some people came in and said to the princess and king, "What are you doing here?" Because the people live to the castle but the king and queen didn't know. They just moved in. And when they moved in the king and queen said you could live here. Then the other group came in and king and queen said you could live here [she repeats this for two more groups that come in]. Another group came and they said you can't come in. There was a knock on the door. It was a little child. "Oh come in." After her another group came and he said, "Come in, come in, come in." After that came a little pile of babies. "Come in." Then others and others. And all the pile of people were standing on the stairways of the house. That's the end.

(More?) Then a scary part came. First came a lady in the doorway. Then a ghost came in and he said, "Woooooo" [she laughs]. The sound of the "Woooooo" was like a person's name. Then came a scary part [with actions]. Then a wicked witch came with his broom and a cat and a broom. Then the wicked witch said, "What are you doing? This is my property." This was her house. Then all the people came in and said, "This is our property too and the wicked witch's." Then came more of them and more and more and more. Then some people said, "What are you wicked witches coming in? This is our property not your property." Then some other people came and said, "This is ours 'cause we got it first. 'Cause the owners gave it to us first." Then a pumpkin came hopping in. And a cat meowed and she was all black. And then her children came in and they were all black. They would jump all around and lay around. Then came a whole pile of little baby pumpkins. They said, "Ho ho you chickens, you can't catch us." And that was the end.

2. 11/28/73

The people are going to the market driving in the car. Just when they passed the store they saw a jack o'lantern. They drove by and there was the jack o'lantern. "Hey mom, I saw the jack o'lantern." That's the end. [She is laughing and giggling as if it's a put-on.]

3. 11/28/73

This is about Goldilocks. She was going to give her grandma some food and when she went her mother said, "Don't talk to strangers. Just walk along." And she met a wolf. "What are you eating?" "I have some goodies for my grandmother. She lost a tooth." The fox ran in and put the grandmother in a closet. When Red Riding Hood opened the door there was grandma. "Why do you have such big ears?" "They're good to hear with." "Why do you have such big eyes?" "They're good to see with." "Why do you have such big teeth?" "They're good to eat with." She ran away from her grandmother. She wouldn't do that again.

4. 5/16/74: The Bean Bag

The bean bag was a friend to a child. Children was sitting on it. The child was very happy. The bean bag said to the child, "I love you." The child gave the bean bag a present. They played together. The end.

5. *10/25/74*

Once upon a time there lived three bears. And one day there was a child born in the middle of the wood. And the mother and father tried to name her Goldilocks! One day as Goldilocks was going she stopped by a little cottage. She knocked on the door. There wasn't an answer. She opened the door and there were three bottles of porridge. And that's the end.

6. *11/22/74*

Once upon a time there was a little girl named Ann. And she was deciding to go to the park. But once she did there was nobody to play with so she went to her friend's house and there wasn't nobody there. The end.

7. *2/20/75*

Once upon a time there was an old woman and an old man. And the mother made a cookie out of the gingerbread. When she took it out of the oven it ran. It said, "You can't catch me because I'm the gingerbread man." Till he came to a bear. The gingerbread man said, "I ran away from the little old woman and the little old man, and I can run away from you."

8. *3/14/75*

Once upon a time there was a little bear. And he wanted to go to a place to eat. And he didn't find any place to eat. So he went to his friend's house and his friend's house said he could. So he ate, and when he was finished then he started to make another bowl, and he ate the second bowl and then he stopped eating porridge. And he got full, very full. Then he decided to go outside, and when he got outside it was raining. And then he went back inside. The end.

9. *11/27/75: The Story of a Little Girl*

Once upon a time there was a little girl. Her name was Gabriel. One day Gabriel went outside. She looked at all the pretty flowers and she picked some. She brought them back inside and she put them in a vase. Then she sat down and she looked at the flowers in the vase. Her mother came in and she said to Gabriel, "Why are you sitting there staring at the flowers in the vase?'' Gabriel said, ''I just picked them and I like to stare at them.'' ''Well, why don't you come in the kitchen,'' her mother said, ''and bring your flowers and you could have some lunch.'' Gabriel said, ''All right.'' It was the next day and she had to go to school and she wanted to bring her flowers and her mother said, ''I'll put them in your lunchbox so when you eat your lunch at school you can put them on your desk.'' The end.

Annette

1. *1/7/74*

A lion. Once was on a train and he ate someone up. He just killed them and threw them onto the tracks and the train runned them over. Then somebody else thought that he was alive and they put down a rope to make him climb up, but he wouldn't. That's all.

2. *5/16/74: The Flower*

I knew a flower once, in my grandmother's garden. It was called a rose. It was a pink rose. My grandmother liked it better than any flower she had. The end.

3. *9/27/74*

This story has a funny ending.

Once upon a time there was a king. He was dying in this bed. He was surrounded by all the people in his kingdom. He had three children there was the first son, there was the second son, and there was the third son. There were all princes.

The king said, ''Bring me my first son.''

The first son said, ''Yes father.''

''Since you like nature so much, all the farms and all the animals in my kingdom are yours.''

''Thank you, thank you, father.''

''Bring me my second son,'' the king said.

And the second son said, ''Yes father.''

''Since you like buildings, all the castles—the east castle, the west castle, the north castle, and the south castle—are yours.''

"Thank you, thank you," the second son said.

What about the third son? There's nothing left.

"Bring me my third son," said the king.

And the third son said, "Yes father."

"Bring me my magic goblet, the one with rubies and diamonds all around it."

[And here, Annette holds an imaginary goblet: before she started the story, Annette had looked around for a paper cup or "something." Finding nothing, I suggested we "pretend," a suggestion she readily accepted.]

"When you want a friend, drink from this goblet. It will make you kind to your enemy. But do me a favor. Don't drink from this side. Drink only from this side of the goblet."

[Annette points to opposite sides.]

"Please tell me, father, why."

"Because if you drink from this side, it'll spill all down your clothes!"

[dramatic pause from Annette]

And who would do a dumb thing like that!

4.   9/27/74

This is the first chapter.

Once upon a time, there was a girl named Nattie. She had a mother and father. No sisters or brothers. She was lonely some of the time. She liked to take walks. There was a place that interested her. It was a castle that once had kings and queens. Some of the furniture was tooken off.

Now there were people to show them around the castle. You pay money. Nattie went to it, but she didn't pay: there were lots of grownups around, so I guess they thought she was somebody's child.

When she was in the Duchess's bedroom, she saw something that interested her. She leaned against a wooden wall, something started moving. It was a secret passage. She went down these stairs—the round kind, you know. In the old days, there was no lights. Then she saw a little hole: she was a really small girl who could get through it.

She went through it and saw a pond. She didn't know if she was inside or outside. She just stood there.

[When Annette said that's the end, I asked her if she would tell me the next chapter next week. She said that this was all she knew. So I suggested she make up an ending. After some hesitation:]

Well, she didn't know if they had closed down for the night. So she went back up the stairs—she found that she was inside—and they were still open. The end.

[I asked where she got the story: "My friend told me this." Perhaps the problem was that Annette forgot the ending her friend told?]

5. 11/4/74

[Annette's father told her this story]

Once upon a time there was a king and he was dying in a glass bed. And all the people in the kingdom were around him and he had three children—the first, second, and third son. And they were around him, too. And the king said, "Bring me my first son." And the first son came over and he said, "All the farms and animals in the kingdom are yours. Bring me my second son. All the castles in the kingdom—the north, south, east, and west are yours. Bring me my third son." And the third son came over. "Bring me the magic goblet" (a long drinking glass of gold and covered with diamonds and rubies and all that junk) and he said, "This is yours and it will give you a friend if you drink from it and will make you kind to your enemy (and that's never good). But never drink from this side of it [points to one side of cup]. Always drink from this side of the glass" [points to other side of cup]. And the third son said, "Why? You've got to tell me why I can't drink from this side." The king just said, "This side, not that side—'cause if you drink from this side of the goblet it will spill all down your coat!"

6. 11/4/74

[Annette's friend told her this story.]

Once upon a time there was a little girl that lived with her mother and father but she had no sisters or brothers and she was lonely most of the time so she mostly took a walk. There was one place that really interested her—it was a castle—and it had guards and some furniture was left out and some rooms were open and some rooms were closed down. You had to pay money to get in, but she just walked right in because they thought she must be with her mother or her father 'cause there was other people there too. When they got to the duchess's bedroom there was something that really interested her there and she went around to the other side of the bed and she leaned her hand against a wooden wall and something in the wall—she must have touched a knot or something—and something in the wall started moving. And she opened the door. There was a stair-way (twisting kind) and it wasn't going up, it was going down and she went down the stairs and she must have gone down a thousand stairs or something and it was really cold down there. And then she saw a crack of light (there was no electricity, so how could there be light?) and then she saw a little hole, and it was lucky she was a small girl because she could crawl right through the hole, and when she crawled through she didn't know if she was through the hole, up the stairs and back home or they may be closed down for the night or should she go to the other side of the pond? There was no boat or anything and she·couldn't swim. She didn't know what to do—she just stood there. [Storytaker asked her to make up an ending.] Her parents came and said, "Where is my little girl? She's here somewhere." And the guard said, "She's here somewhere. You'll get her tomorrow." "But she's our little girl and we want her back now." And they waited 'til tomorrow. And that's all.

7. 12/10/74: The Eight-Day Camel

[Annette's father told her this story.]

Once upon a time there was a man and he needed to go to a state. And it was an eight day trip. And he had to have an eight-day camel because it was an eight day trip. So he went to this place where there were eight-day camels and he got an eight-day camel and the man that owned the place, he said, "When you get to the well you have to let him drink and then you have to brick him." And before he left he said, "The guy said to brick him." He thought it must be a joke. So he went to the well and he drank and then he rode off on the eight-day camel and it stopped in seven days. Not eight days but seven days. And he had to crawl all the rest of the way. And then he said to the guy, "Bring me that eight-day camel." So he brang him the eight-day camel and said, "This is a seven-day camel!" And he said, "Well, did you remember to brick him?!" "Well, I didn't know what 'brick him' meant." And he said, "Oh, you forgot to brick him. Around the well there are bricks. You take two of them and you whack as hard as you can on his tail." "Doesn't that hurt?" "Not if you keep your thumbs on the outside!"

8. 3/18/75

[Annette says she made up this story herself.]

Part 1: The Fart
Once upon a time there was a fart. He lived in fartland. And everyone there laid farts. But the one who laid most of the farts was that little fart. How can a fart lay a fart? [she asks herself].

And one day the little fart said, "I'm too little to lay all these farts. And how come I laid them? I laid them because dey're widdle farts."

Part 2: Fart Moves to Poopland
And then the little fart said, "I think I'll move to poopland." And he moved to poopland and he didn't make a poop he laid a fart 'cause he was a fart.

And the fart was SOOOOO big that it popped him and he was all just bits of sort of like a broken balloon. He was being punished because he moved to poopland.

And he became a fart-ghost and moved back to fartland and laid BIG farts, and became a big fart-ghost.

9.   *3/18/75:   The Gobi Fish (A Scarey Story)*

[This storyteller is hesitant to tell her own stories. This one was told to her by her brother. Note: This story was told very quickly, so the words are not entirely those of the storyteller, but the basic plot is covered.]

Once there was a man and he told his son he would go fishing with him tomorrow and he did. So they went fishing and while doing so the man's hat fell in the water. When he caught his hat the man was bitten by a fish which, he noticed, had two heads. Next day he went to the doctor who, when told about the fish, said the man had been bitten by a Gobi Fish and that it was a magic spell. The man didn't believe the doctor and laughed so hard his head almost fell off.

The next morning when he woke up his wife started yelling at him. "What have you done with my husband you ugly creature, you beast!"

"But I am your husband." The man fled to the bathroom and locked himself in. When he looked in the mirror he was all black and furry, had two pointy ears, and teeth like Bugs Bunny, only they were sharp.

So he put on a dark coat and went outside. But it was so hot he threw off the coat and started running. Some kids who were playing with pebbles started throwing the pebbles at him. One great big kid threw a great big stone at him. So he turned on the kid and pushed him down and walked on him until he was flattened and covered with footprints, two big footprints in his face.

Everyone in the world heard/found out. The president of the U.S.A. heard and sent twenty soldiers after the monster. The soldiers were walking along and they heard a sound of teeth gnashing. [Storyteller just makes this sound—does not say in words what it is.] When they looked around there were only ten there. And you know what that meant. So the president sent one hundred soldiers who bombed and stabbed with swords and shot fire on arrows etc. But he wasn't dead 'cause he was a monster, only wounded. Then they did it all again and he was dead.

10. 4/29/75: *About a Fart*

Once there was a little fart and all he did was [fart noise] lay farts. And then he went to Pee-pee-land and he heard the baby pee-pee. And the baby pee-pee went, "Pee-pee, pee-pee" [spoken very softly in high voice]. And then he met the Mommy pee-pee. And the Mama pee-pee went, "Phee-phee, phee-phee" [with Boston Brahmin accent]. And then he met the Father pee-pee and the Father pee-pee went [in a deep voice], "Pee-pee, pee-pee." Then he met the King of the Pee-pees. And the little fart said, "Do you know the way to Fart-land?"

And the King of Pee-pee-land said, "Pee-pee, pee-pee, pee-pee."

Then the little fart said, "I don't understand that." And the little fart just walked away and tried to find himself back to Fart-land. And he found himself in Pooh-pooh-land. And he met a baby pooh-pooh. [Same routine with all the various types, Ma, Pa, and king, in Pooh-pooh-land] 'til he wander to Burp-land . . . [Same thing again.]

. . . And the King of Burp-land said, "Burp-burp, burp-burp" [in loud majestic fashion]. And that was so loud that it bumped him [the little fart] out of the palace and he didn't understand it. And he got himself to Fart-land. And he found not Mommy and Daddy but three kings. And he saw three fathers and three mothers. Then he met three babies.

And there was so much racket in Fart-land that he went to live in Pooh-pooh-land and the Pee-pees were there. . . . [same in Pee-pee-land and Burp-land].

And he went to live in Candy-land. Little fart was just right for Candy-land and he turned into a candy.

Brian

1. 10/15/73: *Pirates*

Pirates found a treasure full of diamonds. A police boat saw the pirates. The pirates won.

2. 10/15/73

Once upon a time there was a millionaire that liked to be fancy. It was a very fine night with a full moon. But little did he know that it was Halloween. Something happened. There was a big puff of smoke. There was a vampire, an evil magician, Dr. Frankenstein making the Frankenstein monster, Count Vampire, Count Dracula, a devil, and a witch on a broomstick flew by the full moon. He didn't know what was happening. And then the vampire struck! And then the witch came down and cast an evil spell on the fancy man, who was rich, and that spell was to turn him into a frog. And the creeps lived happily ever after and the fancy man was a creep, too.

3. 10/15/73: The Mommy Book

Once upon a time there was a giant monster. When he was asleep his mommy came in. She woke him up because she wanted to tell him that dinner was ready. The giant ate the first bowl of cereal and then he ate ten more. He got so fat that he blew up the whole house.

4. 10/15/73: The Very Rich Man

Once there was a very rich man who was very fancy. One day he was going out in his very fancy clothes. It was a beautiful day. Some robbers came and planted a bomb. Then there was a treasure chest in the hole that was made by the big explosion. Then the very rich man was richer than before. He lived happily ever after.

5. 10/15/73: The Moon in Very Hot Places

When there's a full moon, where the mountains are, wolves and coyotes howl, "Woof—ooo—ooo—ooo." The bats go out in the hot places when the full moon is out. They also sleep in caves and old houses. In the old days, when they did things improperly, they were dumb. They thought vampires lived there. There are really vampire bats, but not vampires.

6. 11/28/73

I like vampires. I'd like to make a vampire story. I go to Florida. One night in Transylvania there was a full moon out and there was an old house up on a hill that had a crooked road leading up to the hill. And in the house lived a vampire and his name was Count Vampire. He went out to find someone to suck blood. His or hers blood. He went down the winding roads of the mountain. After a puff of smoke he turned into a bat. He flew over Transylvania. He came to a house. There lay three pirates. The captain was named Brian. The two first mates were named Don and Rita. The second mate was Ron. The rest of the crew were named Murray, Daniel, Albert, Tom, Ken, Neil and Zachary. Count Vampire didn't like to suck pirates' blood. Only ordinary people. So he went and made friends. They went out and had some tea at his house. He went and sucked people's blood. The pirates helped by cutting off people's heads. Then they all went out for a sail on the pirates' yacht around Transylvania.

[Names are those of classmates.]

7. *1/9/74*

[To set the scene: The class is down in the library and the librarian has announced that Brian is going to tell the class a story. He is seated on top of a desk and the whole class is sitting in chairs in a circle around him. This puts him about a foot above the rest of the group. He starts off saying, "Now, no laughing, because sometimes it makes me embarrassed . . .]

Once upon a time, in the *rumbling* roads of Transylvania, there was a mountain with a castle on it with a curvy road creeping up to it. And inside . . . guess who lived inside of it? Count Vampire. Now his wife Roberta and Louis the vampire and Daniel the vampire . . . ["How many vampires?" asks one girl in the audience.] There's another two—there's lots of spooks in this story. And Michael Smith the vampire. And then there is Michael and there is Ursula the witch and Count Dracula and then one night, Count Dracula ran down the road and there was a big puff of smoke and he turned into a *bat*! And then Roberta the vampire turned into a bat. The strings on her dress turned into bat wings and then Louis and the rest did the same. Then Count Vampire stood up on the house and with three strokes of lightning he turned into a bat. Then they flew over Transylvania and came to a cottage and Count Vampire turned back into a vampire. Roberta the vampire woman's hair turned into a *parachute*! [The whole class laughs wildly at this.] I told you not to laugh! ["That's all right," says the librarian, "That was a funny thing you said." "You're good at storytelling," says a girl from the audience. "Yeh!" cry out a large group of kids. "My father's much better," yells out a boy. But he continues:]

Then they put their capes and arms to the sides of their bodies and they flew up to a window and the window got broken. And guess what

138

was inside? Twenty grim pirates! The captain's name was Captain Alan. [They all laugh at this. "It's a nice name," the girl adds. The boy stands up on his chair. "Up here there's not much noise!" But Brian continues again:]

The first mate and the guards ran. Now Louis, Daniel, and John [he laughs, looking at John] and there was Brian [Brian laughs], then finally Mitchell and Tom, who was the last mate, and the vampires only liked ordinary blood, not pirates'! They loved to drink good guys' blood only. Then they all went to one house and first on the way they sucked the people's blood that the pirates had cut off their heads. Then they all went home.

8. 5/16/74: The Monster's Wedding

Once upon a time there was a butler. He wasn't an ordinary butler. He was a half vampire, half ordinary person, half monster. He was making a monsteress for the monster, his son. His helper, Igor was helping him, but when Igor saw her he said, "I want girl." The butler said "This is for the monster. Now bring him." Igor made a face and stuck out his tongue. The monster came in and saw her and he fell in love, too. The butler and Igor went to a hotel with their vulture. They checked in at the counter. They asked for a room for the wedding and for the guests. The wedding supper was spiders, pigsfeet.

9. 10/22/74

Once upon a time in the rumbling roads of Transylvania there was a mountain with a crooked road. There lived Count Dracula and his wife and a few other vampires. One night when the moon was full, Count Dracula and his wife and the other vampires turned into bats and flew. His wife stood on a cliff and light flashed three times and the linings on his sleeve turned into bats' wings and then they flew and sucked people's blood. The end.

10. 11/15/74

Once upon a time four American astronauts crashed on an unidentified planet. They didn't know it was really earth. After 2088 years, their space ship calendar registered April 5, Eightieth Millionth. Taylor, the senior astronaut, prepared to leave the ship. They got on land and they experimented with some plants. While they were leaving somebody stoled their plants. They saw a footprint in the sand. Then they said they knowed that there is life on this planet.

They found people who took their clothes. And Taylor, the senior astronaut, fell in love with a beautiful young girl who was mute. Suddenly a band of gorillas came from I don't know where. Along with the Chief of State, Dr. Zaius, Taylor, the senior astronaut, was captured. In Central City in the ape's jail hospital Taylor's throat was injured. He made a paper airplane to show how he got to this planet. Dr. Zera became fond of Taylor and she came to visit him in his cell. Meanwhile, Dr. Zaius and General Erko, the leader of the soldiers, were discussing some business. "I'm tired of playing 'catch me if you can,' " said Erko to Zaius. Zaius said, "I've been trying to catch them." And then Erko said, "Let's kill them!" And Zaius said, "We have to give them a chance!" "No, Zaius, we have to kill them. They might carry some kind of poison!!"

Meanwhile in the cell, Taylor, the senior astronaut, tricks the guard. He escapes. He captures Dr. Zaius. He tied him to a rock. But he didn't know that Erko was behind a rock holding a dagger. Erko cut the ropes and freed Dr. Zaius. Then they clobbered all the astronauts and took them to jail. Taylor started yelling at the guard when the injury in his throat was all better. The guard silenced him by forcing him with the gun. Upstairs, Zaius was looking at the charges against the astronaut and the charges were taking food, killing animals for feed instead of fish, and also getting clothes which they didn't know was his regular clothes. And then just as the astronaut was about to slip the keys from the sleeping guard's belt, Erko came, woke the guard up. Then Erko shook the astronaut and threw him down on the floor. That night when Zaius and Erko went home the astronaut was about to sleep slipped the keys from the guard's belt. In the morning he heard the sound of trembling hooves on the ground. It was Zaius and Erko coming in. And when they saw the astronaut trying to slip the key from the guard's belt he put three guards there and himself. Erko did that. And he put bells all over. Then the astronaut was going to pretend to sleep walk and was taking the keys from the guard's belt when Erko asked the Lieutenant to get the coconut made spotlight and asked to open the window to get the sun in. And then Erko told them to get that sticky stuff from inside the trees to make it shiny. And then they shined it on the astronaut and the astronaut knew that if he didn't wake up they'd know he was pretending because of the light. And then suddenly Zaius came and said, "He has committed serious charges, but we will give him a chance and we'll keep him in jail for the rest of the year. And if he doesn't try to slip the keys he will be freed. I will leave him in the hands of you, Erko."

Then, Taylor was so upset he was about to punch them all when the guard put another gun on him. And then he went, "Bl, bl, bl, bl," with fingers and his lips. Then Zaius said, "He may be too afraid of us so we will have a tribunal."

The tribunal began. And then judges and Erko said, "He's guilty, he's guilty." Then Zaius hit the gavel on the table. "Dr. Zera been experimenting on the astronaut and we shall see if he's like us or not," said Zaius. "He does not have hair going out of his skull on to his head, and he does not have the same type mouth like we do and he does not have a bone in the middle of his ribs with a sort of type screw. And he cannot be brown or gorilla black or regular color. And here are the charges against him," said Zaius. "He took food without being sure that he could take it. And he also stoled clothes and he also kidnapped me," said Zaius. "And he also tried to slip the keys from the guard's belt. He is guilty. We will have him in jail for a year." But then, Dr. Zera said, "Please free him." And Zaius hit the gavel on the table and said, "No, he has committed serious crimes." Taylor said, "I object, I object." The judges and Zaius talked. "He is guilty," said the judges. And Taylor was getting so mad he was going to throw a knife at Zaius but he got dragged away by the guard.

Later than night, Zaius had Taylor come to his office. Zaius said, "I am not as mean as all the others. I've only tried to save you from being killed by Erko. But I had to put you in jail." Taylor said, "No! You're trying to put me on a hunger strike." And Zaius said, "No. If I hadn't put you in jail Erko would have killed you." Then Taylor yelled, "No, it's not true! You want me to die of hunger." Zaius said, "No, I'm just trying to save you from death and a fate worse than death." Then Taylor said, "No, it's not true. You and Erko are monsters!" "No! If I had been killed would you have been saved from Erko or anything?" said Zaius.

Then Taylor spit in Zaius's face. Zaius was getting sweaty and wiped his forehead with a handkerchief. He called the guard in. "Bring Taylor back to his cell and if he tries to do anything, beat him to death!" Then Taylor said, "You're doing this because you are afraid!" "Taylor, you're the one who's afraid," said Zaius. Then Zaius said, "If I had been afraid I would have done 'bl, bl, bl.' "

11. 2/24/75: *Robin Hood*

In England the real king had left on a crusade. His evil brother Prince John was ruling the land. Robin Hood had left his home with his friends and had gone off hiding in Sherwood Forest. Prince John was taxing the heart and soul out of the people. I don't mean one penny a day, I mean a hundred pieces of gold a day. Robin Hood stole back the money. The more money Prince John took the more he lost.

One day Sir Guy of Gismen met Robin Hood. And Robin Hood's slave killed the royal deer. Sir Guy of Gismen said, "I see your friend killed the royal deer." Robin Hood said, "He didn't kill him, I killed him." Sir Guy was about to clobber Robin Hood when Robin Hood took out a bow and arrow, and Sir Guy and his men rode away.

Then Sir Guy said, "Prince John will hear about this at my meeting." At Sir Guy's meeting he told Prince John. Then Prince John said, "Why did you not kill this fellow?" "For he had a bow and arrow." Prince John asked, "What was this fellow's name?" Sir Guy replied, "Robin Hood of Locksley." Prince John said, "I believe I've heard of this fellow."

Then Robin Hood was knocking at the castle door. Prince John said, "Let him in." He came in and said, "Hello Your Grace, hello Your Highness, hello my dear lady." The Pope said, "He should not be here." Maid Mary, with an angry face, said, "Why did you let him in?" Prince John said, "Because he has good sport. Duke of England, give him your seat." The Duke of England said, "But Your Highness, this man speaks treason." Prince John said, "For heaven's sake, let him sit down. Pass him some meat." Robin Hood said, "Will you pay the ransom?" Prince John said, "No I won't." Robin Hood said, "Why not?" Prince John said, "Because I want to be king." Robin Hood coughed up the meat. Prince John said, "Don't you have the stomach for honest meat?" Robin Hood said, "I do, but not for traitors." Prince John said, "You call me a traitor?" Prince John called for his guards.

Robin Hood scaled the castle wall and a guard took an ax from another guard. Robin Hood ran out of the castle and said, "There's a traitor at the door, close the gates quick."

Then they held the gates closed tight. Then finally Sir Guy came to the door and said to the guards, "You dummies."

Robin Hood and his Merry Men rode off. Sir Guy and his men rode after them.

Robin Hood was going to play a trick on Friar Tuck. His men warned him that he was the most dangerous Friar in the country. He could handle a sword like nobody could.

He did the trick, they had a fight and then they were friends. And he did the same with Little John, except not with the trick.

Robin Hood was captured and Maid Marion fell in love with him. Then when going to hang Robin Hood, King Richard returned, made Robin Hood a baron, married him to Maid Marion, Prince John was banished.

12. 3/21/75

Fifteen hundred years ago in the horizon a great pirate ship sailed. The captain's name was Long John Silver. His crew was a drunken crew. One day they spotted the ship. They attacked the ship. The captain stayed on board and he sank the ship. And his crew was so drunk that they put on their bathing suits and swam back to the ship. One was so drunk that he got in his tube and got out his rubber duck. And they all sang, "We all live in a yellow submarine . . . " The last one sang, "Row, row, row your boat . . . " The first one was dancing with a shark. Then he asked, "Are you married?" Then he found out it was a shark and he cried out, "Help, shark! Help, shark!" Then he swam underwater and found a sunken surfboard, and he surfed with the tide. Then one saw a sword fish and they started duelling. When they came back the captain hit each of them on the head. The captain slapped them on the face and they said, "Thanks, I needed that." Then the captain said, "Oh boy."

They were on a course for Treasure Island. They were looking for the map. They found it in a tree. They found the treasure and they went back to the ship and that was the end.

13. 4/18/75

Once there were three little pigs, and they were so messy that their parents decided to move away while they were at school. "Move across the street, they're not allowed to cross the street." When the children came home from school one said, "Something's missing, our furniture." Another said, "Our parents." Then the landlord came knocking at the door. Then the three little pigs said, "Not by the hairs of our chinny chin chin." Then he said, "Let me in or I'll blow the house down." Then he blew the house down.

Then the first one said, "We don't have any money." The landlord said, "I'll eat you up." So he ate him up.

The other one said, "Let's play baseball, landlord." The landlord said, "I'll eat you up." And he ate him up.

The third one said, "I'll show you for eating up my brothers." So he took off the landlord's shoes, which he hadn't taken off in years, and held them up to the landlord's nose. Then he took off the landlord's socks, which he hadn't taken off in years, and held them up to his nose. The landlord fell down dead from the stink.

The moral of the story is, "Walk softly and don't carry a big stink."

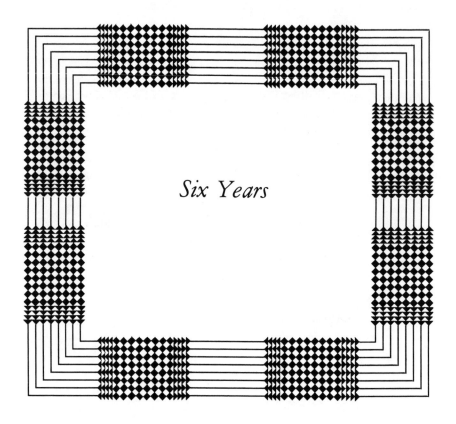

Six Years

Carl

1. *1/9/74*

One night I slept on the floor with my dog Ruff, Ruff. And I was sleeping with my dog on the rug. But the rug started to open and then I went down into a Wonder World. I fell into a bowl of lava. And when I fell into it, I could swim in it and it hurt just a little [he pinches me a little on the arm] and my dog fell in and got burned. And then I jumped in to save him. 'Cept when I got there, it was too late. But then one day I got out of the road and I went into this house across the lake and bats were going around it and the doors were opening and closing and the windows were going like this [he claps his hands together twice]. And I went into this house and I saw a mirror all around me. And then hands started coming out of the mirror and started grabbing my feet and then my hands and they were pulling me. Then I got out of it. Then I went upstairs, but

144

these stairs were creaking and creaking and creaking. And a voice said, "Who goes there?" And I said, "Who is that?" And the voice said, "I'm the goblin of Christmas." And then the monster started coming at me with a green hand, and he touched me, and said, "You're it!" [A boy who is listening to his story says, "I think he was just a friend playing tag."]

2. 1/22/74: Hong Kong Story

Once in Hong Kong there was a man whose name was Ching Kong. He went for a walk, but he had a brother who wanted to kill him. He hid some men where Ching Kong was walking. They had ropes and Ching Kong pulled the ropes out of their hands and there was a fight. There were twenty bad men and Ching Kong. But there was three helpers who offered to help but he didn't want any help. He said, "It's family business. I'll do it myself." So he went out and he saw some of his brother's men. He choked one guy, he jumped on the other guy, he kicked another guy, and he gave another guy a kung fu chop in the back of the neck and killed him. Then Ching Kong went for another walk, and they caught him. But he had long pointed nails, but the bad guys cut off his hands so he couldn't use them. He shot those little nails at those bad guys. He got them in the stomach and he was hurt a little bit. The bad brother got a man that was fat and strong—stronger than Ching Kong. He charged at Ching Kong with his fists and he jumped over a whipping guy that had a whip. Ching Kong won the fight, and all the bad guys were scared of him and they all ran away. The end.

3. 2/4/74: True Story

One day there was a man called Cropsy and he lived five years ago. His wife went crazy so then he decided he would go crazy. But he was worried about his son, so he put his son in a camp. And one day his son tripped over a rock and broke his head open and he went crazy too. And Cropsy went up to that camp and the boys were going swimming and he was hiding behind a tree. And when the boys came to dry themselves off he killed them . . . because he thought the camp had killed his son. But the camp counselor slept in a high hill on the top of the mountain in a tent. And Cropsy went up after him. Cropsy had a knife, a gun, a pistol, and a butcher knife, and a kitchen knife. And he chopped off his toes first. Then he cut his heart open, chopped his tongue off and took his eyes out and used one of the eyes for his eye that had come out. The end.

145

4. 2/15/74

One day, in my camp last summer, the counselor told a scary story about a wolfman that was alive five years ago and he lived right in the cabin that the kids were all in. Now the kids and even I and Ronnie were in that camp, and we loved this counselor. And so the counselor said, "If you don't stay here, I'll open the door where the wolfman is." So all the kids, even me, started running out and some of the kids were hiding under the cabin. Some of the kids were hiding in trees and throwing coconuts down. One of the kids said, "The Dracula strikes again!" And he was pretty fat too. The kids went inside and the counselors were lying down dead, and the door was open where the wolfman was. So the kids went down to the pool and said to the wolfman, "Mr. Wolfman, will you take me for a ride?" So the wolfman said, "See my pinky, see my thumb, see my fist, you better run."

So the kids started running and the wolfman chased them. But the wolfman couldn't run; in fact he couldn't even run at all, because his legs were tied up. And ten of the kids were sneaking in back of the wolfman and they tied his feet up. The wolfman broke out and chased the kids, but they ran twenty-five thousand times as fast as him. And then the kids ran into the nurse's office and the wolfman ran after them. And the wolfman said, "Hello Mrs. Wolfman, would you like a shot?" "Yes!" So me and Ronnie got army rifles and tanks and machine guns and we got all the kids and started shooting from planes and then fifty-thousand, hundred billion, billion, billion, infinity, four hundred, ten hundred million wolfmans started flying in the air!

So then the wolfman said [he makes a chewing sound], "What's up Doc?" Because he got hypnotized and all the other wolfmans got hypnotized and they all fell dead. The end.

5. 4/4/74

A long time ago, there was a black lagoon. This wasn't just any ordinary black lagoon, it had a creature from the black lagoon. His arms were hairy and he had the sharpest nails in the world. They were like a pin point. One day, a man went fishing in the black lagoon and the creature from the black lagoon sneaked behind him and choked out his blood. His nose was bleeding and then he dragged him back to the black lagoon and ate him for dinner.

Then a witch came. Then Frankenstein came. And they were fighting the creature from the black lagoon. And the witch died. Then the two monsters became old buddies and they lived happily ever after. One of them even had a handkerchief to blow his nose. The end.

6. 6/4/74

A long time ago, me and my friend saw this cave and in the cave there was a black, white, green and purple monster. He had black and blue eyes with catsup on them. And we didn't know he was in there. So we made a club house out of the cave and the monster came out and he wrecked our club house up. And we had nitroglycerin. We threw it in the cave with dynamite and then we lit a match and we *flew it in*! The monster blew up.

And his aunts and uncles came over to see what happened and they took over the world. Armies, airforce, rifles, tanks, machine guns everywhere! The monsters could fly, so they needed the airforce. And more monsters came. The lizard man came. The salamander man came. The three-headed monster came. Godzilla came. Frankenstein came. The creature from the black lagoon came.

[A boy interrupts, "Oh, you got those flying monsters from a movie, right?" "No," he answers, adding, "F-u-c-k y-o-u." He spells it out for emphasis.]

And then the scariest monster in the world—stronger than a junkyard dog, badder than old King Kong. I'm talking about bad, bad Leroy Brown; baddest man in the whole damn town. Meaner than a junkyard dog, bigger than an old King Kong. [He's quoting from the song "Leroy Brown" by the late Jim Croce, which the storytaker points out here at the risk of receiving the same reaction as the interrupter did above.] And then Godzilla and King Kong have a fight. I'm talking about bad, bad Billy Jack [the movie *Billy Jack*]. Then I'm talking about good, good Leroy Brown, goodest man in the whole damn town, badder than a Billy Jack, stronger than old King Kong . . .

["What happened to the story?" the storyteller asks him as he sings away.] Ah, let me tell you a story about a man named Charlie who rides the MTA. Let me sing you that song. [He sings it:] Oh, let me tell you a story about a man named Charlie on a bright and soggy day, etc.

7. 9/20/74

This is a true story.

Once I was living in a house up in the country—like a desert. During the night I was up. There was a house people moved out of three or four years ago—like a ghost house, spooky.

I called my friends and we went up to the house . . . and the gate opened by itself . . . no that's not true . . . we opened it. We went up to the house and opened the door. The lights were shut off and we went in and turned on the lights and went up the stairs and went into the bedroom.

We heard a cat go "ah-ooo"; we didn't know what it was and got so scared that we ran down the stairs so fast that the stairs fell down. Someone came out of the stairs. It was a skeleton.

We ran out and to my house and got some sticks and put them in the oven. And took the fire back to the house, and burnt the skeleton.

I asked my friends if they wanted to have a fair with tickets to make money . . . and it'll be our spook house.

We sold tickets and people went into the house. They came out but their hair was standing up. We went away from that house and it got spookier and spookier. And the skeletons came from the grave.

[Here Carl started singing, or rather, chanting:]

Look through my window and saw me asleep
They stuck their hands through
They took my arm and threw me outside.

I was in my room and took my shotgun
and shot 'em through the nose
and they ran away; never to come back otherwise I'd cabam them.

8. *12/4/74*

Once on a ship there was a seal named Salty. He wore a sword and he wore a saddle and he wore a sack and he was the captain of the ship. And there was a whirlpool. They went down and hit a rock in the whirlpool and they came into a land that time had forgotten. And a bunch of cave people rescued them right in the nick of time. Tyrannosaurus rex came and the cavemen took their spears. They set fire onto the spears and they scared the tyrannosaurus rex away. The tyrannosaurus rex got his friends but Salty the seal was very brave. He took his sword and his saddle and his sack and he went out to that tyrannosaurus rex and jumped on his back and stabbed him in the neck. So all the crew went back and took the ship and they wanted to go back to time and get all the people to come back and go look at the place time has forgotten. So the people didn't believe him because they know there is no such place that time has forgotten. So the cops put them in jail. And Salty the seal stayed in the place time has forgotten and had a happy life with the cave people. The end.

9. 2/21/75: *The Planet of the Apes and Company*

Once there was a gorilla named Orko. He was the general of the guards. He made them work like slaves. He never gave them any food. One day they all ran out on him. They stole food from the guardhouse. Then Orko found out. They burnt all of the houses in the planet, they killed all the other guards. They tried to kill Orko but it was too late. The bomb had already blown up. The bomb was planted behind Orko's house. Orko died.

10. 3/21/75: *A Magic Clock*

One day a man bought a clock. But I know what you're thinking now, this wasn't an ordinary clock, it was a magic clock. I'll tell you how this magic clock worked. It fixed every other clock in the world so it was always correct. Like if there was a clock saying one it fixed it so it said three, if it said four he fixed it to say one.

So once upon a time a man come and opened up the clock. He said, "There's something strange here. There's nothing in this clock. No turning vowel, no clutch, no alarm system, no digestive system, no nose, no mouth."

So one day another man came and bought a nose for the clock and put it on. And he bought, ah . . . a face and put it on. So the man opened up that same ol' clock and saw there was nothing in it. He said that's strange. So as soon as the man bought the nose, mouth and face the clock could speak. "I make all the other clocks wrong. Why can't I do anything right?"

So the man put the pieces in [clutch, etc.] so the clock could do everything, eat and drink, etc. So that's how the clock became magic.

11. 6/25/75

One day there was a book about colors. But there was one color missing the book always wanted. One color that it didn't have.

One day the man that owned the book threw it away and a little boy found it. And the little boy was wearing the color that the book always wanted. So then the book felt so happy that it just threw all the other colors out and just put in that one color. Then the little boy threw the book out 'cause it had just one color.

Then the book had another problem. He needed *all* his colors back so another little boy could find him. He had to go all over to look for his colors. Until he saw a little dog that was purple, green, black, white, yellow, orange, brown, black, gold, silver. Then he found all of the colors and put them all back in the book. But there was still one space left. Pink, his favorite color. Ohhhh, that pink!!!

He found the pink! The pink was so happy he just kissed him again and again and again. That's the end of the dumb story.

Clem

1. 11/28/73

Once upon a time there was a Martian with a space ship. He went down to earth. He missed his mother and father a lot. So he said that he wanted to go home. But he couldn't because the temperature wasn't right there. So he went to the country. His mother and father came down to the country and saw him sleeping on a rock. They picked him up and got into the spaceship and they went over and lived happily ever after.

2. 2/3/74

Once upon a time in a castle that was haunted there was an old man and an old woman and two babies just born. When the babies said, "Gaga," the mother wasn't there. When they said, "Gaga" again, the father wasn't there. Next time it was the castle not there. But he was there. The baby went, "Wawa," and he wasn't there. And then the rocking chair disappeared. Then the mother and father came back and the castle came back. Then the rocking chair came back. And they lived happily ever after. But the ghost came and scared the baby and the baby went, "Wawa." The end.

3. 5/22/74

Once upon a time there was a little kittie cat. He hated Rollarman. He went to have a vacation with a little bunny rabbit. The bunny rabbit had pink and white colors. And the kittie had a little red bow. The Rollarman had a fight with the kittie. The kittie won. He stepped on the Rollarman, he scratched him all over. He played a lot with balls. He liked to skip with his best friend the bunny rabbit. He went to his house. It was time for supper. He was just on time. After dinner, he went with his friend the bunny rabbit to play in the park. They played cops and robbers. They were both cops. The Rollarman was a robber. The end.

4.   6/21/74:   *The Bell and the Bird*

Once upon a time there was a bird. That bird had a bell. The bell had a very nice ding dong. Once they were going to school together. And of course the bell goes to music school. Then the bird went to singing school. Then there was a boy. And the boy was big and tough. He wanted to beat the bird and the bell up. Then the bell knocked him on the head. And the boy learned a lesson. The end.

5.   11/18/74:   *Snoopy and the Red Baron*

Snoopy was playing with Charlie Brown and decided not to play with anyone and went to his airplane which is his doghouse and flew it and he saw the Red Baron coming and he shouted, "I'll get you Red Baron," and started shooting his machine gun. The Red Baron said, "You'll never get me," and he [Snoopy] shot him down. Then Snoopy said, "Yippee!" "I got him, I got him, I got him!" and the Red Baron said, "Help!" The end.

6.   12/10/74:   *The War of the Planet of the Apes*

Cornelius and Taylor were running from the gorillas and the orangutans. Cornelius had a wife, her name was Zera. They were chimps. Zaius tried to find them but he never did. The gorillas never found them. One night they found a big treasure. They opened it up and saw Irkus's hat, the general of the army of gorillas and his clothes. Well, Cornelius disguised himself as Irkus in his clothes and hat and put on a mask so he'd look like a gorilla and ran over to Zaius and tricked him and said not to hurt Cornelius and Zera and Taylor. Zaius did not know he was disguised as Irkus. Lucius, his father, who was the biggest boss, said we must kill him, but not hurt Zera or Cornelius, only Taylor. He sent out a band of gorillas with Zaius leading them. Suddenly all of the humans tried to attack all of the apes. But the apes attacked them and shot them and stabbed them. Cornelius took off Irkus's suit and went to Zaius' house. Zaius gave hm a big, big, big dinner, fit for ten million chimps. So they never got him again. The end.

151

7. 2/14/75: *Planet of the Apes versus Count Dracula*

Cornelius was walking in the woods and he saw Count Dracula. He yelled for the soldier apes and Zaius. They all came running and Cornelius said we must get that vampire. So they all jumped on Count Dracula.

Then Cornelius's son came over and bit Dracula on the heel and Dracula yelled, "Help!" and Cornelius shot him. But that didn't work so he stabbed him with a stake in the heart.

Then they took him prisoner and put him in the cell and fifteen gorillas were guarding him. Cornelius said, "Get away gorillas!" and he broke in the jail. He wanted to see what color Dracula's blood was but he had none. Then he said, "It's a monster!" and he killed him. Then six hundred vampires came and fought the gorillas and they were going to kill General Orko, Cornelius and Zaius with a stake until every gorilla was laying down on the floor in the mountains. They were tricking the vampires cause the vampires didn't know they were not dead.

Cornelius yelled, "Now fight like apes!" and they killed every vampire in the whole place.

Then after six years vampires were born and one vampire was left and told them the story and no vampire ever dared to go near the planet of the apes.

8. 5/6/75: *Star Track*

Once there was a starship called the Enterprise. And the captain was Captain Kirk. The first officer was Mr. Spock, the chief Medical Officer was Dr. McCoy, the chief engineer was Mr. Scott. And they were flying over some stars and suddenly a star went up and fell on the bridge. Then the bridge shaked a little and then it went orbiting around a planet and Captain Kirk said, "Beam Mr. Spock and me down."

So they tried to beam 'em down but they couldn't. So they put them in the shuttlecraft and the shuttlecraft crashed on the planet. And Captain Kirk said with his communicator so he could talk to them, "It crashed so we can't get up again!"

Mr. Scott forgot that the beam wasn't working and tried to beam them up. While he was beaming he was almost up but then went back to the planet. Then Mr. Scott remembered and he tried to fix it and he did and he beamed them up. And suddenly, they saw the Klingon ship's head. Then they saw all of it and the Klingon ship started throwing beams at them. But the starship put its head up and shot their beam and knocked the Klingon ship in half and the Klingon ship went running down and crashed on earth.

And then the authorities burned it but they saved the captain of it and put him in prison for the rest of his life without his clothes on so he'd freeze to death. And they put the five hundred air-conditioners on. So he just freezed in an hour and died. Since he was all frozen they put him in the fire and when he melted he realized that he was in a fire and he died.

9. 6/25/75

Once upon a time there was an alligator and he met a frog and the frog was eating an apple. And this worm popped out of it and by accident the frog swallowed it. The alligator took the frog to the doctor and the doctor was an owl. And the doctor said, "All ya have to do is take two of these and you'll be better." [Clem didn't know what two things the frog took when questioned.]

So he took two of those and suddenly the worm popped out of his mouth.

Charles

1. 10/10/73: *Things That Scare Me*

One thing that scares me. On a rainy day, there's a V and it's lightning on the shades. Another thing that scares me is the Pirates' Cove at Rye Beach. When I go to bed, the shades look like monsters.

2. 6/10/74: *The Astronaut*

Once an astronaut went to space. He met a creature. He shot him. He died. The astronaut died. The creature died.

3. 9/31/74

[Taken from a "Star Trek" adventure which Charles saw twice.]

The Bellox Nix invited Kirk, McCoy, and Spock down to the planet. And when they came down they beamed down to the street. And when they were talking two gangsters came over. And they said, "Put you hands on your head and shut up." And then two girls came and they said, "Where's the laundry, we haven't done it in a week." And one of the men said, "Write to Bella." And the girl said, "We did, he sent the letter right back." And then the girls left. And Kirk said, "What does the boss do? Girls aren't safe around here." "If anyone kills them they get arrested."

They went in the building. On top of the door it had a sign which said Bellox Nix Government of Southside Territory of Chicago Mobs. They walked up the steps to the dimly lighted second floor and opened the doors of a big room where Bellox Nix was playing pool. And then Bella said, "Glad to meet you Captain." And then the gangsters took out the phaser he took from McCoy and Bella was about to shoot the phaser and Kirk said, "Don't shoot that, you could break off the wall."

"That good, eh?" "All you have to do is give me about one hundred of these and you can ask me all the questions you want." Then Spock said, "Fascinating, but quite impossible." Spock stepped over to a book, the title was *Mobs of Chicago* and said, "May I ask you where Crackle is?" "How do you know about Crackle?" [asked Bella], "He already knows about him, boss," said one of the gangsters in a stern voice. And Bella said, "Hey, that's the book," and Kirk said, "I know it's a book."

[Commercial]

Kirk entered the room with Spock and McCoy. There were four men playing cards. Kirk said, "That isn't the way earthmen play it." One of the big men playing cards said, "Okay big man, take the cards and show us how it's played!" "If a person gets a jack he slaps it but he doesn't get the card if he's playing on Friday." Kirk made sure that the man's card lay on the floor. "I'll get it," said the man. "No, I'll get it," said Kirk. The man bent down to the floor to get his card. At the same time that he bent down, Kirk put his hands under the table and shoved up. When the man came up he was knocked unconscious. Then Kirk and McCoy went to the building where Bella lived to the room where the pool table was. Bella was not there, but the two gangsters were. Kirk spoke to one of the gangsters, "Give me your uniform." "Hey, wait a minute Kirk," said the other gangster. "I mean you too," said Kirk.

[Commercial]

Kirk and Spock got in the car. Kirk tried the lever in the car which was the way Earthmen started cars. Nothing happened. "Perhaps this lever would work," said Spock. "Press the lever on the floor, I'm sure it will start the car." He pressed the lever, it started; the car went, then it stopped. The car stopped, then it went. The car stopped, then it went. They had went twelve blocks when Kirk put on the brakes. In the street a boy with a cap and a jacket was playing with a knife. The boy stopped playing—"Where'd you get those pointy ears—you look like a vampire or something." "I would advise you to stop talking," said Spock, "It can be quite hazardous." "You sting Crackle and you'll be nudged by every person in the street," said the boy. "But I can fix it for you." "What do you need from it?" said Kirk to the boy. "A piece of the action," said the boy. "You don't even know what the action is about," said Kirk.

Then the boy ran right into the street waving the knife around. His father and another gangster were guarding the doors of Crackle's house. He ran up the stairs to them, but then fell down on the platform on the top of the steps. And he said, "Daddy, daddy, I hurt myself. Daddy, daddy, I hurt myself." "What'd they do to you?" asked Kirk, running up the steps with Spock. "Hey listen," said one of the gangsters. Spock gave the gangster a Vulcan neck pinch. Wearily the gangster fell down. He and Spock ran in. Then Crackle and a woman appeared on the stairs. "Well," said Crackle, "I was wondering how I could get you back. And now you deliver yourselves right back to me!"

[Commercial—continued 10/5/74]

Bellox Nix was sitting in a chair. Spock was pointing a machine gun at him. A man was beamed down, "Mother," he said and handed some money over to Spock. "Hey Captain, that ain't bad," said Bella. "Watch out where you're talking," said Spock.

A lot of the gangsters and other people were standing around the room. It was crowded. Kirk was talking when one of the men in a terrified voice screamed. All of the people rushed to the window. Dr. McCoy went, too. One of the gangsters pushed him aside. "I'm standing here," he said.

Two torpedoes came down on the old time cars. Then three more came. Then four came. Kirk opened his communicator. "Shut your damn communication device," said one of the men, not knowing what it was called. "Well, at least can't I say goodbye?" asked Kirk. He licked his lips. "Fire phasers," he said. They fired phasers. Two men fell to the ground. They were leaning on cars. "Oh no!" said one of the men. "They're not dead, they're just unconscious," said Kirk. "But they could be dead if we wanted them to."

The men went back to the table. Kirk climbed back in. "Now where were you?" said one of the men. "He was talking about the Federation," said someone. "No I wasn't," said Kirk. Bella interrupted. "Listen, we can't get things arranged around here. With a boss like you we could get many things arranged." "Oh no," said Kirk, "Bella, you would be the boss. Crackle, you would be his assistant." And pointing to another man he said, "You can be a security guard."

[Commercial]

Kirk and Spock were on the *Enterprise*. They were not in the gangster's suits anymore. "Well at least we don't have any problems," said Kirk. "The question is," said Spock "I would like to know how you would explain to Starbase that every year you are sending a shuttle craft to collect the planet's cut."

"Jim, I don't know how serious this is," said McCoy. "What, Bones?" said Kirk. There was a brief silence. "I left my communicator in Bella's office." "Where?" asked Kirk. "I'm not exactly sure," said McCoy, "but I think it was in one of his drawers." McCoy began to argue with Spock. "Please," said Kirk, "Gentlemen, we had a war, let's not start another one." Kirk smiled, but the *Enterprise* just sailed away. The end.

4. 11/26/74: *The Deserted West*

Kirk and Spock were on the *Enterprise*. Uhura turned around in her chair. "Captain," she said, "I'm not picking up Star Fleet, but gun bullets." Kirk said, "Scott, you have the con. Spock and I are beaming down." They went to the transporter room, Scott followed them. Kirk and Spock walked onto the transporter platform and then they were beamed down.

On the planet there was a lot of gas. The gas was up to their boots. There was a lot of squares up in the air. But suddenly one of the squares got coloring. The minute it got all colored it said a word. Then the next square was colored yellow and said another word. At last all ten of the squares were colored. But after eight of them had lighted up and colored like fire crackers, the two others did not color. And this is what they said, "You are caused responsible for the death of all us color psychs. We are going to choose a time and a place and a special kind of danger for you." "We come in peace" said Kirk.

"Click, click, click," and then there was a "One, two, three." There was no more gas. But there was a tall house. Passing the house there was a tall man. He had a diamond necklace around his neck and around his hat which gentlemen usually wear, striped trousers, and some brown shoes. He was holding a gun in his hand and chasing a banker. It was the Sundance Kid. Suddenly the banker fell down in a cactus bush. Kirk had ducked. "Spock, is this a duplicate of history?" "I don't know," said Spock, "all I know is that if we walk into a restaurant for food just in case Butch Cassidy is there I think you had better sit down without moving a muscle." "I'm getting hungry now," said Kirk. "This place does look deserted." "Well, we can always beam up," said Spock. "And what do you propose to beam up with?" asked a stern voice. Kirk turned around. There on the steps of the tall house stood Butch Cassidy and the Sundance Kid. But the Sundance Kid did not have his pistol anymore. Butch Cassidy had his. "I'll get mine," said the Sundance Kid. Kirk tried to fire his phaser. It had gone dead. Butch Cassidy shot two bullets. On the last bullet Kirk fell down. He looked around for Spock, but he was gone. He walked back into the house. Above him on a branch in a tree, Spock was hanging, watching all the time. Then after he had walked into the house and Spock was safe, he let go and jumped to the ground. He took Kirk with both hands and dragged him to a cave.

[Commercial]

After he had gotten cold water he brought it back to the cave. He had dumped half the water into Kirk's mouth when he heard horses galloping. Butch Cassidy jumped off his horse. Spock knew that there would probably be a hole on the other side. He climbed up to where Butch Cassidy was. Butch Cassidy sighed. At that moment, Spock had jumped off the top. Butch Cassidy turned around. Spock jumped over him as he turned and gave him a Vulcan neck pinch. He went into the cave only to find Kirk had gotten well again. He was perfectly fine. Spock told him to get out of the cave. Then he showed him the knocked out Butch Cassidy. "Your uniform, Captain. Now pretend that you have caught me and when you ride say nasty things about me. Sneak your pistol out of your holster and try to shoot some of the people. I will take one of their uniforms."

The Sundance Kid was sawing a piece of wood. Kirk was riding. "Hi, my old buddy." He took out his gun and sneaked out a bullet. He fell to the ground. Spock jumped off and took his uniform, but his horse was missing. Suddenly Kirk said, "Look." There was the Sundance Kid's horse neighing in terror. He had seen the exchange for the clothes. "We'll have to spend a long time persuading him that you're the Sundance Kid," said Kirk.

An hour later the horse thought that he was really the Sundance

Kid. "Butch Cassidy must have recovered from his rest," said Kirk. "At five o'clock it will be logical for him to kill us," said Spock.

[Commercial]

Two hours later it was five o'clock. Spock put his face next to Kirk's. "Our minds are the same. The bullets are not real. We will stay alive." They walked over to a fence. They could see Butch Cassidy and the Sundance Kid with their guns walking towards them. They were just about to pull back their trigger when there was a loud noise, "Click, click, click." Then, "One, two, three." Then they were back on the *Enterprise*. Kirk found him back in the bridge. "Turn on the screen," he said to Mr. Scott. Scott turned on the screen. There were a lot of squares on the screen along with dark space. They were all colored up. "That time and place and certain kind of danger was not very dangerous. But I will destroy you, I will destroy you!" Kirk licked his lips, "Fire phasers," he said. The squares disintegrated. "Mr. Scott take the *Enterprise* out of orbit. We're going back to earth." The end.

5.   4/11/75

A spaceship was going past a planet. It was sending off rays. The ship's shields were shielding the rays but one of the shields was broken. There were 561 crew on this space ship and the rays were going through the broken shield. Five people were killed. The gas was coming through the engineering room. It upsetted six of the engines. There was eleven engines in the whole engineering room. The engineering man fixed up two of them. They did not find out that the gas was spreading on the spaceship until they found eleven thousand pounds of it were on the space ship but by then it was too late. Seven men went down to the planet with the rays. They turned it off. But rays were coming in at different directions. They destroyed half of the whole space ship. They destroyed half of the engineering room. There were eleven engines in all. There were only eight left. Two of the most important engines were destroyed but the ship did not notice. They did not know the ship was changing course. It was in twenty thousand hours it would be at the rays. Two hours passed. Thirty hours passed. Ninty-nine hours passed and they had ten hundred hours left. The astronauts on the planet did not see the ship going away. Then they noticed it was too late. They knew that they could not get back to the ship now. In two hours they were starving. The next day at eight o'clock a beast on the planet killed them. Finally the space ship discovered that they were going toward the rays. Meanwhile on the ship some men were talking. The Atlantic beast must have killed them they said. "What's the Atlantic beast?" asked one of the crew members. The Atlantic beast has claws and ivory teeth. He is worse than Moby Dick. He could turn his body as flame and he could turn over this whole space ship with just his back and burn it. The worst part of it all he hates men with astronaut suits. "I'm going to the engineering room," said the engineer. He was picking up readings of the beast. He could not figure out what it was so he did not know its danger. He kept on staring at the readings but he stared too long. The rays were going into his body. He was becoming one of the beasts. He could not survive it. The rays were killing him. An hour later he was dead. There was exactly eleven hours till the ship entered the rays. Eight hours passed. There were two hours before the ship entered the rays. It had entered the rays. One of the men survived. The last survivor of the ship did not want the mission to succeed. He disconnected the computer. The computer told the ship all the information it needed. He wanted to spoil the mission. Before he could disconnect anything else he was transformed into a house on earth. He walked into another room. He felt like he was floating in space. He saw the star shining and then he was dead.

6. *4/18/75: Special Flight*

A space ship is a big thing that goes in space. This space ship was going to Jupiter. There were only thirteen men on it. There was a Quangle-Wangle, an Elephante-Sante and an Orang-utan Sang-utan, a Monkey da Donkey and a Stupid Woopid and there were the So-On-Low-Ons. When they got to Jupiter the Orang-utan Sang-utan played cards with the Monkey da Donkey. The Monkey da Donkey got an O-C-Rang on his card and the Orang-utan Sang-utan go a So-See-Sang-See-Tang. When they finished playing cards they beamed down to Jupiter. The Orang-utan Sang-utan beamed down to a jungle on Jupiter. So did the Monkey da Donkey. The Stupid Woopid beamed down to the sky and his leg got stuck in a cloud and the Orang-utan Sang-utan climbed up a tree and reached up to get him down. Since the Orang-utan Sang-utan had reached up to get him down and since he only had three hands to hold on to the tree (an Orang-utan Sang-utan needs four hands to climb up a tree) he lost his balance and fell in a thorn bush and his pants got stuck in a thorn bush. The Elephante-Sante beamed down and when he saw the Orang-utan Sang-utan stuck to the thorn bush he went over and pulled and tried to pull him out. A few feet away there was a tree with some glue on it. He stretched so hard that the Orang-utan Sang-utan pushed him so he'd get off the thorn bush. The Orang-utan Sang-utan pushed him so hard that he pushed him a few feet away into the tree and the Elephante-Sante got stuck on the tree. The Monkey da Donkey beamed down and saw the Orang-utan Sang-utan stuck to the thorn bush and this is what he did. He pulled and he pulled on the thorn and he had such a tight grip that his nails, sad to say, got stuck in the thorn bush. Then the So-on-Low-On beamed down with some scissors. He cut the thorn which were holding the Orang-utan Sang-utan. Then he gave the scissors to the Orang-utan Sang-utan and the Orang-utan Sang-utan climbed up the tree with the glue in his hand and then he went down inside the tree and cut the point which had the glue and the Elephante-Sante fell down in the tree then the Orang-utan Sang-utan spent two hours trying to get him out and on the third hour he finally, leary deary, got him out. Then the Orang-utan Sang-utan climbed up the tree to where the Stupid Woopid was stuck in the cloud. He cut the cloud in half and the part that he cut fell down to the ground. They cut the cloud into pieces and the Stupid Woopid got free. The Orang-utan Sang-utan went over to the thorn bush with his scissors and cut the thorn bush. Now the Monkey da Donkey was so frantic that he was pulling really hard and when the Orang-utan Sang-utan cut the thorn bush he went rolling over and over and bumped into a tree. He bounced off the tree and went high in the air. The Orang-utan Sang-utan was standing near the tree. All of a sudden the Monkey da Donkey fell on top of him and the Orang-utan Sang-utan did not know what had happened to him. When he got off the Orang-utan Sang-utan they beamed back up to the space ship. They went back to earth and beamed down in the jungle, and the Orang-utan Sang-utan and all his friends will be back with more adventures in another book.

7. *4/25/75*

One day the Orang-utan Sang-utan was walking with the Stupid Woopid. The Stupid-Woopid saw an airplane. He went inside. He pressed a lot of buttons. When he pressed one button the airplane was not on the ground anymore. The Orang-utan Sang-utan climbed up a tree and reached out for the airplane and poor Orang-utan Sang-utan was holding on for dear life to the airplane. Meanwhile inside the Stupid Woopid looked out the window. He wanted to get a closer look. Suddenly he wasn't on the airplane anymore. The Orang-utan Sang-utan jumped off and the Stupid Woopid and the Orang-utan Sang-utan went to the space ship and got ready for another space voyage. The end.

Deirdre

1. *11/9/73*

Once upon a time there was a bear. The bear was unhappy because he was
jumping on rocks. And once he was not very happy because he couldn't
find a rock to jump on. He found something he was hunting for. He tried
to get away. He got stung. So he found some honey in a can. He saw a
man who set the trap with it. But he didn't go near. He jumped with it
and stuck his head in. He tried to get away from the bees. The man did
not help him; he was scared of bears.

2. *9/30/74*

Once upon a time there lived a little mouse. He sniffed a lot with his little whiskers and pink ears and tail. He could run very fast with his pink
feet front and back and then he could fool the children at school. He
went to P.S. 3 day and night and Kathy wrote about him. [Other
children were playing with the class mouse in the room.]

One day he was walking out of the school and he smelled a yucky
smell because the children had bottles with spoiled food in them. [Also
in room.]

One day Mouse heard fourteen bells in the school—ding, ding,
ding, ding, ding, ding, ding, ding, ding, ding and five more after ding,
ding, ding, ding, ding. A fire! He was crawling in the flames under the
table back and forth [she crawls under table] until his legs would not go
another feet. His feet were prickly like in the summer in the morning
when the grass is wet. He found some bread on the floor and some jam.
He said, "What could it be?" He sat and thought and thought and
decided it was jam on toast for breakfast. Yummy, yummy I must call the
grocery store. The bread was toasted by the fire.

One day the mouse was walking and found fourteen gallons of jam
and fourteen loaves of bread. He ate it all up and got very fat, but he
loved it. He started walking again, very glumpy and full.

He lived for fourteen thousand million trillion days after that
without getting sick and two times a day he ate that much and one day he
got so full from eating fourteen plus thirteen loaves and twenty-four
times jam, he just died!

His aunts and uncles and cousins were not alive to put flowers on his
grave. Russia wasn't there, China wasn't there, even the U.S.A. wasn't
there. The end.

[Storytaker: Draw the most exciting part of the story.
Deirdre: The picture is about when he ate all the jam.]

3.   10/4/74

Once upon a time there lived a little boy and he lived in a land called
Loggadoggajogga. In Loggadoggajogga, little boys had long noses and
they looked like a pretzel and they could even write with them. The little
boy went to school and the teacher told him to write a story. The little
boy used his nose to write and the teacher thought it was very strange.
Then the little boy, Mr. Glue, said, "I will take my nose and find a piece
of paper and a bottle with a top and will write on it and throw it in the
water so I will be rescued from Loggadoggajogga because it is burning up
in two pieces." Then the people got in a boat and went zoom so fast that
they drowned in hot bubbling lava. They were dead, dead, dead, and
med.

Then the little boy went home pushing a chair with his nose sticking
out. He thought he would die so he got up on the chair to keep his feet
out of the lava. His nose got him in so much trouble he asked the teacher
to cut it off. Then he grew duck wings and he couldn't wear his clothes,
dresses or pants, he could swim in hot lava and it didn't hurt him. Then
he got tired of being a duck so he asked the teacher to cut him all off so
he became a parrot and he was beautiful blue. He asked the teacher to cut
him off again and he changed to a fuzzy long-maned lion, but he looked
funny so he asked to be cut off again and he became a chair. The kids
were bouncing on him because he was a chair that talked so the kids cut
him off and he became a bird and flew to his mother who he told, "I was
a person, a parrot, a lion, a chair." His mother cut him off and he got a
duck wing and a parrot wing, lion's hair and feet, a duck beak, a parakeet
beak and a lion's mouth. He looked crazy. He was named the king, the
people started cutting off themselves, but they didn't get as pretty as
him. Duck-Parakeet-Bird-Lion flew over with his funny wings. "Cut me
off and I shall make you better," said the old king, "Won't it hurt
you?" He said, "I got cut off for a lion, a bird, a parakeet. . . . " He
turned to a rabbit and then he asked the king not to change him
anymore, because he liked being a rabbit.

4.   10/11/74

[handwritten by child]

Captr 1. The mouse from outer space.
The mouse that came from outer space.

Hi! I'am the mouse from the other world in Joopatre. [Teacher corrected spelling.] Jupiter is a fasanting world in Jupiter I go ear skating but there are dajrs [dangers] too. Like when you are skating you might slip and you could break a bone and I would think you would die. So in Jupiter be careful because you can hurt hoursalf. Also in Jupiter you can go slipiripring but I wood think that you wook hate yoursalf so be carflle thats the sakind time that I told you abot darnjer so stil be cafl in Jupiter. [Teacher stopped correcting after Jupiter.]

Captr 2

Okay now lots got too sam Iksiing [exciting] parts of my umfandrs [she didn't know what word that was] hmmmmm lat my think . . . ow yes I was a sals men in the odin das. I sled [selled] hats and othr clothing. Than one day I want to got pad [paid] one they sad toy canot gat bad [and they said that I cannot get paid] becas you do not wrk a nofe. [because you do not work enough.] One day mues [mouse] was walking in the farist and he saw a brd [forest, bird] and stop to lok. Lok at it, he stard and stard intil hes eyes got sore and than he want on woking [went on walking].

Captr 3 Going to the moon.

Muse want to the meeon. mues was going to the moon frst muse had to go to the rbit and than he staterd the motr [started the motor] eand was on hes way to the moon and when he got thar he saw so buetiyefol moon he was glad he came that he livd ther for many years and so som buty for thengs and wan he got bak an the rth he faut strang bat aftr a fuw awrs he falt got agan and but one day he falt ille and for many mor das and wiks he dad and one day he did sarow kam [and when he got back on the earth he felt strong but after a few hours he felt good again but one day he felt ill and for many more days and weeks he died]. [Big] THE END

5. *11/22/74*

Once upon a time, in a land called Green there lived lots and lots of green rabbits and the land was green like the rabbits. Popcorn was green.

One day a very, very old rabbit was walking in front of a house. He saw the house move. He saw the house jump and bump. He got scared of a bull that pulled the house. So he jumped on the house and the bull did too. So did the house so where were you?

I was on top of the rabbit which was on top of the frog which was on top of the horse which was on top of the car which was on top of the Indian which was on top of the ground.

So the house went on with the bull chasing him and he would rather not be there and I would rather not be there either. So where shall I be, here or there, I think I must be where I want to be. I'll be in the sea, I'll fit in a fish but I won't let him eat me, I'll be a fish. So he swam and he paddled and he splashed and he paddled some more until his legs could just go another inch.

He was surprised to see many living things under the water. He saw many fish, a frog, a turtle. The turtle always bothered him. He saw a doggy swimming in the water to get his bone to drop and he called out to that dog.

He knew how to speak dog language and animal so he talked to the frog and turtle. (If I cough don't put it in.) [Deidre had just gotten some paperback books and she was leafing through them.]

One day he said, ''I think I don't want to be here. I'm tired of talking animal language and doing what everyone else does under the sea.''

One day he saw a little lion walking by. He said, ''What is your name?'' ''Well, my name is Tiggy, what is yours?'' [has lion hand puppet] ''My name is Georgy,'' said the ghost. ''Where are you going?''

''I'm looking for someone to play with.'' ''Will you play with me?'' ''Yes, but I'm not very real.'' ''That's okay I'm not either, I'm only paper.'' [She sings a song—''Miss Merrimac:'']

Miss Merrimac, mac, mac
All dressed in black, black, black
With silver button, button, button
All down her back, back, back
She asked her mother, mother, mother
For fifteen cents, cents, cents
To see the ants, ants, ants
Jump over the fence, fence, fence
They jumped so low, low, low
They stubbed their toe, toe, toe
They never came back, back, back
To Cucumbo, bo, bo

Miss Lucy had a baby
She named him Tiny Tim
She put him in the bathtub
To see if he could swim
He drank up all the water
He ate up all the soap
He tried to eat the bathtub
But it wouldn't go down his throat

Miss Lucy called the doctor
The Doctor called the nurse
The nurse called the lady with the alligator purse
The measles said the Doctor
The mumps said the nurse
Nothing said the lady with the alligator purse
A penny for the Doctor
A penny for the nurse
A dollar for the lady with the alligator purse

"Let's play some more." "All right, Tiggy, what shall we play next?" "How about playing ring around the rosy?" "Yeah" [sings ring around the rosy.] "Let's do it again" [repeats]. "Let's play climb the wall." "Neat, climbing up the wall, one, two . . . [sings and makes up words]. "Sliding down the fence, one, two, three, four, five. Down again we go together." "Let's play look alike." [She sings song:]

I have a pink nose
You have a blue one
I have yellow hair
You have a purple one
We have some curly hair.

Dumpy dumpling sat on a wall,
Dumpy dumpling had a great fall
All the kings horses and the
kings dumplings couldn't put
dumpling together dumpling

[She keeps singing, making up lyrics.]

"Let's play scary look alike—yeah."

One is a lion
Two is a tiger
Three is a ghost
And four is a goblin
Five is a witch
And six is a monster
And seven is a great big pumpkin head
Eight is a scary thing
Nine is a big thing
Ten is a thing I will not know
But do you know your numbers?

165

Yes, I do—Ten, nine, eight, seven, six, five, four, three, two and
one.
Now, how about again
Let's go down one more time—one, two, three, four, five, six,
seven, eight, nine and a ten.

[She goes up and down stairs as she sings.]

"Let's go have a chocolate cream sundae—yeah." "Let's go and
play with the bulls." "Yeah." "Oh-oh, I'm dead." "So am I—goodbye
and that's the end of our story."

6. *1/30/75: Cheerful the Little Mouse by Deirdre*

[handwritten by child]

Cheerful was a littel mous that livd dawn the lan in a hawl!! Insid a had
to cars and a tabil far plats and far cups and far sasars. He had a bad and a
blankit and plow. He had a kicin and a dask with a car! Outsid in the bak
he had a gardin and a sin that sad do not entor and in the front outsid he
had a sin that sad cirful cas that was hes nam.
    Cirful ha frands at he was stil happy far he had aloot avrything he
wantid and day he sad to him salf I wad lik to hav a car a mous sis car a rad
one with blow fanders and 4 sits. Wal Cheerful that abawt this far a fuw
das and fawn it was to bad he cad not hav a car ow boy he was so unhappy
he ha naver bin so unhappy in his lif! Then the hal yer he was draping
arawnd the haws he was so anhappy! Then it was nit and he want draping
into his bad and san he fal aslip in bad The and of cheerful the littel
mous.

7. *1/30/75: A Berthday Book for a 8 yer old cild!*

[Pictures on cover with labels—things to open, party hats, things to pop
and play with, blowers. Handwritten by child.]

Hary Hary I am 8 today. I am haveng a party today today and all hav
funn blowing the blowers and eting kcac and waring the party hats and
poping balowns and opining the prssants. (Pictures 1 Blosing the blosers,
2. eting kak, 3. and waring party hats, 4 opening the prisints) But bst of
all having so mac fann then wan all the kids go I can hav so mac fan! And
then my mater wad say tim to go to bad and I wad say I do not wannt to
and sh wad say cam on and we wad hav to go the end of a Berthday Book
for a brthday cild.

8. 4/7/75

Once upon a time a tree lived in the forest. He liked the birds and sparrows and the other trees and the flowers and the nice cool grass below him.

But he'd rather have someone to talk to. He thought about this for a few days and thought he shouldn't be a baby about it, and [Deirdre laughs] soon closed his sleepy eyes and soon was fast asleep.

In the morning he said, "Birdy, birdy, I want to play with you." "Oh no, how could a little bird like me play with a big and ugly tree like you."

"I am not so ugly. I'll say you, you dumbell birdy. I'll say you might as well skate and live by yourself 'cause you're seven weeks old now.

One day a man came with a big saw and sawed the poor lonely tree up for firewood. The end.

[Comments: Deirdre was very talkative and animated during the storytelling session. While telling the story she sat cross-legged on top of a desk. She wanted to write the story out by herself. She told the story very dramatically, almost acting out all of the parts. She spent some time thinking about the story before she put it down on paper herself. She seemed to enjoy the experience very much and laughed at several points during the story.]

9. 6/9/75

Once upon a time there was a guinea pig. His name was Butterscotch and he was a very naughty guinea pig. And one day he got out of his cage and his owners got very worried, and he didn't get to eat for four days. But one day Butterscotch's owner found him and he didn't run away again. But one day they were going on a trip and he wouldn't come out of his cage because he didn't want to go into that other cage. So it was a problem and he squeaked and squeaked until he was out of breath and he got very, very tired so they took the other cage instead of that other cage. He was happy in that new country, of course he'd never been there before, but he got used to it fast. A week later they had to go back to their old country and he got bored there. It was very boring in that old place but it was alright for him, but he didn't like it at all and he ran away again even though he said he wouldn't run away again. This time he didn't get to eat for 14 days. But one day, he found another guinea pig and said, "What is your name?"

"My name is Black Butt." After a while, they were friends and he introduced him to his mother and he recognized something and said, "That's my mom! And where is the other guinea pig?"

"You mean my brother?"

"I remember you, you're my brother Butterscotch."

"Yes!"

His mother's name was Tanner. Tanner said, "Butterscotch, you're home!"

She was very happy to see him home again. The end.

10. 4/12/76

Once upon a time there lived a bunny rabbit named Muffin. Muffin was a white, fluffy rabbit and Muffin loved to hop around the trees.

One day Muffin decided to take a walk away from her family. So she did. She took a long, long walk, far away and she got lost. She met a hungry, old fox. And he said, "Ya better scat before I eat you like a rat!"

So Muffin did and she ran as far as she could until she pooped out. It was getting cold and dark and she thought she better get home. So she started hippity hopping along the dark, steep, scary roads trying to get home. She didn't even get half way 'til she bumped into that fox again.

"How dare you meet me again!" he screamed. "Why'd you follow me?" "But I didn't," she said. "I just happened to have met you." "So that is," the Hawk says. "If you meet me again," he said, "I'll drag you to my den and eat you like a rat, like I said!" "Oh dear," she screamed. And scared she hippity hopped away.

So she was going along very cheerfully now, hoping she wouldn't meet that nasty old fox, until she met something else. When she met that thing around the tree it wasn't exactly around it, it was sort of up. It was a scary looking hooting owl. The hooting owl was going, "Wwhhhhhhhhooooooo, wwhhhhhhhhoooooo," with its big eyes wide open.

The bunny thought, well, owls are supposed to be very wise. Maybe I'll just hippity hop away and he won't see me. So she hippity hopped away and the owl, luckily, didn't see her.

So she was making her way again happily—hopefully—and then met something else. A lion sprang out from one tree. She was hoping he wasn't chasing her. Well, he wasn't. The lion was just chasing a poor, little, old field mouse.

Muffin decided she'd better take a rest before getting home. So she cuddled up in a little hole in a big oak tree. "Wwwhhhhhhhhooooo, Wwwhhhhhhhooooo," an owl cried. She didn't like it. She decided she needed some comfort in her little hole. So she went for a little hay. Brang it back and slept on it cheerfully.

After a while she decided she shouldn't sleep, she should go. Then she decided she should sleep not go. So she decided that from both things she was arguing the best thing was to go. So she was on her way again.

She was almost home when she met that fox.

"Oh, oh," she said. "Oh please Fox, I don't want to be eaten so please let me go home and I'll never harm anyone that you want to eat ('cept for me)."

"All right", said the fox, "but this is the last time."

So she said, "Thank you big, old, nice, gray fox, see you sometime again hope-notfully!"

She got home and everyone was asleep 'cept for her Mother who was crying because her poor little Muffin was gone. She ran up and said, "Mommy, mommy I'm back!" And she told her the whole story.

Denise

1. *11/2/73*

Some boys were playing baseball. A man came and said they couldn't play there. "Why can't we play, we're in our own backyard." "Okay, I never knew it was your backyard."

Then mother came home and said it was time to come and play inside because it was going to rain. So they came in and played inside. Later they went out. Played more baseball.

2. *11/12/73*

Once there was two bears. And they went to the country and they got a country house and they went swimming. Once they went swimming and they got lost. And there was a nice whale that picked them up and brought them back to their house. Then he said, "Goodbye," and asked them next time if they got lost to come with him to his house. And they went to his house next time they got lost and lived happily ever after. And they got rid of their country house and went to live in the whale's house. The end.

3.   *12/8/73*

Once upon a time there was a robot, and he could do magic. When he was near someone he got very scared so he found out a way to make magic with his head. And when he made magic his head would go down inside his body. And everyone would get scared because he looked like a monster with no head. And one day he found another monster that could do the same thing as him.

4.   *12/8/73:   From a Hardy Boys Book*

Once there was two boys, Frank Hardy and Joe Hardy. One was fifteen and the other was nineteen years old. And once they were going to this house in the country, and their Aunt Gertrude was scared of this guy in the woods. And they went in the woods where their father was 'cause there was this house and this old man who was kind of crazy. Then he (the crazy guy) was getting very, very crazy. And the Hardy boys weren't getting scared. They were getting unscared. And then the crazy man showed them his laboratory; and then Frank and Joe Hardy went with the man . . . then they followed him to the laboratory. And in this laboratory Frank and Joe saw this electric thing and it looked like a tree but it wasn't. And then they started to go up like they were in an elevator. And when they got all the way up the thing stopped and they were in the top of the house. And they explored. And then the Hardy boys found an electric elevator and went down to the man's laboratory—he was sleeping in the laboratory. Then they (Frank and Joe) asked the man to look around—(he said) "But you have to come with me if you want to explore." And they went with the man. And they found the tree and the tree was growing by electric wires. And then the man brang them two chickens made eggs by electric; and there was electric in the air—lightning. And then they heard a big kaboom, and found out that the kaboom was from all the electric stuff. Machines going . . .

Frank and Joe left the house, and said goodbye to the man . . . and the man came with them to their house. And they go home and the man has all his luggage and clothes 'cause he is going to sleep over. And the father comes home and they introduce him to the man. Then they go to sleep.

The next morning they get up and go for a walk and the man talks about his life. And they go back to his house. The man tells them to go to bed. The next morning the man finds some people and traps them. He puts them in the basement. Then after a while the boys hear the man calling them 'cause he was fighting with the men in the basement. The

old man gets a cut in his head. He feels better after cutting his head
'cause he was crazy. Now he gets better because of the blow on the head.
Then he tells about his life and they let him stay at their house because he
didn't like his old house all alone in the country—nobody liked him . . .
everyone thought he was weird and was scared of him. And then the boys
let him stay at their house. And the Hardy boys got a medal and they all
lived happily ever after.

5. *12/2/74*

Once upon a time there was a dog and he loved jumping and playing.
One day he was jumping and playing so much that he forgot where he
was going and he bumped into a tree. And it seemed like the tree had
said, "Ouch," and the dog said, "I didn't say ouch," and the tree said,
"I said ouch, you bumped into me," and the dog said, "Who said
that?" and the tree said, "I said that," and the dog kept on saying,
"Who said that?" He didn't know that trees could talk of course. Then
another little dog came along and said, "What's the matter?" and the
first dog said, "I don't know who said ouch." And then the other little
dog said, "I bet I know who said ouch. The tree did!" And the first little
dog said, "That can't be. Trees don't talk." And the tree said [deep
voice], "They can't?" And the first little doggie said, "Who said that?"
And the tree said, "I did." And the other little doggie said, "Yeah, the
tree did." And the first little doggie said, "I don't believe you," and the
other little doggie said, "Let's go up and see if the tree said it." So they
climbed up the tree and they fell inside the trunk through a squirrel hole.
But they had fun in there because they could play around and scream and
yell as much as they want. And no one ever saw those two little doggies
ever again. And they lived happily ever after inside the tree. The end.

6. *4/11/75*

Once there were two dogs and their names were Mimi and Tasha and one
day Mimi and Tasha went into the forest with Tanya and they played in
the trees and when they were playing in the trees Tasha got stuck in one
and Mimi and Tanya got her out. The end.

7. *4/18/75: Another Adventure of Mimi and Tasha and Tanya*

One day Tasha and Mimi and Tanya were walking in the forest. It was a
very hot day and the sun was so hot that it made them hot even when

they were walking under the trees and they kept on walking 'til they came to the middle of the forest and they found a farm in the very, very middle of the forest and they went in the farm and there were two people inside and the people gave them all a drink of water and the people's names was Jim and Ruth Bradley and they lived there for three weeks and they had a lot of fun. When they had to leave they were all very sad but still they knew they had to go when they met Tanya's mother and father they ran to them and they got into bed 'cause they were so tired and Tanya's father read the Hardy Boys and they went to sleep. The end.

8. 5/2/75: Another Adventure of Tasha, Mimi, and Tanya

One day Tasha and Mimi and Tanya were walking in the forest and they found ten tigers, but the ten tigers were very nice tigers and they made friends and they had fun. After a while Tanya, Tasha, and Mimi had to go home and the tigers said, "Goodbye," and Tanya, Tasha, and Mimi said, "Goodbye," and Mimi, Tasha, and Tanya said, "We had a good time," to Tanya's mother and father, "and we met ten lions and they were nice" and they met the ten lions again the next day and they had just as much fun as they had the day before and they had so much fun that they asked Tanya's mother if they could stay overnight at the lion's house for the night and Tanya's mother said they could.

Doris

1. 10/19/73

Once there was a little girl named Red Riding Hood. Once she went out to give her grandmother some food because she was sick. On the way, she saw a big bad wolf. And he jumped and jumped and jumped. And after he got to granny's house and got dressed like granny. And little Red Riding Hood knocked on the door and granny said, "Come in." Then after little Red Riding Hood said, "What big eyes you have." "The better to see you with my dear." "What a big nose you have." "To smell you with my dear." "What big teeth you have." "To eat you!"

2. 11/28/73

There was a little girl named Jan and she once went out skating. And she fell into a hole and all her friends were helping her. And at last she got

SIX YEARS

out and she went home. She ate supper and she went to bed and her mother kissed her goodnight. The end.

3. *11/28/73*

Once upon a tme there lived a girl named Julie and she had a birthday today [she did at school]. I killed her. I really didn't. I went to jail. I loved it in jail. It's not really true. The truest thing is that she had a party. We ate a lot of candy. And I said, ''Fuck you'' to her. That's the end.

4. *5/19/74*

Once upon a time there lived a girl named Maura. And she always wanted a dog. And her mother said that she can get a dog when she goes to Italy. And she got one. The end!

5. *10/29/74*

Once upon a time there was a kitten and that kitten had a baby kitten. And one day that baby kitten ran away so it got lost. And it died. So it got buried. The end.

6. *11/19/74*

Once upon a time I saw a mummy. And that mummy had some money so he went to hide and that mummy died. So I stoled his money. The end.

7. *11/19/74*

One day it was windy. I went out to play and I saw a cat. That cat was stupid. That cat was so stupid that I walked away from him. The end.

8. *1/31/75*

There was once a little girl that had a dog and that little dog had a little puppy. And that little puppy had a doll. And that little doll had another doll. The end.

9. *1/31/75*

Once upon a time there lived a dog that was very bad. And her owner was very mean, and her child pulled the dog's tail.

10. 1/31/75

There once was a little girl, and that little girl was a very little girl, and that little girl had a very little puppy. And that little girl had a little kitten. And they lived happily ever after.

11. 3/14/75

Once upon a time there was a fart and his name was Farty and he farted all over the place and he had a brother and his name was Farty too and he had a brother and his name was Farty too. He had a sister too and her name was Francesca and she farted all over the place too and his mother and father were named Fartica and Fredica and they all farted around the place and everybody said, "Eh, you smell." The end of the farty story.

12. 3/14/75

Once upon a time there was a girl and a boy. And they lived in a house in a far, far, forgotten corner. And the girl had a dog and the boy had a cat. And the dog and the cat always chased each other around just for fun.

And one day the girl's dog got lost. And so did the boy's cat got lost. And the girl and the boy went out looking for the two pets. Mother said, "It's lunchtime." And the girl and the boy did not hear. At last they found the cat and the dog. And they got home and it was five o'clock. The end.

13. 3/14/75

Once upon a time there was a koala bear and he ran away from his cage. And everybody screamed, "Help! Help!" And the owner said, "Help! Help!" himself. And hunters went looking all around for him. And at last they found him and put him back in his cage. The end.

14. 6/19/75

Once upon a time there was a fart and that fart had a fart. And the fart that had a fart had a fart. And the fart had a fart, fart, fart.

15. 6/19/75

Once upon a time there was a dog. And then the dog got lost. Then the little girl found the dog. Then the little dog had some little puppies. And then the little puppies grew up and then they had some puppies. And then the little puppies grew up and then *they* had some puppies. Etc., etc., etc. The end.

Poem: Here comes Spring
I hear the birds sing
Spring, Spring, Spring.

Seven Years

Eddie

1. 2/20/74

This is how it started. Do you know Michael in our class? He had this monster and was trying to destroy the British. But then the Americans were also trying to destroy it. And the Germans were trying to destroy the sea monster, too. But then the Americans changed their minds. They found out that the British would have been destroyed and even the whole world would have been destroyed by that monster. And then the Americans called up the Germans and the Germans caught the sea monster, because they wanted the world to be all right. And the reason why they wanted to stop the sea monster, because they really wanted to destroy the one on land. So they dropped a hydrogen bomb and the land monster and the sea monster were destroyed. Then they brung it to the museum to make a model of it, using all the bones. And that's the end.

2. 2/20/74

The Americans were attacking the people in India and India thought they should use tanks, so they used tanks. But by accident, they shot some people who were in a balcony instead. So the people in India said, "The only thing to do is to go through our escape hatch and go through the tower and then we fire our rays 'til we run out of rays. Then we start shooting our guns and then we have to reload. But we have a lot of bullets. But also if our other ray breaks, Rajah has another ray still, even though that ray still isn't as strong. But one of them has a shield. That's the only problem. So we have to make a robot. Why don't we try to make a robot in our laboratory?"

So the next morning the robot was finished. "Now," said the captain, "we have to give the robot a name. Why don't we call him "Monstra". We better measure him first and give him also a shield so he won't melt." While Rajah and all the other people fired rays and bullets, "And just in case, give the robot a solar-charged battery, so he'll never run out." And um, the next morning they made some controls for the robot and then the robot was finished and then they sent the robot out. And the robot destroyed one of the planes. But he couldn't destroy the one with the shield. In the nighttime, while the Americans were asleep, the captain said, "Let's attack America at night, because of course they won't be awake. Because they'll be tired and asleep. But just in case, we better bring some tanks and battleships."

Then there was this giant horn and they blew it and all the people went running into the tanks and also everybody grabbed a rifle and then the captain grabbed a rifle and the remote controls for the robot. And while that was going on, they got ready with the battleships. And they brought a lot of ordinary bombs and time bombs and the captain went back for just a second and grabbed a disguise, so he would look like an American. And he grabbed a time bomb and put it into a clock and then he set it 'til morning. Then they got to America at nine o'clock and the bomb was set for ten o'clock. So they said, "I'll go into one of those buildings and I'll give them a terrible shock." Then he went upstairs to the tenth floor and he gave the man the clock and he said, "Here young man, take this clock. You might need it." Then the American said, "Want some coffee?" And the captain said, "No. Goodbye. I hope you have a good time." Then he went out of the building and then he found out it was nine-thirty. Then he grabbed his robot controls and got in a taxicab and said, "Taxicab, could you please take me to Rockefeller Center?" And it took him thirty minutes to get there. In the morning, he woke up and he found out that he was in jail, and he knew that the bomb had blown up. So then he took the controls out of his pocket and said, "Monster robot, I am in jail. Please get me out of here. This is your captain speaking." And the robot said, "Grrr, grrr." And then another hour later he heard a rock falling, then he knew that it was his robot. So then he said, "That's right, Monstra, right in here." And then the robot stuck his hand into the building and pulled out the jail that the captain was in and the captain almost forgot that he could use the robot's controls as a walkie talkie. So he said, "All tanks, rifles, and battleships, destroy all America!" And then he also knew that Monstra could fly. So he said, "Monstra, up, up and away," and then the robot took off and they went all the way back to India. And they lived happily ever after.

3. *3/21/74*

It's about one of my pictures. No, I got it. I'm attacking an army, so here's what I'm going to do. I'm going to make an army truck that's made of stone, steel, wood, and plastic and glass. And it's indestructible. And the Jupiter 2 is attacking him . . . [A boy interrupts, "Nothing's indestructible." He continues.] How do you know Jupiter 2 is not indestructible? But luckily, the army truck has six cannons, seven rifles and four machine guns. Four of those things that shoot out of tanks. And um, bazookas and six bazooka guns and. . . . But, luckily the Jupiter 2 didn't get destroyed, because when the army truck fired his guns, the Jupiter 2 shot his force field and all the guns bounced off the force field and destroyed the army truck. But it's good that couple of people are still alive in it and luckily Jupiter 2's force field has a hole in it. So Don West is in the front of the spaceship, driving the spaceship. But the guy with the gun, sneaking up on Don West. But Don West saw him. So, he gets a laser gun and he shoots it at the guy. And the guy goes, "Ahhhhhhh." And then he said, "A hole in one." Then he opens the hatch and runs off of the spaceship. He takes away the machine gun and shoots the remaining people. But John Robinson is captured. But he just left the general alive and he said, "If you don't tell me where John Robinson is, I'll shoot you with this laser." And then the general told him that "He's in the cave up on the planet Era and he's in the freeze machine and you'll have to get there. But he's not dead, but he'll remain frozen for two hundred years. But he won't get old. And besides, here's the map." Then Don West said., "I'm going to take you to prison." Now Don West brings the spaceship back to skyland and he says, "Are you ready for countdown?" And then Skylab says, "Roger." And um, then, um, he said, "Give me some power to bring me to planet Era, and give me machine guns, bazooka guns, lasers, and ray guns, and don't forget tanks, and army jeeps, and bring force fields." And then the countdown's starting "ten, nine, eight, seven, six, five, four, three, two, one, blast off! Prromm! Boom!"

"Now, I'm at Mercury now. I better go up before the sun destroys me." And once he goes above the sun, he say, "Oh, no, here comes twenty supernovas." "They're like big comets and shooting stars. I'll put on our ten force fields." And then he said, "I'll put . . . Shut all air locks, man the lower decks! Get the robot, we need the robot. Okay, robot, destroy those supernovas. All permative, that means yes."

"Now . . . I'll shoot my lasers. Open up one of the air hatches. Oh, no! The robot's floating out in space," said Will Robinson (John Robinson's son). "There he goes to the planet Era. Let's follow him. Hey, look. Look at that gigantic building over there. Look at that giant thing. That must be where John Robinson is captured." And then Don West says, "Give me a space helmet, keep on all force fields, Maureen Robinson. Give me a laser and give me a long line of rope." And then Will Robinson says, "Be careful of those supernovas." "I will."

Now he's down at the planet Era. He found John Robinson in the control room. Then he started watching. He started to fix the clock so all the people could become unfrozen. Then, but then, Dr. Smith was down at the planet Era and he was in the freeze center and when he saw this guy doing cat's cradle, then he pulled the lever. But the guy used the cat's cradle to choke Dr. Smith. But then Dr. Smith said, "I'll make a bargain with you. If you take that cat's cradle off my neck, since I have a spaceship, I'll bring you back to your home planet." Then he said, "Okay," the guy said. And then the guy took one of the guy's clubs who was frozen and he smashed all of the things that made them frozen.

But then—while that was happening—the guy with the cat's cradle said, "Stay on the pedestal and the guard will freeze you." Then Dr. Smith said, "It's freezing." "I'll get you out of here." Then he ran off the pedestal and then the alarm went off and then the guy who had these robots came into the room where the computer was. He saw Don West and captured him. But he didn't see John Robinson. And now, um, he put him on this thing that was chained to the wall and then the robot shot the freeze gun at him and he was frozen. But for just one minute, he became unfrozen and then John Robinson cut the chains from Don West and then after he did that the guy with the cat's cradle and all the other people came and they said, "We're going to destroy the spaceship." And then John Robinson said, "Just give me a minute and then you'll be free." Then he took out a couple of screws and then the clock began to move and it moved to number two hundred, which meant two hundred years was over. So, then the computer said, "You are all free now," and then they all yelled, "Yeh!" So Will Robinson came down and went into the other spaceship and when the guy with the cat's cradle gave him the rope, he took off. (That's the longest one I did. That's because I got most of it off "Lost in Space".)

4. *5/1/74*

Once upon a time there was a man and he had a brother. And the man who had a brother was very greedy. And one day the brother found a cave and it contained pearls, gold, and silver, and jewels. And the brother picked a big huge bag of gold. And when he got home the man said, "Tell me how to get to the cave where you found the gold." Then he said, "Okay." And he told him the magic words, which were: "Open Sassafras." And then the mean man went to the cave but that day there was a guard there. And he cut off the man's head. And then the brother came to see what took so long for the man to come home. And then he brought a pistol with him. When he got to the cave he saw the guard and shot him. And this time he didn't only take one bag of something. Then he took a cart and donkey and he put a lot of sacks in it. And when he came back home he told his mother that he hit the jackpot. And he lived happily ever after. The end.

5. *6/21/74: The Creep*

[handwritten by child]

He had a ten foot nose. And a smelly button. And a twenty foot eye. And he was green. And he came from Mars. And he was fat. And big eyes. The creep.

One day I went to the candy store and bought some gum. When I came out of the candy store and saw the monster and I blew a big BUBBLE.

6. *11/25/74*

(This story is going to be about a monster called Pleisaurus.)

One day I was on a boat on a lake and all of a sudden I saw this giant head stick out of the water with big teeth. He took his tail and hit the side of my boat and the boat fell over. I had to swim to shore. When I got to shore, I told my friends but they didn't believe me. So I told them to come with me on my boat and I would show them where the monster was. We got on the boat and went out and the head stuck out of the water. This time he didn't hit us with his tail, he dived back into the water. I put on my diving suit and dived down after him. After I got down three hundred fifty feet, I saw the monster and the monster charged at me. I got out of the way just in time.

I went on the surface and got a spear gun and went back down. Just as I was about to shoot, another monster came up behind me and grabbed with one of his tentacles. I aimed my spear gun at him and shot him in the eye luckily so he died. When I got loose of his tentacles, I put another spear in my spear gun and the pleisaurus charged me. I hit him in the flipper and he reached out his neck and almost bit me.

I took out my walkie-talkie and walkie-talkied my friend and he came down in a submarine we had on the boat and he aimed the gun and it hit pleisaurus's long neck. Pleisaurus sank to the bottom of the lake and I swam back up to tell my friends and this time they did believe me.

The next day, I came down to the lake and saw at the edge a big hairy monster named Bigfoot. When he looked up he saw me and I ran back to my house and got in my helicopter and took off and pretty soon I was ten feet over Bigfoot. I lowered my net and I captured Bigfoot. Then I took off and when I got to the center of the river, I dropped him and he drowned. I never saw him again.

The next day, I went down to the river and I didn't see anything for the first hour. Then it was three o'clock and I saw a fin that looked like a shark's fin, but it was a giant shark.

The shark was a whale shark because the only kind of shark that doesn't attack man is the whale shark. I jumped in the water and when I was a couple of hundred yards behind him I set up a net and then I went home and took my helicopter again and when I got just over the other net I dropped a line and it attached to the net and then I went in front of the shark and put another net down with a string. I pushed the button that dropped the submarine into the water and I operated the metal bars to attach a heavy nylon to both of the nets. Then I pulled the submarine backwards and the nylon string closed the net on the shark and then I raised the submarine back to the helicopter, raising the nets, and I put the shark in the Atlantic Ocean because it wasn't supposed to be in the lake.

Then I went back to my house with the helicopter and parked it in the garage. I went in my house, had supper and went to bed. The next morning, I got up and went to the far side of the lake. Then there I saw an animal that was part chicken and part crow and I heard it say this funny thing like, "Blah, blah, blah." And I knew chickens and crows didn't sing that so I wondered what it was. I picked up the chicken and carried it to my house and the next day I brought it to the Museum of Natural Science and they said they didn't know, but it might be something from long ago. So I took it to the Museum of Scientific History and asked them what it was. They said it dated back one hundred million years and it was a Chapachowwa-wa. They said, "You should hand that bird over to us. We can use it in a very important experiment." So I handed it over to them and I went home.

Then I took my gun and my dog Bismarck out to hunt some geese because there were very many around here. So I went out and I shot four birds, then I came back to my house and I ate one of the birds and I gave one to my dog to eat. Then just as we were about to go to sleep I heard this funny sound go boom, boom. I looked out my window and I saw this big monster that was fifteen stories high. I got dressed and took my gun and dog and went outside. Everyone was running and saying, "Run for your life, Godzilla is coming!" So I asked somebody, "What's all the commotion about?" He said, "Godzilla is coming." I looked at the monster and aimed my gun and shot a bullet, but it hit the stomach unfortunately, and it bounced off and hit a building. Then I hit him in the toe and he fell down and then I shot him in the eye, but he was still alive so I ran in the house and called the police and the army. And they brought all their military weapons and they shot at Godzilla and he died a half an hour later. I felt very tired that night, so I went back to the house and fell asleep.

The next day, I was lucky 'cause there was no monsters around. I went to the lake with my fishing pole and threw the line in the water. I felt a big jerk and found it was a big whale trapped in the lake. I pulled him in but left him partly in the water. I ran back to my house and got my helicopter and flew right over the whale and dropped a one hundred ten feet stretcher and slipped it under the whale. I made the helicopter hover and I parachuted down and unhooked the hook and I pushed the button that made a ladder come down from the helicopter. I climbed up the ladder, then I made the ladder come back up and I carried the whale to a place where they needed one for tricks. I dropped him in the tank and took the stretcher out from under him.

I flew the helicopter to Europe for a vacation. And I heard tell of a flying monster that was in Southern Europe so I took my helicopter from Iceland to Southern Europe and I saw the flying monster. I pushed a button that made missiles shoot out and hit the bird in the mouth. He lost his balance and he was falling and almost hit the ground but flew away. Just as he was over the Mediterranean, he fell in and then I pushed the hold button on the helicopter and dropped the submarine and it fell into the water and I went down six hundred seventy-two feet and I saw the monster who was still alive. I shot a missile and hit his stomach and he died. I attached a metal arm to him and went under the helicopter and pushed the button that made it raise up to the helicopter. And I attached four hooks to the monster and carried him away to the Natural History Museum and dropped him.

I said, "Here's a present for you." They said, "Thank you." They called the police and asked them for one hundred twenty tow trucks to move the monster. So they got one hundred twenty tow trucks and it took them an hour to pull the monster into the museum. While they were doing that I flew my helicopter home and had lunch. After lunch I went outside with my gun and my dog. We were going to hunt today, pheasants. So I shot three pheasants and I went back home and put them in the oven and cooked them and an hour later I ate them and gave one to my dog. After that I was ready to watch TV because my favorite program the horror movie was on. So I turned on the TV and I heard a sound of clanking of chains. I looked upstairs in my attic and I saw a monster ten feet tall and it weighed as much as a Sherman tank. So I got my gun and shot the monster in the head and it stunned the monster. I put him in my truck and drove to the Museum of Science. They said, "What are you doing here?" I said, "I have a monster." I carried the monster into the Museum and they put chains on him so he couldn't get loose.

The next morning, I was very tired so I slept late. I got up at eleven o'clock and ate some cereal and went out to play tennis with my friend. He heard the cracking of leaves and he knew it couldn't be anybody because no one came around here. We saw this hairy big ape standing on his hind legs with three inch long teeth. My friend moved just in time because the monster jumped where he was standing and fell down. We ran in the house and I got my specially armed mini-tank that was ten feet long. I aimed the big missile and hit the monster in the stomach and he died. I loaded him on the truck and took him to the Museum of Natural Science.

When I got there I said, "I have something else for you." He said, "What is it?" I put the monster in a car that was just big enough to fit a person in and the car moved at five miles per hour up the stairs. I took the beast out and the man said he was made by Mr. Victor Frankenstein. So he put him in a cage next to the other monster I brang in a long time ago.

7. 12/4/74: *Freaky Goes to the Bathroom*

He was just about to go to the bathroom. He is entering the bathroom, he is in the bathroom. How can I get in to get the toilet when the toilet isn't even there. I think I went to the wrong room. Look at the toilet, I found the toilet. Now, how do I get up to the toilet. I'll go and get my ladder. This looks like the Mediterranean Sea. I might as well dive in and go to the toilet. A matter of fact, this is the Mediterranean Sea. I'm probably going to get into women's lib that proves that girls can get into the bathroom. I flunked the human race. How can I get into the human race, I am not a human. I'm only five inches tall, how can I get into the bathroom if there is one? Oops, I forgot, this is a leaf race. A bug-eating fish is here, oops, he got me. I'm in a food chain, I hope something doesn't crunch us up like potato chips. I can look through his eyes, here comes a shark that wants to crunch up this fish. Here he comes—crunch, crunch, crunch. I can go to heaven if there is one. I'm not all crunched up, I crunched up the shark, now I'm eighteen feet long. I might as well go to the bathroom, I hope he comes out of me when I do. The end.

8. 12/12/74

We were playing this football game between the Jets and the Miami Dolphins. I was the wide receiver for the Jets, I ran to the 22 yard line of the Miami Dolphins. Joe Namath threw me the ball, but I fumbled it, but I picked the ball up and then I went back to the 50 yard line. We set up and I ran to the 32 yard line. Joe Namath threw me a pass. I caught it and ran to the 22, 18 someone tackled me. Set up on the 18, this time Jerome Barkum went out to the 10 yard line and I blocked protecting Jerome Barkum. I caught the ball, went back to the 5 yard line then I ran to the 4, 3, 2, 1 and made a touchdown. Jets were winning, 7-0.

Larry Csonka had the ball then me and Jerome Barkum ran and I grabbed the ball but Larry Csonka jumped on me and intercepted the ball. Then we set up on our own 32 yard line. Riggins ran out to the Dolphins' 5 yard line. Joe Namath threw his strongest pass, Riggins caught it and we got another touchdown. Then in the third quarter the Miami Dolphins made a touchdown. 7-14, Jets were winning. It was our ball, Joe Namath threw the ball, Jerome Barkum caught it, ran to the Miami 28 and was tackled. We set up on the 28th yard line. Joe Namath gave the ball to Riggins, he charged into everybody, knocked them down and was almost tackled. Riggins threw me the ball and I went from 28, 26, 25, 10, 5, 1 and got a touchdown. Score 20. Our good kicker, Number 5, kicked and now the score 21-7. In the fourth quarter the Miami Dolphins made a touchdown, 21-13. It was our ball and Joe Namath threw a pass to Riggins, he missed it, incomplete. Jerome Barkum ran to 43 yard line of Dolphins and Joe Namath threw him a pass, Jerome Barkum caught it was tackled at 32. First down. Then it was the Dolphins' ball. Their quarterback threw a pass to Mercury Morris. Jerome Barkum tackled him and then threw another ball, it was caught by their best player, Larry Csonka. Riggins grabbed Larry Csonka by the foot, but Larry Csonka was still running, but very slow. I jumped on Larry Csonka and he fell down and Jerome Barkum also jumped on him. Five minutes to go, Dolphins' ball at our 32 yard line. Riggins tackled, our ball on 45 yard line. Then Joe Namath threw a 10-yard pass to Jerome Barkum. Barkum ran to 22, another first down. Then we went to the 22 yard line of Dolphins. I ran to the 3 yard line, Joe Namath threw the ball to me, I made a touchdown with a minute to go in the game. Score 27-13. Miami Dolphins' ball on the 3 yard line, ran to the 23, tackled. Quarterback threw Larry Csonka the ball, ducked Riggins, Jerome Barkum grabbed his foot and Riggins jumped on him. They threw the ball, Mercury caught it and ran to the 16 yard line where he was tackled. Seven seconds to go. Larry Csonka ran 10 yards with the ball but was tackled by me and Barkum. Miami Dolphins' quarterback threw pass to Mercury Morris, tackled by Jerome Barkum at the 3 yard line. We won the game, 27-13.

9. *12/12/75*

There was this robber who robbed the First National City Bank on West 3rd Street. The police were after him. They sent four helicopters, one police car, three guys and one armored car. One guy went in a manhole, one guy put a roadblock on the highway. One guy was on a concrete block and another was hanging by his feet upside down and shooting a machine gun at the robbers. He hit one of the tops of the guy's car and gave the guy a concussion and the guy was knocked out. Then the guy in the manhole jumped onto the guy's car and smashed the window open and threw the bad guy in the back. He drove home in the bad guys' car which the police said he could keep. He drove home and his house was being robbed. He shot the robber in the kidneys but the robber didn't die. The robber shot two shots and hit him in the finger. The policeman shot a bullet in his head and got killed. The next day the policeman came to the police station and brought his car with him, his new car he got from the robber. He asked the officer, "Did you put that bad man in jail?" The guy said, "Yes."

He got in his car and went home. He went to the pet store and bought a watch snake, a cobra. One day while he was outside a robber came and the king cobra hanged from the chandelier. When he got under it the king cobra bit him with his poisonous fangs and killed him in a few minutes. Then the king cobra went back on the chandelier and waited to see if any more robbers would come.

Then the policeman came back and saw the dead guy. He walked the guy to the hospital to see if he was alive. Then he came back home, had some dinner and he went to sleep.

The next day, he woke up at six-thirty in the morning, had breakfast, got dressed and he went to the police station, got in his patrol car and drove on the West Side Highway to see if any robbers were around. He saw one robber and he called the helicopter which came and hooked the robber's car and carried it away to the police station. They shot bullets at the car so the guy couldn't shoot bullets back at him.

The guy in the helicopter lowered the car slowly and unhooked it and pulled the rope up. He lowered the helicopter and came out with his pistol out of his pistolholder and shot the bad guy in the stomach. Then the guy in the highway phoned the armored car because there was a bad guy he had caught and he wanted the armored car to take him to the police station because he was too busy. So they came and got him. When he pushed the guy out, one of the guys shot a machine gun at the bad guy's foot and he fell down. Then they brung him to the police station and they questioned him at the court and put him in jail for seventy-nine years and put the other guy in jail for one hundred sixty-eight years.

Then the guy in the helicopter went over the West Side Highway and caught a crook and took him back and gave him a life sentence because he had done many bad things: 1. killed sixty-eight people; 2. robbed one hundred twenty-eight banks; 3. robbed houses; 4. steals animals; 5. steals jewels; 6. steals thirty-two policeman a day and has been known for poisoning and kills judges and juries and uses illegal weapons such as shotguns, machine guns, pistols, knives for killing and uses a huge graveyard for his hideout.

10.   1/25/75

Once way deep down forty thousand miles in the earth there lived these creepy shaped monsters like a twenty foot scorpion, a one hundred foot tall sloth and a giant monster called Rodan. Rodan owned all the monsters. He sent them up to the surface of the earth to attack the people. First he sent the one hundred foot tall sloth up, up, up to the top of the earth. There was a skiing lodge in the Appalachians. When he saw the lodge it was too big for him to push down so he opened his mouth and flames came out and hit a car and the car blew up and blew up some of the building, killing a person inside. He hit the roof with his paw and the ceiling caved in and squished everything. The people sent out an army to attack the sloth.

The front of the army was blown up. They were near a place with a lot of oil tanks. The sloth shot fire and the tank got a hole and started on fire. A man fell into the fire and was badly burned. They sent a fire squad and lowered one of them into a tank and he got the guy and they brought him to the hospital. The fire squad went after the sloth and shot fire into his mouth so he couldn't blow his fire, but he was still strong. Then the sloth took his paw and smashed the fire kitchen and it blew up and killed three people. Then the fire squad retreated and reported to every army in the world that the giant sloth was attacking Tokyo. All the armies attacked. The Hungarian and Chinese army were destroyed. After the African army was destroyed the one hundred foot sloth was killed. When he was killed they had five hundred helicopters attach five-inch thick ropes to him and then the helicopters dropped him in and there was a big explosion and three people were killed, but at least the one hundred foot sloth was killed.

Then Rodan sent out the giant scorpion. A person didn't know it, but the scorpion was behind him and he grabbed him with one of his nippers and poisoned the guy to death. The guy died in six seconds.

Then they sent out a giant army that shot very high electric voltage—one million volts. When the monster came close they turned on the current, but that didn't stop him. Then there was an explosion and the ground was blown up, but the monster was still there and he shot a beam at the electric squad. [stopped for lunch]

11.   1/24/75

[handwritten by child]

The score was 3-7. The raiders were beating the jets. Because the raiders quarterback threw a pass to Mike Siari and he got a touchdown and the extra point was good and then the jets got a field goal. And in the second period the raiders got a safety then the score was 5 to 7. Then after the second half the raiders got a field goal. Then in the third period the jets got a touchdown. Then the jets got another touchdown with six seconds to play. Then every body started cheering.

12.   3/3/75

[a dream]

Once I got a B-52 bomber and flyed over Europe, over Asia, all the way to Australia. When I got over the North Islands of New Zealand I dropped a

H-bomb. Blew up two inches of the island and just those two inches were burnt and one man who was there was squished. It was Michael's Uncle Robert. The bomb didn't explode cause someone put the wires but it was 1,850 pounds so it smooched him good.

13. 3/3/75

He was at the bottom of a ninety-nine story building and I was at the top so I dropped a million pound piano and it smooched Uncle Robert's head down to his socks.

An ant came along and said, "Get off our ant hill." And then he gave Uncle Robert a bop on the nose. The end.

14. 4/27/75

Once there was a spaceship called Vostok 8. The Russians sent the rocket to check the Martian atmosphere and blow up the American spaceship that was on Mars, but the Americans heard about it and so they sent out a spaceship called Apollo 33SK that was armed with phaser banks and sidewinder missiles. The spaceship took off on April 28, 1975, 2:32, its destination Mars.

The Russian spaceship by now was almost past the moon so the spaceship had to go warp 10, the highest the spaceship could go without retrorockets. But luckily the spaceship did have retrorockets, so it could go warp 18. So halfway past the moon he turned on warp 18 and in three hours they were past the moon.

Vostok 8 was already halfway there. The Russians didn't know that the Americans knew their secret so they were going at warp 3 which is thirty kilometers per second. The American ship was moving three hundred kilometers per second.

They saw the Russian shuffle craft getting near them so they fired their phasers and exploded it. It had no passengers, it was controlled by a remote control operation station. When the Russians found the Americans were following them they went at warp 9 and now they were only nine million kilometers apart and getting closer every second. In two hours they would only be fifty kilometers apart. So the Russians knew this and so they tried to throw them off the trail. At three hundred kilometers apart the Russians fired a sidewinder missile and blew up half of the bridge and the American ship retreated and then blew to smitherins because the gas tank got on fire.

The Russian ship was badly damaged so it had to go back to the Soviet Union to get supplies.

188

The American ship had eighteen shuttle crafts and took up all of Kennedy airport and the shuttles were armed with phasers so powerful they could destroy the world.

The spaceship took off going at a speed of 1,532 kilometers per second. By now the American spaceship was way ahead of the Russian spaceship and reached Mars in two hours, letting out all its shuttle crafts to protect the spaceship on Mars and destroy the Russian spaceship.

The American ship on Mars sent three shuttle crafts to help the other American spaceship. By now the Russian spaceship was past the moon. Luckily they knew only five shuttle craft could fit on that ship so they would be outnumbered nineteen to six. Everything was locked on target. One of the shuttle crafts approached the Russian spaceship and was blown to smithereens. The American shuttle craft fired phaser banks at the Russian shuttle and the Russian ship crashed.

There was a spaceman on top of the Russian ship and he fired his little phaser gun but it bounced off the big earthship. The American ship fixed its biggest phaser and blew him up and then the Russian ship retreated three hundred thirty kilometers. But the earthship wasn't going its fastest speed and kept up with it. The Russian shuttle craft blew up seventeen of the American shuttle crafts, but one of the Russian ship's phaser banks blew up so there was only two Russians and one American ship. So they couldn't fire their phaser banks for awhile 'cause they needed to save the ship's energy so they fired sidewinder missiles, but they both had force fields up.

They both turned on their phasers at the same time and turned off their force fields and fired. The Russian ship blew up and the landing gear of the American ship caught on fire and the gigantic American ship shot a blast of water that could fill the Atlantic Ocean in one minute. And put out the fire but one guy on the shuttle craft drowned.

Now the Russians were outnumbered two to one so the American ship purposely blew up their own shuttle craft so it would be a fair fight 'cause they knew they would win. Then the American ship shot their strongest blast of water that could fill the Atlantic, Pacific, Antarctic and Indian Oceans. And filled the Russian ship with water and fired their phasers, but the Russian ship wouldn't catch on fire because of the water. So they turned on their heating system and in five minutes all the water was gone.

The Americans fired ten sidewinder missiles at the Russian ship and blew it up. Then the big American ship called the American ship on Mars and told them it was okay to come back.

The American ship returned to earth, but by mistake they landed in Times Square, killing three people.

15. 5/19/75

I dreamt that I owned a spaceship and I was the captain and it was called Apollo 25. It was from Canada and it was supposed to go to Orion. There was three hundred fifty-six people on it. Its fastest warp speed was warp 8. Its slowest speed was impulse. Its mission: to find life on Uranus and on the five moons. It was supposed to land in the Dead Sea and there the PT boats would take it onto land and a helicopter would take Apollo and the crew back to Canada—Montreal. The very day that the Mets were going to play the Expos so they wouldn't miss the baseball game. On May 26 they took off, in two hours they were speeding past Mars' atmosphere. All of the sudden, the spaceship hit an asteroid belt and one person died, but there were few dents. In a few hours they were speeding past Saturn, one hour later they reached Uranus. All of the sudden, the ship started being pulled down to Uranus very fast—that proved there was life on Uranus. They landed and sent out one of their men. All of the sudden, they saw a phaser beam, then they sent out the whole crew. They saw a clawed to death body and a monster walking away. I ordered the lieutenant commander to fire his phaser and the monster turned around and the whole crew fired their phaser and the monster disappeared. Then all of the sudden, someone yelled, "Someone was clawed to death by the monster." We sent out one of our commanders to catch him and the next day we found him choked to death. We sent out fifteen men and they followed the big footprints to a big dome. They tried to walk through it but there was a force field that even their phasers couldn't penetrate. Then they all shot their phasers at once and made a hole and they saw the monster. One of them stabbed a knife in the back of the monster and killed him. Then they all went back to their spaceship and went back to earth and told all the countries not to send their spaceships to Uranus.

Edna

1. 4/11/74

Once there was a girl and that girl was lost. And she met a tree and she said, "Tree, did you see my family?" And the tree said, "No." So the girl went on walking. And she met a house. And she looked in the window and she knocked on the door and somebody opened it and she was surprised, because it was her mother and she went in the house and she ate something to eat and then she went to the park and played in the sandbox. And then she went home and then she ate dinner and went to bed and when she woke up and she got something to eat and then, ah, she ran to school. The end.

2. 4/24/74

Once there was a little girl and she went to the park and she saw her friend and they played together. They made a castle out of sand and the girl had to go home and so she went home and she had dinner. And then she went to sleep and she had a dream: Her dream was about a baby who knew how to talk and that baby knew how to walk, and that baby drew a picture of a baby. And that picture of the baby drew a picture of another baby. And then her dream was all over. And she woke up and ate something and then she went back to sleep. And when it was morning she ate breakfast. And she went to school. And she ate lunch. And she played with her friends. And she played a game called checkers. And her friends went home and she played with her cat. And then she ate dinner and she went to sleep. And when she woke up she realized something . . . that it was her birthday. And she got dressed and she went to school. And she came back home feeling happy. The end.

3. 10/25/74

One day there was a dog and the dog was tired because it went to the park and was playing a lot. The dog went home and cooked dinner and then the dog went to sleep. When the dog got up it went to school and it was a hard day. It was very hard because they had to write all day. And then it went home and played a little bit and then it cooked dinner and then the dog went to sleep for a long time. The next morning was Sunday and the dog was happy, the dog went to play and played a lot till it got dark and then went home to sleep and the dog got up to get dinner and the dog went to sleep again. It was a tiring day. The end.

4. 11/22/74

One day I saw a rabbit and it was fluffy. Very fluffy. It was so fluffy that I wanted to take it home. And then I saw a cage and I put the rabbit in the cage and ran home. I told my mother I found a rabbit and she was happy. And then she gave me a bigger cage so we can keep the rabbit and I was happy. I played with the rabbit, fed it and then I had to go to sleep. The next morning I played with it and I had to go to school. I wanted to bring it to school so I did and the rabbit got sick. So when I got home I told my mommy that it got sick. My mommy said, "We'll bring it to the vet." And it was okay. The end.

5. 3/28/75

Once upon a time there was a rabbit who wanted to eat radishes, but he didn't know how to get any. He tried to sneak in a garden, but somebody caught him. He tried to hunt for some, but he couldn't find any. The person said, "Get out of here."

His friends ate carrots and lettuce, but he liked radishes. He was lonesome and hungry. His friends gave him some lettuce and carrots, and he ate that instead of radishes.

Elizabeth

1. 11/9/73

Once upon a time there was a wise old man and he was a bad wise man. And he lived in a very dark forest and there were very vicious animals. And the most vicious animal was the mountain lion. And he lived on an old tall mountain. He was very lonely. And one day, he found a monkey in a tree. And he roared at the monkey and the monkey ran away. Then the mountain lion got angry, so then the wise old man came out of his house and said, "Shut up! You stupid lion." And then the lion was furious. Then it was midnight. And a coyote came out of the forest and yelled, "Ooooh!" And the wise old man woke up. And said, "Is that you, stupid lion?" And the coyote got off the rock and ran away.

The wise old man did it to all of the animals until they all ran away. But then he got very lonely when all the animals were gone.

One day the old man thought and thought until he had an idea. And his idea was to yell to the other animals so they would come back. And the wise old man could have a better time. A year later, the wise old man gave up. And the wise old man fixed up the town and it was nice again. And there were fields and the wise old man bought him some farmer's clothes and he was a farmer. And he took care of the animals. And the sky was blue and the grass was green and they lived happily ever after in the country. The end.

2. 12/7/73

Once upon a time there lived a bunny and her name was Mrs. White-tail Bunny. And she lived in a deep hole in the woods. And then, one night she heard a voice and she screamed, "Help, help, help!" And then the voice went away. And then she had a very nice sleep. And then in the morning it was raining and raining and raining. And she called the weatherman and he said, "It was going to be a tornado." And she was so scared, she jumped up and down and all around. Then it was time to eat breakfast. But the tornado blew all the food away. It was like birds flying in the sky and she had no food left and she looked for her money and it blew away, too. And then the tornado stopped and it was sunny again. And then she got on her bathing suit and she went for a swim. And she got knocked over by a strong undertow and the lifeguard saved her. And then she was singing, "Put your finger in the air, in the air . . . da, da, da." And then she got into her car and she rode home singing, "Jingle Bells, Jingle Bells, Jingle all the way . . . da, da, da, da."

And when she came home she sang, "Santa Claus is coming to town." And then it was four days 'til Christmas and those four days passed. And she was so excited that she wiggled her little white cotton tail and then she went to sleep. And then in the morning she said, "Oh, it's the twenty-fifth, tra, la, la, la." And she looked under her Christmas tree and saw twenty-five hundred million presents. And she opened them and piled the bunch of toys and paper all up. And then there was a big wind and all the paper flew away and she said, "Thank goodness for that!" And she fainted and then she woke up and then she fainted and then she woke up and she blew out of her hole. And she said, "What in the cotton pickin' world did I do?" And then she came back in her hole and woke her baby bunnies up and she had cookies and hot chocolate. The end.

3. 1/15/74

Once upon a time my father went to drive a dune buggy. He got into an accident and went "Kerplunk." He wasn't hurt, so this was my dream. When my father was in the hospital, to myself I said, "Jump into the ocean and jump into the sea and then you will meet me." And then I felt something, and my ears grew, and I looked just like a bunny rabbit. And I said, "What day is this?"

Of course, I looked at the calendar and it was April 14th; that was Easter Sunday. And then skipping along "Tra la la," I sang a merry song. "I am an Easter Rabbit, Hooray, Hooray!" I went on and on 'til I came to a kid's house. But I didn't get to see the sign to his house, because I was so excited. Then do you know what it said—"Dead-End Kid." Of course I went along anyway. But soon I woke up and my daddy told me, "This was all a dream." The end.

4. 4/2/74: *The Tale of the Poptail Cubs*

There was once a poptail cub. And he went to the movies, and what did he hear? It was a little song: "I'm a little teenie cubby [sung] and am watching the movies . . . boopity, boopity, boopity, boo." And she made this little poem: "I'm a poptail cubby and I go trippity, trippity, trop." And then she found something that amazed her. It was a big, big, big, big gigantic birthday cake. And she said, "I'm going to add something to my poem." HAPPY BIRTHDAY!!!

So that's the story of the little cubby that went to the movies . . . Ta-Taaaa [accompanied with dramatic gesture signaling the end.]

Poptail Cubby Song [Based on a song written by Elizabeth]
[sung merrily]

I am a tiny little cubby and I'm watching the movies
I am a tiny little mommy and I live in the zoo
My mother broke my arm and my tiny leg too
Boo-Boopie-Doo

5. 6/18/74: *The Strangest Creature*

[handwritten by child]

One stormy night I looked out my window. And I saw a strange shaped creature and I was scared. And he was green and yellow and had red and pink hair and he had ten eyes. Boy! When he went away I was really glad. But still I knew another creature wood come and ! He did. A green haired Pok-a-Doted five head squared creature and ! a yellow body. OOO I was scared. The end!

6. 10/7/74: *The Land of the Lost*

Once there was a dinosaur. The name was Grumpy. And he was always grumpy. In the case of his grumpiness was because there were three people that always used to fool around with dinosaurs. So then Grumpy got real mad and came into a cave and started growling. And in this growlness the three people by the name of Holly, William, and their father. Well, they went into this particular cave and the children started playing with big old Grumpy. Then after that they found these apes. The big apes started climbing on the big apes. So then finally, the big apes started growling with Grumpy. They jumped off the 2022 feet of apes and they got seriously injured. Of course there was no doctor but their father was studying to be a doctor before they landed in the Land of the Lost.

Then it became night. In the night big old Grumpy came banging thru the cave, Awakened the children, and as petrified as the children were, they stayed in place. In the morning they woke up and started dancing through the stream and then found this boat and went back to where they lived. Of course this was all a dream so they were happy again.

7. 11/13/74

Once was a cat that lived in a nice house. It had a five, four rooms, upstairs and downstairs and two bathrooms and it had a backyard.

So one day the cat sat near the fire on the rocking chair playing with yarn. Then the cat got off the chair and fooled around with the dog. Teasing him 'cause he was chained to a pole. Then the cat got tired and ran upstairs to the little girl's room and she was scratching the rugs and the chairs. Then they caught her.

It was near bedtime. She had supper and climbed up in the closet on a little shelf and that's where she slept.

The next morning, she met a girlfriend and they played all day and then she went to bed and that's the end.

8. 11/20/74

Once there was a hill on top of a mountain and there was a cave on top of a volcano and there was rocks on top of the volcano and then on those rocks there lived a bunny. And he lived in a hole with his family. He was jolly and happy every single day and then one day he was sad and he was really sad. ''Why?'' his mother asked. ''Because I got a cut on my lip.'' ''Oh,'' said the mother, with a mad grin. ''How did it happen?'' asked his brothers and sisters. ''I touched the point of the volcano.'' ''Oh, oh, oh!'' said the bunnies. The end.

9. 2/5/75

Once upon a time there was a little girl who got a Yorkie dog named York. The dog had brownish, greyish hair, blue eyes, narrow sweet face. The little girl felt good to have a little dog. The dog could do lots of things; bark, sleep, jump, lick. And that's it.

10.   3/3/75

Once there was a little fox. A fox and a little bear. The bear's name was Brownie, and the fox's name was Reddi. The fox's name was Reddi because he was always ready when you needed him. The bear's name was Brownie because he went with the brownies on hikes. One day, there was a brownie hike and Brownie was sick. He was very, very, very sick and he told the girl scouts he was very sick and they told him if he was sick one more time they wouldn't let him go on hikes. One day he was sick again when there was another hike. He went over to Mr. Fox's house and he was as ready as he could be. Brownie said, "Can you dress up like me and you be me and I will be you for the day?" "Okay," said Mr. Fox and Brownie gave Mr. Fox some fur to put on as a costume and then they looked in the mirror and saw that they were just alike. Then when Mr. Fox came home Brownie was all well again. "I am glad to hear that you are okay now," said Mr. Fox. "Oh, I am just fine," said Mr. Brownie. "How was the hike?" "Oh, just fine," said Mr. Fox. "Did they find out that you weren't me?" "Of course not," said Mr. Fox. "What did they do on the hike," said Brownie. "Oh, climb rocks, and played in the grass. I am so relieved you are better because those hikes are a little too steep for me." "Oh, same with me," said Brownie. "Good night," said Mr. Fox. "Good night," said Brownie. In the morning, Mr. Fox came outside and saw it was raining. He went inside and got his umbrella and went to Brownie. "It is raining, can I stay for the day?" "Oh, of course," said Brownie. "You are very very kind," said Mr. Fox. "Thank you," said Brownie, "So are you. Tomorrow, I will take you on a hike, but not climbing hills and trees." "Oh, fine if it is a sunny day."

In the morning, they looked out the window and the sun was shining in their eyes. Let's go out and dig a hole and put water in it and they did. Let's get wood and make a diving board, so they did. They swam and swam all day. "That was a fun day we had wasn't it?" said Mr. Fox. "Yes indeed it was. Well, the sun is shining now, do you want to take the hike," asked Brownie. "It's getting a little too late, maybe tomorrow." "Fine," answered Brownie. In the morning there were beautiful clouds in the sky and the sun was shining like gold. "Oh, I am going to run over to Mr. Fox," said Brownie. "Mr. Fox," Brownie yelled, "Rise and shine, it's a beautiful day." Mr. Fox ran out and they played all day. "Wasn't that fun," they both said. "Why, we'll see you tomorrow and tomorrow we will definitely go on the hike." "Bye-bye," said Mr. Fox, "Bye-bye," said Brownie. "See you tomorrow." They opened the door to their house and made their supper. And in the morning they definitely went on the hike through the lakes and streams and grass. The sun was shining like gold and diamonds. The end.

Emily

1. *12/3/73*

Once upon a time, there was a monkey and he lived in the forest. One day, a little girl went out to take a walk and she saw the monkey. But she always wanted a pet and she saw the monkey and she thought that she could keep the monkey, but probably her mother wouldn't let her. So she went home and asked her mother if she could keep the monkey and she said it was all right if you go back and get it. But don't get lost, 'cause there's a mean wolf in that forest, don't forget. And she gave her some cookies so she wouldn't be scared and she went to her Grandma's and shared it with her. And suddenly the wolf came in and her Grandma screamed and called the hunter. So then, she went to get her mother and she ran so fast her barrette fell out of her hair and the cookies fell out of her basket. And suddenly her mother came and her father came home from work and said, "What's going on here?" Then her mother told him so fast that he couldn't understand it. So he asked the hunter and said, "What is going on here, hunter?" "Never mind, I've got to scare the wolf away," the hunter said. And so he scared the wolf away as fast as he could and got his breath and told him what had happened. And so the family was safe and sound for ever and ever and they ate cookies and juice and invited Grandma over to eat with them. The end.

2. *4/17/74*

Once upon a time there was a very little rabbit. He was the littlest rabbit in the forest and the biggest rabbit used to, and still does, call a little tune like this:

> Tot-Tot littlest rabbit
> You are the littlest rabbit. . . .

And he got very sad.

3. *4/17/74*

[Round story with Jill]

Emily: One day a hamster was born

Jill: In the middle of the forest, and he grew up in the forest.

Emily: And then when he got older than he was now he ran away to the city.

Jill: And when he got to the city he found out it was his birthday and he was three years old.

Emily: And somebody found him and said, "This looks like the hamster I lost, but it isn't. Today was the birthday of the hamster I lost."

Jill: And the hamster said, "So it's my birthday, too." So he took him home and put him in a Habertrail cage.

Emily: And they had a birthday and they celebrated it and they gave him hamster food and hamster cake. And he was full of hamster food. And he ate it all up. The flavors of the hamster cake was corn and peanuts, apple and tomato, and soybean, and sunflower, and alpha.

Jill: And after the cake with all the hamster foods in it, it (the hamster) went to the bathroom so many times it got kind of sick. And the person who owned her took her out and took her to the dinner table and put her on her (the girl's) seat. And it went to the bathroom on the seat.

Emily: And when she picked her up she [the hamster] threw up twelve times. And she went to the vet and she asked the store man what was wrong with her. And he said, "She has a sickness and a disease, and it's called *Tropicana.*" And she gave her medicine that didn't help, 'cause hamsters carry diseases if they eat too much . . . and they grunt. And if they're born in the forest and come here [city]—there's disease in the city, they can catch 'cause they're used to the forest and not the city. "But this one is not allergic to anything," said the store man. "I think it ate too much."

Jill: And when she ate too much she had this very, very bad sickness. She died. And there was another one she [girl] found—this one was called "Happy" and the second one was called "Laura." And they got a new one called "Ruthie."

Emily: And then suddenly the girl remembered that she lost two hamsters—not only one. And she found them. And one of them was named "Pom-Pom" and one was named "Ribbon." And one of the hamsters she found died of constipation and the other one remained [Ribbon]. And she brought her with her into school yesterday.

Jill: And today a girl brang in a hamster and it was in Room 305. And she was playing with it. And they were playing with their friend and their hamster. And they were playing so happy that they took her out of the cage and showed her to the teacher and she jumped when it was "Show and Tell" and she said, "That's a nice hamster."

Emily: And she showed it to Gil. [Brings in hamster in cage and shows it to storytaker.]

4. 5/16/74: *The Strangest Noise*

[handwritten by child]

Once I was asleep. But then! I heard a noise. It was strange to me. Because I had never heard it before. Well sort of the same as last year. But not really. I think it's a monster. But I couldn't see it. It made a noise like this "ekkekekk", and this "oooowwice", and "Lika Lika Lika"! It sounded funny. Oh no! Not again! Another sound like this! "oeokeeo wee-o wee-o wee watto ne naw ukuk nukei brain me meeee oeea nee reee lacta." But before my little eye I saw a little book. But when I opened it it said "Monster Trap Magic." I closed my eyes and I dreamed a dream, so magnificent, so touching, that, that, well, O.K. really. But, um, a, well, a, I was Blech! Then, fast as a bee, I woke up with a surprise. The end.

5. 11/22/74

Once upon a time, there was a little girl named Suzie. She wanted to go out and play with the other little children.

Suddenly, she jerked and heard a scream. It was probably mother. She always screams when there's a mouse in the house. She picked up some dirt and said, "I'm tired of just playing by myself in the dirt. I want someone to play with."

So she went to every house in town and down the road to Mrs. Creaky's town. She said, "Go to the candy shop and there will be a nice man. He'll tell you where there's some nice children to play with."

So she went there, to the candy shop. She saw a little, little man. He had a queer voice. "I know where you go. Up the road, put your heels together and I'll snap you to some children."

She put her heels together, closed her eyes and she saw two little girls and one little boy. He was actually the smallest there. He was two years old and the others were his sisters. One of the sisters was named Kathy, the other sister was named Jane. Then one day Jane said, "I have to go home" and Kathy, the youngest sister, and the little boy (his name is Jack). Jack and Kathy were the smallest.

Jane said, "We have to leave now for a birthday at Little town. We could ask our friend if you could come." "Well," she said, "I can only come if I ask my mother. Come down the road with me and I'll ask."

"Mother, can I go to my friend's friend's birthday?" "Yes, you may," she said. So she did. She lived with her friends 'cause she found out her mother died and her father. She was so sad that she died. The end.

6. *12/12/74*

Once upon a time there were three little mice in a hole. In the hole, they had matchbox beds and pieces of cotton for pillows and material for the pillow cases. One day, the cat moved in. He said he had to go out to the supermarket to buy some food. So he said, "I'm going to buy four bananas and a slice of cheese," and then he heard a little giggle. It was the mice he heard. He didn't know who it was because, "Cheese," he said, "just made someone giggle." He saw a hole in the wall and said "cheese" again and he heard the giggle come from the hole. He put his hand in the hole, and he felt two little mice on his finger. He walked outside, onto the grass, he took the telephone with him because it was a portable telephone. He called the owner of the house and said he does not want to rent it anymore and he died cause the mice were poisonous. The mice figured out; mice are better than cats. But one day the mice found out they were poisonous and died because they thought they were going to be sick and die so they killed themselves. The end.

Engel

1. *12/3/73*

Once upon a time there was this funny guy. He wasn't any drunk or anything—just a little crazy. What he did was, when he drove a car, he would blink the left blinker and it would turn right. And when he went to dive in his swimming pool, he would make a belly flop. When he came out of the water, he said, "Ouch!" After he said, "Ouch!" he went to the car with his wet bathing suit and started to make a fire in the fireplace. But the bathing suit kept on dripping and he never got the fire started. After he took a special kind of fan and he took the wrong one, because one gives hot air and the other gives cold air, and you can't tell which one is which. And so, he took the hot one and he said, "Oh, I think I have the right one!" And he did. But the fan that he took was burning hot and so he had to go to the refrigerator and get some ice and put it all over himself. The end.

2. 1/24/74

Once upon a time there was a man and he could lift up one ball and two packages of baseball bats. But he had a little trouble going to the baseball game. But when he got there, he put on his baseball suit and went to the ball game. After he got there, the umpire was mad at him. The baseball player who had just come was mad too. And so they had a fight. But the umpire won. The baseball player knocked the umpire on the head with a bat. But the umpire was *still* winning! The umpire had the whole fence to hit him on the head. But the baseball player ran away. And he just made it, so he stopped. But the umpire was chasing him, so he ran and so he got tired out and so he stopped and looked behind him, but the umpire was still running! And so he stood up and started walking.

But he got tired and the umpire was still chasing him. And so the baseball player started to run again! But there was a pool nearby. So he dived in and he was so tired from running that he could hardly swim. And so his grandma's house was nearby. He went to the shed that they had there and came out with a tractor. And he shifted the gear into rapid and he turned down the cutter and went towards the umpire. And the umpire was still running and the cutter cut off his shoes. But it was a cold day, so the umpire started to the warm pool again and jumped in. The end.

3. 2/12/74

Once there was a man. And he went swimming. But when he came out of the pool to go home—he always made a fire when he got home—he made a fire but the match kept going out because his bathing suit dripped. Now he's really mad at himself for dripping on the match, and so he didn't like that. So he started to undress himself and do it the right way. But after he did it the right way he forgot about how to dive, and so he learned how to dive. And then he forgot how to undress himself. And then he learned how to undress himself and forgot how to dive. And then he remembered how to dive but forgot how to undress himself again. And on and on. . . . The end.

4. 6/10/74

Once upon a time there was a boy who was so interested in pop-a-wheelies that he, instead of calling them "pop-a-wheelies," he called them "daddy-wheelies," because it's Papa. And one day, as he was walking in his backyard, he saw this motorcycle. After he saw this motorcycle popping-a-wheelie, he saw a racing car doing a pop-a-wheelie. And more and more cars and more and more motorcycles came and pop-a-wheelied. And then the boy decided to jump on the back of one of those motorcycles and take a ride. Then they went to a racing stadium. Then the boy held on to the luggage rack and the race was on. And he put on his seat belt and he says, "You can do it, you can do it!" And he said that so much that the driver heard it and so he slowed down. When he slowed down, he slowed down at the right time, because he was past the finish line and he won the race. So he got a prize and he looked what was on the top of his car and sure enough he wasn't there. Because he went so fast that he flew off way back to Germany! The end.

5.   6/18/74

Once upon a time there was a boy. He loved to go fishing. He saw a frog. The boy had always wanted to have a pet frog. So the boy took his net and tried to catch this frog. He did not have any luck. But when he saw that they were really lizards, he flipped his wig! It was five-thirty and the boy had to go home. He went into the shower. He brushed his teeth and went to bed. The end.

6.   10/1/74

Once upon a time there was a beaver. He lived with his mother and father. Every day after dark he would watch his favorite TV show except on Saturdays and Sundays because on Saturdays and Sundays it wasn't on.

One day he was passing by the baseball field and he saw lots of other beavers. He decided to go to the manager of the baseball team and ask him if he could be on the team that he saw. And when the manager beaver answered him he said, "Yes you may be on the team that you like." So the beaver chose his team and told the manager which team he wanted to be on. Then he went up to catch up with his mother. Then when he got home his father was on his desk and writing about a story he was going to make for the beaver. Then the beaver asked his father what he was doing. Then the father said, "I'm making a story for you." And then when the beaver heard his father say that, he said, "What is the story about?" And then his father said, "It's about you." And then the beaver ran out to play. And then he came home, ate dinner, took a shower, brushed his teeth and went to bed.

Then the next day he bought a baseball suit and then he went to a baseball field with his glove and he forgot his helmet. Then he remembered his helmet and he ran back home and got his helmet and then went to the field again. Then he said, "I'm all ready," to the manager. Then he went to the team that he wanted to play and he played. His team was called "Lightning . . . Lightning Bolts." The score was 15 to 14. The Lightning Bolts were losing. Then someone hit a high fly and he ran all the bases and that was the end of the game, and it was a tie. And then the little beaver went home and told his mother about the baseball game and he took a shower and went to bed.

Then the next day he went to the baseball field again. This was practicing day. When it was the little beaver's turn he hit a high fly and he ran the bases and sledded into home. Then he went to his friend's house and said, "What do you want to do here?" And the little beaver said, "You want to go out and practice on our own?" And the friend beaver of the little beaver said, "Why don't we do that!" "I'll get my bat and ball," the little beaver said. "And I'll get my catcher's glove and the bases." And so they fitted the bases in place and they started to play. And then the friend beaver said "We need a pitcher and an outfielder." And then two of their friends walked by. They just came back from the baseball practice and said they were playing baseball. "Maybe we can play." And so the little beaver and his friend came over and said, "Can we play with you?" And then the little beaver said, "Yes." "One of you will be an outfielder and one of you will be the pitcher." And then the little beaver said, "It's getting late. We have to go." Then everyone agreed to this and went home. So the little beaver brushed his teeth and then took a shower and then went to bed . . . because he played after dinner. The end.

7. 11/13/74

Once upon a time there was a sheep. Every time somebody wanted to have their lawn done, he would do it; he would eat their grass. And on holidays he would make a circle with a star in it and on very special holidays, he would make circles which come in, in, in until they come to the very middle. One day the master of India, which is the president, he did not want the sheep to mow the lawn and so he took a box and went into the park and put a little umbrella up and people came with their money and put it in the box. And they did not know that the money was for a lawnmower to take the sheep's place. So when they saw the machine, they wanted the sheep back so nobody ever came to the park again. So the president of India said he wanted that sheep back. So all of his men went to look for the sheep but they could not find it. So the family that liked the sheep the best set off to find the sheep and the boy in the family thought he could remember by the look of him and the father could tell by the eyes and the mother thought she could tell by feeling the skin. And the boy saw the sheep and he jumped on his back and shouted, "I found him!" And so they took him back to the park and he would be there and whenever you would think of him you would remember the holidays and the grass and the designs.

8.   *1/23/75*

[handwritten by child]

I would like to be a screwdriver but I would have a headache by screwing so many screws. It would be so fun lying in a tool chest. But on the other hand I think would be fun, I would know how many time be used but three time a day would be enough for one day.

9.   [no date]

[handwritten by child]

One day I met a mouse. His name was Charlie. Charlie the mouse lived in the country, his best friend was a salamander, his name was Mr. Claw. I didn't tell you that Charlie was a robber Shhhhhhh! I don't want you to let anybody hear because if the police hear Charlie will arrest him. If I told him that the police were trying to get him he would get mad. So here is the story. Once Charlie took a walk. He saw the police so he hid behind a rock. The police walked right past him. He knew he was safe now. He burped. The policemen turned around. There he was choking to death. The police ran but he was quick. Soon the police gave up, but Charlie thought they were still trying to get him. He ran and ran and ran and ran till his feet hurt him and couldn't run. Soon he saw his parked bike. He remembered that his key was in his left coat pocket. He took it out and unlocked the chain. Then he went away but he did not know that the police gave up. So he kept on going. At first he said to himself if I stop and look they will get me. At first he didn't want to take the risk but then he thought: if I go to jail and he would sneak out again. So he stopped. He couldn't believe his eyes, the police were all gone. The end.

10.   *4/14/75*

Once upon a time my name was Engel; I was a soccer player. I was the best in the whole team. I could kick the farest. I could kick the highest. I could kick two inches long. I could kick two millimeters high. I could run very, very fast. I could run eight million miles per hour. The first time I could run it, I tripped over a stump. I fell two hundred million miles up and I landed in S. A. In my grandmother's shower. The shower is on because my grandfather forgot to turn it off. After two minutes I couldn't believe my eyes 'cause I was so soaked. I went downstairs, said hello to my grandmother and grandfather and run really fast down the hill and tripped over a stump in my grandmother's garden. Again, I was over and back into N. America in the soccer field. And then I was running around the field and I kicked the ball two millimeters high and the ball hit me on the head. The end.

11. 5/5/75

Once upon a time there were two mice called Gergels and Wisker. Gergels was older than Wisker. But they were still very good friends. One day they were going on a bicycle ride. They had a bicycle factory that had made them with rulers and tiny tools so the bicycles would fit them. So they went on the West Side highway. It was great fun but eighteen feet is like a mile to them. So they only went a few eighteen feet. So they went down the ramp and then they bicycled to the piers. The pier was empty because everyone was in school. Gergels and Wisker couldn't go to school 'cause all the school pet cats would eat them up. Once Gergels and Wisker tried to go to school but they saw the cats and with their super-dooper rollercoaster they flew down the stairs. When they passed some boys and girls they all giggled because also they saw two mice in a roller-coaster going straight down. When they got off the rollercoaster they jumped on their bicycles and started rolling, rolling. By then it was night time already. So they went into their house, put on their pyjamas and went to bed. When they slept it seemed like five minutes, then they woke up again. That day they went to the Grand Canyon. It took a very long time to get there because they had to stop for gas. Finally they made it. Then they said, "Why don't we try to jump over the skinniest part of the canyon." And that shortest place was a mile. So they wanted a rocket cause they weren't sure they'd make it with a motorcycle. So they were joking. After a while, Wisker said, "I bet I could make it with my motor-cycle a quarter mile across at seven hundred fifty miles an hour." Of course that's straight down. Then it gets very late, they find a hotel because they can't go because it would take too long. So finally they find Howard Johnson's hotel and restaurant. So they slept one night and the next morning started back home. At home they started to go to the museum because it was raining. They saw a marble cat and they looked at it; they stared at it so long they thought they saw it move. They were so scared they ran quickly as they could and went home. Wiskers said to Gergels when they got home, "I'm glad that cat didn't chase us all the way home because then we would have been eaten up. Well anyway we're home now." It was getting very late so they got undressed and got into their pyjamas and went to bed. Early the next morning the alarm clock went off. They said with hope, it's going to be a good day today, and it *was*. The end.

Felix

1. *1/22/74*

A baby was walking down the street making trouble and when the baby saw a man passing her, she said, "You suck your buggers, two times, yeh, yeh." Then they went to a music studio and they heard, "Keep coming in ABC, ABC, 1, 2, 3," And then the baby said, "I can do the whole alphabet. ABCDEFGHIJKLMNOPQRS and TUV, W and XYZ. That's how!" And then the baby said, "I spit at you," and then she spitted in the air. Then the baby said, "ABC my bugger!" Then the baby said, "I think I'm so smart just because I have one tooth out." Then the baby said, "I am Superman, you can't hurt Superman." Then the man said, "You're messing up the whole music studio. Kick the baby out." Then another baby said, "I never saw a baby with a moustache," while putting his fingers on his nose. Then he said, "Me Chinese, me tell joke, me go peepee in your coke." And then the baby that was getting kicked out said, "You're not Chinese, you're American."

Then they saw three ladies kicking their legs up and saying, "Legs, legs, legs are here!" Then the girl said, "I shave my eyelashes everyday." And then the baby said, "I think I'm so great because my teeth don't need to be fixed." Then the baby walked into an A&P Wee-O store and everyone was saying, "Wee-O!"

Then the baby said, "It passed my bedtime, I better find my way home." Then he accidentally walked into a museum while the guard was asleep, and he climbed up a plastic tree and there was a rope hanging on it and he said, "Me Tarzan!" Then the baby swinged out the window and about a mile and landed through the chimney into his house and said, "Me Santa Claus." And then he climbed into bed and went to sleep. That's the end.

2. 2/4/74: *The Adventures of Baby Tiny Tim*

Once there was a baby. He jumped out the window and said, "Me Tarzan." He swung into a museum, knocked down a few dinosaurs, and said, "When I jumped out the window my mommy was in the middle of giving me an enema." And then he said, "I'm not really Tarzan. Hi hippie." He went on climbing and said, "Me go outside to be Tarzan." Then he turned on the TV and heard, "Hey Jerry, what's the story?" And then the baby said, "You're not Jerry, you're screwball." And then he said, "That's the story, Jerry."

And then he heard, "Da-daa-daa-da-da" [sings theme for Bugs Bunny]. And he watched Bugs Bunny. He turned off the TV and went to his grandmother's house to get a frying pan 'cause it was so dark in the house, jumped three times, flew out the window again. Then saw a man in a window and said, "Hi, Harry." And the man said, "So you're a nigger." And he said, "I'm not a nigger, I'm Tarzan. Listen to my yell" [does an imitation of someone doing a very poor Tarzan yell, i.e., very weak and ends in a cough]. Then the baby said, "Woopsi-dazy, gotta go home again."

He went home, got an enema, jumped out to the big big lake and said, "Here I am again. Woopsi-dazy." A man came out and said, "You're a dazy, here." Then he gave him a dazy [daisy]. There was a wire attached to it and the baby said, "What's the wire for?" And the man squeezed a bulb attached to the wire and water squirted out into the baby's face, it was a trick flower.

And then he went home crying, and when he got home he said, "I met a man with funny buggers." He jumped three times, went out and took a walk, got some Pepsi—three thousand gallons of it, drank it. And then he didn't know what he was doing so he went out again, bought fifty cans of Pepsi—at least what he thought was Pepsi, it really was whiskey. And then he said, "I think I'll drink this Pepsi," and he drank it up. And then when he was done he did this [acts drunk]. He went to a drunk party, poured beer on someone's head and left. He turned on the TV when he got home, and the "Night of the Vampires" was on. And the baby said, "You oughta use Listerine for your eyeballs." And then, "Tonight's show is sponsored by . . . Bounty, the super-picker-upper."

The baby got mad, put on a wig, and started singing, "I'm a hippie, I'm a hippie, I'm a hippie." He took off the wig . . . and that's the end.

3. 2/12/74: *Frogenstein Meets Smackula.*

The night was dark and there was a moon, and someone saw something creeping out of the pond. It was Frogenstein. And he started singing,

"There's a little pink frog playing in the water, a little pink frog doing what he oughta, he's jumping right off the lily pad." And then he said, "Me messy, I was just visiting the creature from the orange lagoon, but he's no fun. I think I'll go out. And then he went to the house, picked up a torch from the doorway—'cause there was two, one on each side of the door—picked it up and threw it at the house. Then he noticed a sign near where he was standing that said: "Beware, boomerang torches!" Then the torch flew back at him and he caught on fire, and he was jumping all over the place.

Then Smackula came out and said, "Well, ole pal, what happened to your coat?" And he said, "Those boomerang torches, I never learned what those were for . . . except from the Late Late Show." And then he said, "Look, over there. I see something. What do you think?" "Eeek, Eeek. It's a man. He's got a claw—that won't stop me but it might stop you, and he's got a torch to stop you."

Then Frogenstein got scared and ran away, but Smackula picked up the torch and threw it into the other torch and then a flame of smoke went up and destroyed the sign that said, "Boomerang Torches," to stop him from throwing it at him. Then he took another torch and turned it backwards so it wouldn't hit him but would hit the other guy. Smackula climbed up the lamp post, picked up three bricks, threw it at him, fell down the chimney and that's the end.

4. *4/25/74*

Once there was a baby jumping up and down on his bed saying, "I'm Superman." And then his friend came over and then the baby who thought he was Superman jumped off the bed and said, "Did you burp?" And then the other baby said, "I thought you burped." The other said, "Maybe it was Uncle Howie, he's a hippie," and he jumped on his bed and broke his arm because he forgot he put a board under the bed because he'd been trying to stretch himself around his mother's hand because she had a cut on it. And then his Pampers came off and his friend screamed—the friend said, "I'm a tushie." And then he said, "It isn't whatever you said, it's in between my legs." Then his friend said, "It might be in between your legs but it sure is stinky." Then the friend's pants fell down and the same thing happened to him. And then they both jumped out the window and landed in the Museum of Natural History on top of the strongest dinosaur bones they could put together, and they said, "Soooo, a poo-poo monster." And the friend said, "Are you sure you didn't burp?"

Then they jumped back home . . . and the mother came in pouring a bottle of Ajax down her apron with a half-eaten cockroach dessert. Then she started saying, "Where'd you get that stinky stuff on your bed?" "I don't know. The dog must have—or Uncle Harry," he said. Then the baby said, "You mean Uncle Howie?" And then the friend said, "You mean the guy who just drove off in the back of the police car?" And then Larry came in burping and then the baby said, "So that's who was burping." Larry said, "That Ajax must get soggy in your apron. Don't you want to stop pouring it in there?" Then the baby said, "Burp!" The friend said, "I'm a hippie and a hippie knows the finest hippie is Uncle Howie." And then Uncle Harry came in eating a cheap cigar saying, "Oooh, so-la-mea."

Then the baby jumped out the window again and landed in the city dump. And then they said, "I found just what I've always wanted in the Shitty (city) dump." Then the baby said, "Isn't that thing about to dump that smelly old car on us? . . . I always wanted to have my very own poop toilet." Then they jumped back and they landed on the bed on a tack that made them jump back up and they landed in Mommy's apron. They said, "Now I know what it's like to have Ajax all over you and oily diapers . . . and to pick your buggers." The end.

Moral of the story [contributed by David who was listening]: Never misjudge Uncle Harry's cheap cigars and Mommy's apron.

5.   6/26/74

There was two babies in the White House and one of them said, "Look at that crazy man!" It happened to be Nixon. And Nixon said, 'Boy, you dirty little midgets, I'm going to kill you. I want my Watergate money back. I want my money back. I want a pizza!"

And the baby flew through the air and landed in the car and then drove to New York City and then into the Atlantic Ocean. And an octopus said, "Hey look, a hotdog." Because their weeners were so long, they looked like a hotdog. It's longer than the ocean, so it took five hundred oceans to fit it in.

[At this, William, who is sitting nearby interrupts and says, "You copied!" "No, I didn't," replies Felix. "How can you prove it?" "I don't have to prove it." William insists. "Well, if you can take my word for it, it's all right." "No." "In this case, you can take my word for it," Felix reiterates, "Because you're not me." "Because you're not *me!*" William exclaims. "Well, let's go ahead and continue the story," the storytaker suggests]

Then a boat came along and a lady who was watching, while pouring a half bottle of Ajax down her apron, said, and she was burping. Then she said, "Look, a couple of hotdogs." And Nixon happened to be on it, and Nixon tried to bite off the tip of the weener, thinking it was a hot-dog. And the kid pissed in Nixon's mouth, and he pissed so much it filled up all five of the oceans, and there was no room for all of the water. Then his mother came and said, "Hey, Sweetie Pooh!" Then Nixon just happened to make a poop-oh of his own self. Then the lady, who was watching, went overboard, still burping. And she drank the whole ocean, trying to stop her burps. And then, since it didn't work, she went in front of the boat, and it whacked her on theback, and she went flying through the air.

Then Nixon happened to get the burps his own self. So he threw up. Then he began to stink up the whole place. Then he started to, his hair started to grow so high that he was a hippie. And he started going around saying, "Peace, man." Then he started to grow moustaches and beards and he turned out to have all sorts of combs in his hair. Then he started to get pizzas in his nose, and he began to pick up cockroaches and eat them, and he went to the bathroom of the ship and he found a bunch of cockroaches and waterbugs in it, ate them all up. Then buggers and snot began to drip from his nose into his mouth, and he began to slurp them up, and eat them. Then his ear wax started to drip and he poked his eyeballs out and ate them, copying the saying:

> Little Willie with a shout
> Plucked his sister's eyeballs out
> Stepped on them to make them pop!
> "Really Willie," Ma said, "Now stop."

Then there was a well on the ship and he threw himself down in it and then he copied the saying:

> Little Willie mean as hell
> Pushed his sister down the well
> While the father went for water
> He said, "Gee, it's hard to raise a daughter."

And then he climbed up and went down an elevator, copying the saying, and he couldn't think of the saying, so he went, "Wha, wha." Then he found dynamite and lit it, copying the saying:

> Little Willie found some dynamite
> Stunned as heck
> Curiosity never pays.
> It rained Willie seven days.

And then he remembered the saying and he said:

Little Willie fell down the elevator
They didn't find him
'til six months later.
When they found him
All the neighbors shouted and said,
"What a spoiled brat that Willie is."

(I don't think that's really it, so I just did it.) Then Nixon threw up five times and then he jumped overboard. And then all the passengers said, "What a spoiled brat." The end.

6.   *10/29/74*

Once there was a crazy cross-eyed baby and his mother came into his bedroom pouring a half gallon of Ajax down her apron. Then she said, "I've got a surprise for you, sweetie, hee, hee, hee."

His grandmother came in and squished and pinched his cheeks hard, "My, how you've grown!" [He told me to put exclamation point in.]

Then a big hippie with hair three feet long and a beard two feet long and his moustache was nine feet long.

Then the grandmother gave him a present and left.

He opened his present and then before the grandmother and mother left they said, "Take care!" And he opened it and it blew up and his hair grew stiff and he shouted, "A slingshot!"

He set it up on his bed and he ran up to it and jumped on it and it flew him out the window into the Museum of Natural History and he landed on top of a dinosaur and Nixon just happened to be passing by and the cross-eyed baby had a soggy brown squished up apple with soap on it and a couple of worms and cockroaches and it flew into Nixon's mouth and then Nixon started shouting, "Impeachment, impeachment!"

Ford was there and Ford's hair grew straight and he grew stiff and jumped three feet through the ceiling shouting, "Impeachment, impeachment."

And back out of the ceiling he landed on the museum's chimney and the baby fell down from the dinosaur and his diaper got caught on the dinosaur so he came down with nothing on and Ford came back down as dirty as Santa Claus would be and then he said, "Impeachment, impeachment!" and he jumped up again and this time his clothes fell off and he landed on the dinosaur in the baby's diapers and landed on his butt and he jumped up again, through the window and into the baby's house. And then just as he landed in the baby's house the mother and grandmother came in and pinched him on the cheek and said, ''My how you've grown.''

7. 11/22/74: Burping Nixon

''Well, your old great-great-granddaddy goin' to tell you a story about Nixon. It was back in 1974 when the idea of Nixon being impeached came upon everyone. Nixon fought back like a rat with no belly button, but eventually they got that old fruit! I just got fed up with that nasty old skunk. It was my idea in the first place to impeach him!'' ''Tell me more great-great-great lying granddaddy.''

''It all started out with Watergate when Nixon made his speech. And this is how he made his speech: 'Well, I think that the shortages are here are stupid and they'll be taken care of like that. Use all the oil you want to, old friends.' And just as he said those words, a little squeaky person from the audience yelled, 'And shall we use up all the gas, too?'

''And then Nixon yelled at the top of his lungs, 'Shut up you punk, I was getting around to that!' Then Nixon's face turned red in embarrassment and his overalls slipped down to his knees, then his trousers fell and everyone saw that he had been wearing polka-dotted underwear the whole time!

''And then someone from the audience yelled, 'Hey, Nixon, if you turn your underwear inside out you'll be able to wear it for five more days.'

''And then Nixon just burped and laughed. And then when they got into Watergate this was one of his calls: 'Now you listen here, Bob. I'm going to make a deal with you. You announce that I'll be president for five more years and I'll let you listen to my tremendous loud burp.' And that was the end of the phone call.

''Now, how do you like great-great-granddaddy's old story?'' ''I love it, great-great-granddaddy.'' ''Well, I forget you've got a history test today and that was the history of Nixon and don't forget to tell it!''

Hours later, the great-great-granddaddy said, ''How was your day at school and did the history test go well?'' And placing a dunce hat on his head he said, ''Oh fine, fine great-great-granddaddy.''

8. 12/12/74: Ford

I hate Ford, he pardoned Nixon. Ford was doing his speech and it started like this, ''Ladies and gentlemen,'' and just as he started saying that a little cute kid with funny looking glasses and skinny legs said, ''Can I have your autograph?'' Then Ford said to the kid who asked him for his autograph, ''Shut up your mouth, you stupid baboon!'' right in the speaker.

The audience clapped and laughed disgustedly. That's how Watergate with Ford started. This is how Watergate was. Ford spent all his time in Watergate saying, ''Shut up, I don't deserve this, let me at them, I'm kill them, let me at them, I'll strangle the bum!'' And all the people who were against Ford and were in Watergate said, ''Shut uppa you mouth! Shup uppa you mouth.''

That just goes to show why Ford before he became Vice President or President or anything, was just a crazy old creep who worked in a store.

In the mornings, when he woke up his mother came and had to go, ''This is your eyes, this is your mouth, this is your ass, this is your elbow . . . '' And then when he got to the store someone came in and said, ''This is your eyes, this is your mouth, this is your ass, this is your elbow . . .'' Then in the afternoon someone came in and repeated that and then maybe he could remember until six o'clock. When Ford wanted to know he said, ''Which is what, tell me please, this is my ass?'' [while pointing to his elbow]

The moral of the story is: ''Always be able to tell your ass from your elbow from your eyes from your mouth.''

9. 2/4/75: *Ford's Biggest Speech and Hopefully the Last*

Who will be the survivors of this terrifying story and once again, who cares?

Ford was beginning his speech and someone from the audience says, ''Can I have your autograph?''

He says, ''Shut up, you stupid pinko!''

As Ford started he said, ''What is this world coming to? I don't know, what's this, they're showing a stupid short in this movie theater while I'm giving a speech. What is dis—two spiders making love to each other? This is dirty!''

''I would like to announce that 7-Up has been making its soda too strong. Food prices—they're just delicious.''

Then Ford's dog came along and licked him on the cheek and spit it out. The end.

That's what Ford's coming to.

10. 4/11/75: *Nixon's Monopoly Game*

Movie of the year—three people have died while watching it, twelve of them committed suicide because of it. Here it goes:

"Well, let's see now, looks like I've landed on Free Parking, so I'll buy Boardwalk and Park Place and roll the dice again, forget about your turn. Well, I've landed on a railroad so I'll take five hundred in cash, real cash of course, give me your wallet."

"So I'll roll again, it seems I've landed on your hotel and you have three hotels anyway and I can't pay it up and you can't pay it up and all three of us all together is just enough to pay it up so I'll take all of your money and win the game."

And for the story, Nixon made up this moral: "Want to join me in a game of chess?"

11. 5/14/75: Nixon's Favorite Menu

Unappetizers
Cross-eyed Goose Egg broiled in butter made with mustard, relish, six pounds of flour and plaster from the ceiling.

Our appetizer special: Cross-eyed Chicken's Egg also bacon 100% fat with mustard on it, pickle relish, paint, and a beer.

The beer contains of dirt from our shoe, the stickiest peanut butter you ever tasted, so sticky it glues your mouth shut, and melted mud mixed in the melted metal (that rhymes). That's our special.

Dinner
A hamburger contains of a wrench, a screwdriver, metal from a cavity and a lit lightbulb.

Bun contains of 1% starch, 99% electricity.

Corned beef contains of 100% starch topped with shaving cream.

I like most restaurants. When most restaurants give you a rabbit's foot for good luck—we give you a human foot for good luck, but we mix it in with the food.

More Dinner
Tack tack sandwich contains of salami which is 1% salami, 12% metal and the rest of the percent isn't there.

A bun instead of mustard and relish we give you a tack.

Attack Sandwich is a jolly delicious sandwich. Mustard, snarkle snot and the dolly of your choice. It is such a jolly delight to see the monster fight. It is a jolly delight because a huge monster, a gorilla or lion of your choice, pops out and eats you.

Spaghetti 100% hair, the sauce is 100% mustard. The magic of how well we cook is a demon's secret. Most witches who are making a brew put in one rabbit's hair, but we put in a whole head of human hair so you have hair popping up in your sandwiches and meals.

214

Desserts

One thing about our desserts is that you think that if we just try to make it look good it will taste as good as others. Did you know that black paint looks just like whipped cream and that's just what we put on our sundaes. And by the way it isn't Sunday so why don't you try a Thursday, it tastes just the same.

Our cake special for dessert. Since we favor Nixon so much we decided to break out all of his teeth and put one in each of our cake specials. Since the cake is going to break out all of your teeth you may as well have some of Nixon's cavity-prone teeth.

Did you know that with our restaurant you need a lot of time for two reasons. For one, you have to wait a long time to get waited on and two, we never let you out—that's why it's so crowded in here.

Our Clear White Special—when you try our painted glass you're going to love it when it makes that terrific crunch. And when you try our chewed up magazine we put in it you're going to think it's so good you're going to turn cross-eyed. With that hair that we put into everything we make, you're going to love it.

When you try our terrific dessert, Broiled Brains in Butter, you're going to love it. It contains of broiled brains in butter.

When you try our Bust Your Braces Dessert you're going to love it. It will bust your braces so you don't ever have to wear them again cause you will have no teeth.

There is sixty more desserts, but I won't mention them all and twenty more delicious dinners, but I won't mention them all and thirty more unappetizers. I'll mention some more desserts, but not more dinners or unappetizers.

This lovely dessert is dietetic—get yourself fat with thirty pounds of chicken fat cause if you can eat all of that you'll get fat and that's just what we put in our lovely desserts.

So try our new Nixon menu, you'll turn into a hen—you old slug it to me.

We give you a free gift—a lifetime supply of unwaxed dental floss.

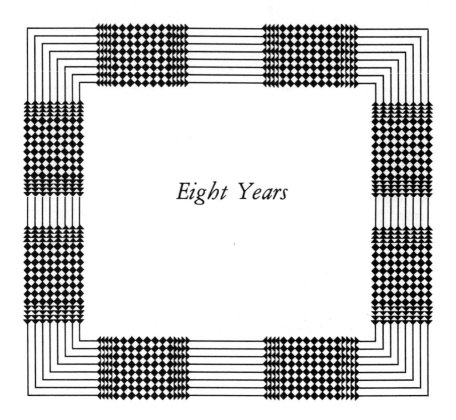

Eight Years

Fred

1. *12/15/73: Speedy the Cheetah*

[handwritten by child]

Chapter 1: The Deer Chase

Once there was a cheetah. The cheetah was his name and he lived in the forest. He was a very smart cheetah. Once in the middle of the night he heard footsteps. He thought it was a hunter he ran up a tree. He said, "yum" because he saw a big deer walking along the path in which he came. So since he was so hungry, he crept down to the top of the trunk of the tree and he waited until the deer got near him. When the deer got very near him, he jumped on him. Then the deer looked around and saw Speedy so he ran like any deer would. Speedy scrambled down the tree and chased him like a bullet and everybody knows that the cheetah is the fastest animal in the world. He came nearer and nearer to the deer. And the deer leaped away like a bullet but Speedy just kept on going on and on and finally he got so near to the dear that he leaped at him and the deer fell dead. And I would say that everybody has to die sometime. Well he did not know what to do with the deer so he went home and his family and told them about it and they went to the place where Speedy left the deer. It wasn't there so they searched for the deer. They found another deer but it wasn't the same one so they brought it home. After all that work Speedy ate it all with his family.

Chapter 2:   The Speedy Race

Once there was a king of the jungle and he was a very smart-so king. Once he said to Speedy that he was the fastest animal in the forest so Speedy said that he would have a race and the winner of the race would be the king. The next day they started the race. It would be 16 miles. They both got in their places and then it started. "On your mark, get set, go!" And they were off. Now as you know, Speedy was in the lead and the king was very much behind. Speedy leaped and was in row 1 mile ahead of the king. The king was just about to give up but then he remembered that whoever won the race was king. Meanwhile Speedy was 2 miles ahead and there was 8 miles to go. Speedy was just about to turn a bend with a giant cliff that was made of big rocks. All of a sudden the cliff crashed in and the king said, "Ha! Ha!" Because Speedy didn't know the short-cut and the king knew it. Now the king was a half mile away from Speedy and Speedy had to find an idea to get over the pile.

He had an idea and so he looked around for a hole and he found one. By this time, the king was very near to Speedy so he ran through the hole and leaped in the air and ran off. Now there were only 4 miles left and he ran so fast that in ten seconds he had run 1 mile. There were 3 miles left. In the meanwhile, the king had 8 miles left and Speedy had 2 miles left so Speedy went to rest on a rock and fell asleep. When he woke up, he remembered about the race and when he looked up he saw the king and he got up and ran as fast as he could and got in the lead. He leaped off and in a limit of 6 seconds he had gone 1 mile and he ran like a bullet. This time was his fastest, 3 seconds 1 mile and he won.

Chapter 3:   Speedy, When He Was Young

When Speedy was young he was very smart and he was very fast. Once he raced everybody in his forest and he beat everybody. Since he was so sneaky he could hide from his own mother. Once he hid from his mother but then went too far from his home and he got lost and he could not get home. He tried to find the place where he came from. Since he could yell so far, he tried to. Way back at his home, his mother heard him and came to the place where he was and took him home. She told him never to do it again. So he didn't. He was very good for the rest of his life, to this day. He lived in the big jungle and he was so fast that in 3 seconds he could run 1 mile. Everybody watched him and learned from him and from that day to this everybody knows that the cheetah is the fastest animal in the world.

2. 10/8/74: The Mystery of Caben Island

[handwritten by child]

Frank and Joe Hardy where speding down baret bay on the coust of bayport. "We better head for home Frank its blowin up a gale" said Joe. "Your right" said his one year older brother Frank. Once they were speding back to bayport the storm struck. Luckily it wasn't a very hevy storm. by the time they reched ther bote house and packed the sluth they were socked head to toe. "We better get home quick" said Frank just when they had just packed. "So lets get movin" said Joe, "the cars right out sied. When the got to the car it wasnt ther "I know a mystery all redy", yep "i ges so but whatever it is it got to wayt intil we get home. "Your right" said Joe. "but how are we going to get home"? "I got it" "Why dont we go to Chets and hill drive us." Chet Morton was a very close friend of the Hardy's. So they walked 20 miles to Chets hoes when they got ther Chet was out in the garden digging up weeds, they were surprised to see Chet werking so hard. Chet had always been very lazy about werk. When Chet saw the coming up the road he said "Ahoy me mates, Chet was always very fun loving giy. Finly after some taeking Chet drove and they whe late so of corse they got yelled at by ant gertrude. The end.

3. 2/12/75: Coming Into The World

One morning when it was very cold, a mother wolf was sitting in her den in a windfall and three little cubs were under her. The cubs were six days old.

The windfall was warm, but not warm enough for the cubs to roam around, since they didn't have a hair on their bodies.

One of the cubs was a sneaky chap. He was always trying to nudge up to the top of the hole that the mother was sitting in, but he never got all the way to the top. This particular cub had sort of a mask on his face.

He looked like a raccoon. The other two were brown with black and white faces.

Within two weeks the cubs could sort of walk but not quite. The mask could walk the best. Sometimes the mask found that his mother was not in the den (of course you and I know she was hunting) so he took care of his two other brothers, because he was the strongest.

One day, for no reason, Mask and his brothers followed their mother out for hunting and, oh, what a beautiful sight they saw! There were white mountains and lakes covered with ice. Once they saw their mother break the ice and plunge her head into the water and come out with a big fish and they sat down and ate it all up. But then when they were resting on the side of the stream, an owl caught sight of them. He aimed for the one farthest away from the mother which was Mask. He swooped down on him but Mask was too fast and leaped away, and the owl just got dirt. But in a very quick motion, the mother wolf was upon it, and they had owl for dinner.

Hunger
That morning Mask followed his mother out of the den. They went down to the river to see if there were any fish. They waited for half an hour but no fish, so they were forced to go into the woods. Very quietly they waited for a rabbit.

They waited for an hour but nope, no rabbit. So again they were forced to go back to their den. This had been going on for two weeks. Bad luck continued through the last winter months. The end of the winter found them weak from hunger.

Spring
Spring brought plenty of food for Mask and his family. See the winter snow had made it so that there were no branches on the trees and had made it so that there were no deer for food, and no rabbits. Mask was getting bigger, and now he went hunting by himself or with his brothers. They often found rabbits or occasionally a deer and mostly they ate near the old creek and they even got some fish there. The end

4. *4/5/75*

[handwritten by child]

Silver was a bear, he lived in north america. Silver had a mother and father, but they wher very old and not strong. Finally they got so weak thet they died, but Silver was big and strong and he new thet he could live by himself.

Garth

1. 5/21/74: The Shadow

Chapter 1

A dark haired man was walking down a street one day. All of a sudden he saw a shadow of something over near the curb. The shadow said, "Help!" It said, "Help!" in a louder tone. It didn't sound like it was coming from the foot of the shadow. It looked like it was coming from the mouth of the shadow. And the strangest thing about it was that it wasn't upside down like most shadows are; it was standing like a normal living thing. The man came over and found that there was nobody at the foot of the shadow. The shadow strangled him! The man fell and the shadow vanished.

After that a man rushed out from behind some boxes where he seemed to be peering on the whole case. He looked at the man and had an expression on his face as if he didn't know what to do. He ran into an empty car that seemed to be glittering right out in front of everything because the moon was shining on it. He jumped in and tore off down the street with a loud cre-e-a-k.

Chapter 2

At the police station the man told the whole incredible story, ending with a "That's it." The captain looked at him like he'd been drinking and was delirious. He said, "Was there any other witnesses?" The man said, "No." The captain said, "We'll just have to see about that . . ." When one of the phone men in the area rushed in and told the same story, not knowing that the man who drove off in the car was the same man in the office. The man on the case said, "All right you two," and went over it with the phone man and the other man. The next day he got a man in the service to go on this mission. "And don't give it up until it's lost," he said. The man walked out of the building with a rather funny look on his face—sort of calm, sort of mystified, and sort of scared. He drove to the woman's house—the woman who was the wife of the man who was killed. When he got in he asked a few questions and told her the bad news. She looked like it was all a joke for a second . . . and then looked like she was going to cry. After she explained it to the children, he brought her down to headquarters for a man to question her.

Chapter 3: The Questioning

The woman said to the first question, "My husband never had any enemies that I know of." She paused for a second and then she said,

"Wait!" Then she said very softly, "He had a cruel boss at his first job. That's all." "Ma'am, where is this boss fellow at right now," said the detective. "He's been dead for fifteen years now," she said. "Yes, I know. But that doesn't explain who it is or about that shadow."

The man walked out of the building and down the street to a cafe. He looked just around the corner to where the whole thing happened. He thought he saw something. Then he saw the very same description of the shadow. It seemed to look like it was going to climb up the lamppost. But the man, to his surprise saw the shadow rise into the air. Being almost in a state of shock, he ran into a building that the ghost flew into. Going up to the eleventh floor he took out a small gun and pointed it at the ghost and said, 'Hold it." It seemed to stop and he shot three times . . . but to no avail. It went right through. It flew out the window and seemed to vanish into the sky.

Chapter 4: The Unveiling of the Dreadful
The man saw another man who seemed to be following the ghost or more or less walking with it. Following them to a car, he knew he could not run after. He made a quick dart and jumped onto the back of it as it tore off. Roaring down the street, finally coming to the outskirts of the town, it roared into a cave that he would have never seen unless the car turned toward it. It roared into the cave and to his surprise it was like a mansion.

Once they got out, he pointed his gun toward the human and shouted, "Hold it." The two of them turned and the man said, "All right, you're probably wondering what I'm doing with him." And he said, "Yes, very much." "It happened a long time ago," the man said, "I was the pilot of a small airplane—not in one of those big companies. It could only take one passenger and that passenger was the man that got killed. He hijacked my plane and took my daughter as hostage. By the time I gave him the ransom and had rushed her to the hospital, she was already dead. I didn't tell a word of this to the authorities or anyone. I made up a likely story and got my revenge." "Oh yes," he said, "I forgot to introduce you to my friend. Meet my partner, the ghost." "You see my friend," he continued, "The ghost has no fingerprints, cannot be registered on film, no radar can pick him up, and best of all no identification at all."

"I think I can get you out of this," said the detective. He coupled them into the car and drove off, reassuring them they wouldn't have to hide away in the cave anymore, and could walk on the street like two regular men again. The ghost seemed very pleased and decided it would be very nice for not everyone to have to faint and stare and scream. When they got to the station, they went to bed and the next day they cleared up

221

the case with flying colors. And the ghost from then on could be of very good use to the fire department, police patrol, private eye service, and was known throughout the city as a very important ghost. The end.

2.   10/29/74:   *My Strange Family*

Once upon a time which wasn't such a happy time, but wasn't such a sad time. Oh, let's just get on with it. (Write that down.) The title is, "My Strange Family."

To start with my brother. The older one has a penthouse bed. In other words it practically touches the ceiling. And my mother often has trouble waking him up because she has to scream up to the bed and when he finally does get up his head usually hits the ceiling and he has to go back to bed!

Now for instance, he has all sorts of strange items which little kids love to dig into and kind of makes you feel like his bedroom is a sweat-shop where your eyes do most of the sweating.

My brother brags over his things and makes bets that his are better than yours and that he has more money because he's won lots of money bets and my little brother has at least thirty pounds of blankets which makes funny forts and things of all sorts. He's quite a big liar, yes he is, he is. He lies about things at home and once he lied that he had a two-hundred year-old coin from Rome. And we said, "You couldn't even find a ten-day-old marshmallow which you could eat and he said, "I bet I could beat your coin collection" and we stuck it out and said, "See." And he went out to his room with a mean looking tramp at three decker speed.

Then my father, he smokes old tobacco and often at night he cackles how the Mets won the Orioles and he screams during football, "That's the way Macgrue!" and things like that and makes himself look fat from drinking twenty-two cans of beer in one night. And we watch boxing fights we scream about the left and the right and when they do do the left and do do the right it's usually the end of the fight. Then he says to my mom, "Good night" and then he goes off and weighs down the bed and makes it look like he's too big for his bed.

And then my mom, oh my mom, sweet and kind. She snaps through dinner and snaps through lunch to eat it, to eat the cauliflower and spinach and when she gets mad, boy does she holler and then my dad comes out and says sweet nasty words and makes her feel like she's just for the birds. She says, "Oh Eric, can't you say something nice" and he says, "Oh, you're just all full of sugar and spice."

She says, "If I'm full of sugar and spice, you're full of pipe and pick,'' and then my Dad gets so mad—he goes in the room and he leans on the old dusty feather mop broom and that's kind of the way it is at my place.

One man was after habit type place.

My room is kind of future bizarre with a tame lizard that's at least three feet long in a cage on a desk that goes from side to side and a picture of a beautiful sea side. And my big neon light (says Garth) and a picture of Joe Frazier's fight and my fluffy bed too and my snazzy lampshade too and I come home from school feeling moppy and slow. Thinking the day's over and who knows, I jump in my fluffy bed and think to myself, "What a bad place for a bed. I'd like to have it in front of the door so when I come home all snoozy and bored and the very darn second I open the door I can jump in bed and stay there that way for the whole sleepy boring real draggy type day.

And everybody does that when they all come home or sit and watch TV. When they come home that's kind of strange to do, but really not quite because do you expect them to all get up and cheer and fight? After a day of hard math, I just say, "Good night."

Our cat, listen here now, our cat such a jeer now. She sits around lazy all soaking up milk and eating her food all sloppy type and crude and ruining her reputation and getting in moods where she feels like just sitting down and soaking up food and she pees on the rug every darn scheduled day in our average old house every average old day.

Our Summer House
Our country type summer house can be quite a bore, after a couple of weeks it's like a la quan snore. Listen, the guys around there are such a bore that you'd rather do dirty house chores. And only one little lake full of lots of boat gases which could fume and even break bullet proof glasses. And brother all he does fish, fish, fish, fish. Never catches a thing except for slimy seaweed fish and once my mother made a dish called slimy seaweed fish with noodles and stroganoff and crisped in a dish. Not one person touched it. They were even afraid to say it was bad. And our dad threw his all away and our mother started crying that we didn't like it and our father said, "It's the wrong recipe, dear," or "the guy who made it must have been some kind of jeer," and he went on like that trying to soothe her in vain, but the shock of actually hating it was too great a pain and all our cat did was sit on pine needle bark and ate up mosquitoes and things like that and got lazier and stupider and fatty fat, fat. And all she would do was play with catnip mouses and chase them into little twig houses which were built there by falling twigs and oh what a scare when she bumped into them nose to nose, hair to hair.

Speaking of scary things that happened around there, they kind of pop up when you're not expecting them there.

Our cat was inside just purring away the whole darn day when a man came over one of our good friends indeed. He came over with some dry ice and that ice was so nice we loved that invention which was called dry ice. He dropped one in water and started such a potion it made us all scared it started such a commotion. Finally my brother was big, strong and brave, stuck his hand in. He says it felt like a grenade went off in his vein and we pretended we drank it. It fizzled all over and just as he was leaving, we were seeing him off. His big greyhound dog made a bark, like a gun and our cat went aloft straight up a tree fifteen feet high and she wouldn't come down. Man you should have seen him fly and we got a big ladder and finally got her down and then that hound wasn't around. Not that he was just barking and not that he was scared, but it took quite a while to get her down—an hour or so and then what a snore. We were all bored stiff by the time she was down and that's why that big old hound wasn't around.

And another thing happened one day or one night. We stayed up till twelve o'clock, no kidding with no fights ('cause we fight a lot you know when we stay up late). And there we are walking home on that dark trail, half scared to death, trees all around us, just one light spot, but knowing my brother, "Listen here, sonny Mac" we were all shuddering stiff by the time we got back. We locked all the doors and turned on the lights every one that was indoors and we turned on the radio full blast and we turned on the TV and found a movie which was nice so we turned down the radio so there was no sound at all. And then we found out that this show was quite a scare, it was about how Martians came to earth one day. It was a fact, it was true, no kidding, no lies, but maybe right in our backyard one lived.

It was tough on the nerves and that's about all I've got to say.

3. *11/26/74*

Once upon a time, oh forget the old corny bit, there was a family. A little boy was jumping up and down on his bed screaming, "Superman," with a mushroom in his hand. His mother came in chewing on some gum with her apron tilted and said, "What is it?"

The little boy said, "Who's making that snuffly noise?"

The mother said, "Don't have the slightest idea, go back to bed."

His mother went away.

All the sudden, his friend Billy jumped through the window. Billy said, "You're in your underwear!" The little boy said, "Let's go for a walk."

His bed collapsed on the floor. Then Uncle Arthur came in with his pipe, snuffling. Then the little boy said, "So that's who was making that snuffling noise."

Uncle Arthur stuffed his pipe full of tobacco and let little junior take a puff. He blew all the tobacco out on his friend Billy.

Uncle Arthur laughed. Billy pulled down Uncle Arthur's pants. Billy said, "Ah, shut up!"

Then Billy and little junior jumped out the window and landed in the Museum of Natural History on top of a mammoth. Billy said, "Did we goof?" Little junior said, "Did you burp?" And he said, "For tickles." Billy said, "I do think we did goof." And they jumped back inside the window and found Uncle Arthur trying to mend his pants back together. They were in the kitchen and Billy leaned on the lamppost which was in the kitchen. The lamppost bent over and touched a mouse trap. The mouse trap sprung, fell on the toy seesaw on top of the refrigerator, but the little wooden boy on the seesaw slid off, wedged open the refrigerator door, rolled into the butter cabinet, rolled all the way around the butter cabinet, came out with an egg on top of his head. He fell on the floor, the egg bounced off with the shock waves, bounced all the way up onto the counter, tipped over the pepper shaker which tipped over and shaked on Uncle Arthur's nose, which made another egg begin to tip. Just as Uncle Arthur was opening his mouth to sneeze the two eggs fell, one in his mouth, one on his head. The one on his head cracked, he swallowed the one in his mouth. And the one on his head began to fry.

Little junior said, "I think we better go now." And they were absolutely right because as soon as they left the egg on Uncle Arthur's head was charcoaled brown and getting hotter by the minute. [meeting interrupted]

4. 1/24/75: My Lovable Family

My weird, lovable family, now let's go back to the weird part. I have a brother who collects anything but other people.

Once he tried and got himself in a lot of trouble. Well, not exactly trouble, you see, he tried and after he tried the person who he was collecting slapped him in the face, took a switchblade out and cut his belt and his pants began to fall down. He ran back inside of the apartment, put a new belt on and began to collect things again.

His room is full of so much junk he can't find the important things, like his baseball cards or his bubblegum collection and stuff like that.

And about my little brother. The one who's six years old and has a schedule for crying every morning, afternoon and night. Once he cried over five different things. He cried over being yelled at in school, he cried over not being able to buy a lollipop, he cried over not being able to watch the movie, he cried over not seeing the whole movie, he cried because after the movie was over he wanted to see the other movie. He'll cry over anything. Either he's smiling or he's crying. He was spoiled and he still is spoiled and he'll always be spoiled. And besides that isn't all about my weird family.

My dad has fuzzy hair and a terrible sense of humor. And he hasn't shaved since yesterday. And my mom paints paintings because you can't draw a painting.

First she buys a fifty dollar camera and thirty cent roll of film and then she goes and gets some gas and then she drives out in the country and she takes a picture of a barn. And then she blows it up, and turns it into a slide and shows it on a projector which she buys. And then she sketches over the lines with a number two pencil which she buys and then she paints it in with expensive paint which she buys and then she copies it onto a frame that she buys. And then she has a show with all her paintings and for every painting she sells, she gets forty percent of the money for the painting. Which all amounts to a losing of four hundred fifty bucks. Ingenious.

And about me, I've got a foot-long iguana. That's where the dream came from. He sits on his heating coil all day and eats his lettuce and water and goes back to sitting on the heating coil. He just sits, doesn't make a move. I've got a big neon sign in my room and all I do after school is sit quietly meditating in my room.

That's all that's strange about my family. Anything strange about your family? Strange!

5. *2/19/75: Execution Dock*

This ain't going to be a comedy. It's going to be a rhyme.

I would rather be in Execution Dock than in school. I know why and maybe you do too. Because in our great classroom nicknamed the Gas Room, when the guards let in the gases it kills us kids by the masses and tortures us to death.

The one way out is up a wall three hundred feet high with spikes sticking out and you'll probably be spotted by an electronic eye if you do.

And if you don't get shot the monsters in the moat with a big long throat will get you. And if he doesn't devour you and kill you with big claws he'll come out with a Viking boat and out will come some paws. He'll lift you up onto the deck and throw you in the brig and take you back to the main land and treat you like a pig.

And then they'll take you to the stretching rack and stretch you till you break your back. And then they'll take you back again to the whipping chamber where they'll whip you twenty times and then the worse torture of all, they'll take you to a room which is so bad it's worse than death. And then they take you and give you the worse fate, they practice up your penmanship and give you a debate about whether you should take the math or history or spelling.

Oh but wait! I forgot to tell you about this. This horrible thing they do. They make you eat their horrible lunches which they prepare in the cafeteria too. These lunches are made out of hamburgers smothered in goo. Until I see you next time, I'll be in the dungeon with my crew.

6. 4/11/75: The Threat from Outer Space

[He starts by saying, "Think, think, think, think, think, think, think," and then miming a whole story with sounds like "Pow, pow, yeh, heh, bzzzt."]

A scientist is working in his labs. His space communication device begins to buzz. He answers it and a strange message comes. They translate this strange message and find it's a threaten that the people of Androlean have decided to move to your planet. Evacuate it at once or you shall be destroyed. [The original message was a lot of different sounds.]

The President and governor know about the threat and it's in the papers. Everyone tries to get away. The President orders the army, navy, everybody to be on the lookout and prepare for the big war. A month and a half from then they get one bleep on their radar that is there one minute the next it's gone. They do not understand how they can get just one bleep. Then they confirmed it was going at twice the speed of light. Newspapers read of the strange signal and then one day, a half a month later, the war began. It started sixteen miles from the Washington Monument. People say the craft just was there, they didn't see it come, it just was there.

It hovered perfectly, not moving up or down, it stayed in its silent hover for six seconds and then let out a stream of bright ray which immediately disintegrated twelve buildings. The craft suddenly disappeared as if swept away by the wind.

The newspaper had a large blowup of the space craft on the front page. The President and all the high officials of the countries read that it was impossible to defeat such a superior force so they agree to evacuate home sweet home. A large quantity of space arks appeared and a planet with the same atmosphere appeared on the radar at NASA. They immediately evacuated but left one small party of people on earth in a highly developed space craft. These people were to see what other civilization of superior beings were like and then to leave the planet.

Garnet

1. 12/15/73: Planter and His Wife

[handwritten by child]

Chapter 1: Planter Meets a Dinosaur.
Once upon a time there was a cat named Planter. He lived in a little hut in a place called Alaska. It is very warm in the spring so he plants all his food for the summer, fall and winter. One day it was the first day of summer and he went outside and took a walk through the forest and he saw a big thing. Planter said, "Get out of my way." The big thing did not get out of his way and said loudly, "I will step on you." It was a dinosaur. The cat said, "Oh yeah." The dinosaur said, "Yeah." Planter ran back to the hut and said to his wife Chubber, "There's a dinosaur in the woods." So Chubber decided to call the police and the police came over in dinosaur suits. Planter forgot it was "National Police Dress-up in Dinosaur Suits" week.

Chapter 2: Planter Goes On A Long Trip
Once upon a time there was a cat named Planter. He lived in a little hut in a place called Alaska. Once he walked into town and went to the train station and got on the train to 6th Avenue, Washington Square in New York City. It was going to be a very long ride so he had to pack his things in five suitcases. (His wife didn't want to camp.) When he came, his wife helped him carry this things to the train. When the train came, Planter got on with his five suitcases and the train left. At 8:00 in the morning, they had breakfast on the train. When they finished breakfast, they heard a sound. It was the train. It stopped and they looked up front. There was a sign saying New York City. They had gotten there in one hour and they were surprised.

Chapter 3: Planter Meets a Talking Can
Once upon a time there was a cat named Planter. He lived in a little hut
in a place called Alaska. One day after he finished breakfast he went on a
walk and found a thing that looked like a tin can. Then he found out that
it was only aluminum foil shaped like a tin can. [illegible] and so he did
not pay any attention, but then the can talked. It said "Do not go away. I
am magic. I can do anything but bad things." Planter said very politely,
"Will you be my servant?" The aluminum foil said, "Yes, but I will not
do bad things, and if anybody in your family calls me names, or doesn't
like me, he shall get turned into a frog." So they never did and the
aluminum foil was happy and they lived happily ever after. The end.

2.   *9/25/74:*   *The country*

[handwritten by child]

every other weekend I go to my country house in Massachusetts. We own
7½ acres of land. About 6½ of them are woods 1 of them is field. My
father loves it up there, My mother hates it, Phillip and me like it. It gets
very cold up there much colder than newyork in winter. in summer it gets
to 110 deggrees there. it is 120 miles away and it takes us approxometly
2½ hours to get there. both andy and marion have a house not more than
30 minutes away. I have a small amount of freind's there and i am usally
very lonly.

3.   *11/22/74*

A wick on top of a candle is burning. There was a round ridge on top but
now it's melted. The flame is made up of three different colors, yellow,
blue, and brown. The melted wax automatically turns hard when you
touch it. As the candle gets smaller the flame gets higher. There is a
round wax buildup. When the candle is lighted the flame gets bigger.
On one side the candle has a big rim but on the other side it's small. On
the wick there is a red spot that disappears when the flame goes over it
but when the flame is not over the spot it turns red. The wick under the
melted wax is white because the wax is over it. The blue flame is partly
under the wax so the wax must dry when it melts into the ditch. At the
top there are three different stages and it looks like three flames. When
you put something near the flame it smokes. Most of the melted wax
evaporated by the heat. You need oxygen, a surface and something to
burn to start a fire. When you blow it out the red spot stays for about five
seconds, probably because of the heat.

4.   12/2/74:   The great home run

[handwritten by child]

here we are at the polo grounds in the playoff series between the newyork giants and the Brooklyn dogers. We are in the final game the series is tied 1-1. the score is 5-4 the dodgers are winning in the bottom of the ninth. The giants are up with runners on 2nd and 3rd. Two out's and Bobby Thomban's up. Wille mays on deck and here's the picth. Strike 1 the count is 1 strike and no balls. he's in to the windup the pitch (crack) a long fly ball it's going back, back, he's at the wall and it's Gone a home run the giants win 7-5 and will go in to the world seires. vs. the New York Yankees.

Inez

1.   3/7/74:   A Little Horse Named Flip

Once there lived a little horse named Flip. He lived with his mother and father, and were owned by a girl. The girl said that she wanted to give away the horses for money. And the mother said, "No!" And her father said, "No!" And then the girl took the father horse away and sold him for money. And then the girl took the mother and sold her for seven hundred dollars. And then she took the pony and she went to the store and she bought another horse just like him for her sister. And then she sold the horse she had before it. And when she sold that too, she had enough money to buy a couple of rabbits. And then the mother and father rabbit had lots and lots of babies, one litter each month. And then after a while she was beginning to have too many rabbits, and she began to sell them for more money. And she gave some of the money to her mother and father. Her father and her mother spent it to get the mother and father horses back. And then the girl thought that the horses had come back by themselves. Except the father and the mother went away for awhile and came back with ten baby horses. And then the girl sold nine of the horses. And when she sold them, the father and mother said it was nice of her to get back the baby one, because they thought she'd brought it back but she had not brought it back. The horses brought it back. And then the girl told them that she sold nine of the baby horses and she kept one. And the mother and father took the baby horse to the back yard and they jumped over the fence that was there, and then they came back with twenty-two horses. And all the horses that were there got away and came back with lots and lots and lots of horses. And then the girl sold one hundred of the horses and she got lots and lots and lots of money. And she bought some dogs. And the dogs went away and came back with more dogs and the girl named one of the horses Flip, because he always flipped a lot. And then Flip grew up to be a beautiful big horse. And that horse Flip, he always came when the girl whistled and then Flip died. The end.

2. *3/11/74: Our Classroom*

Our classroom is a wild classroom because of Milo, Isaac, Darius and Vinnie, Gregg and John. They always do weird things, like Milo got bit on the arm by a dog. That's true. I like our classroom and the people I like in it best are Melissa, Rose, Adina, Samantha, Dara, Dan, Niblets, Survivor and Sniffles and Lisa, I've known the longest of all and Cleopatra. That's our gerbil. Joanne is not nice in the cooking group. She is not nice at all. In our classroom we used to have ten rabbits and one gerbil but one of the rabbits died, and the next day they were all dead except Niblets, Survivor and Sniffles. And one of our gerbils died. We had two. His name was Mark Antony, and we were left with Cleopatra. Samantha is nice because whenever you give her something, she always gives you something better back. Melissa is nice because she lets me play with her all the time, and Rose just came back from her house from being sick. And we might be getting a hamster because the other gerbil died. And we might be getting another gerbil. And Lisa, the one I knew the longest, is really a nice person because she's always generous sometimes. Rose is nice because whenever she's holding the baby rabbit, she lets me hold them. And Dan's nice because he may let me take the rabbit home. And if he does, I'll have to put my cat in the bathroom. And it's up to Freya. And I like Dara because she lets me have a doughnut when she brings them. Deirdre green pepper and me because I brought a whole and a half green peppers. And Gabe always makes all kinds of noisy dumb sounds in my ears, so I hate him. And Dan is still real nice because he doesn't get mad when we're in the classroom before he is. The end.

3. *4/5/74: The Two Kittens*

Once upon a time there were two kittens who lived with their mother, father, brother, and sister. And one was a boy and one was a girl. Once one of the kittens went out in the fields and found thousands of mice there. So he went back home and told his brother about all the mice. Then they both came out because the brother did not believe there were that many mice. And he saw that there were that many mice. So they went back and told their sister and then they all came out because the sister did not believe there were that many mice. And she saw that there were that many mice. And then they started to catch all the mice. All the cats started to chase the mice except the sisters. And the sisters went home and told the mother and father about the mice and took them over. After about a week they chased off all the mice except for two. Then the two mice went home and told their parents, friends and friends' parents about the cats, but they didn't believe it. So the mice took them out to see the cats and the cats started to chase them. Then when the mice saw the cats were chasing them they ran into their houses, and never came out again. The end.

4. 5/15/74: *Two Little Kittens*

Once upon a time there were two kittens and they lived with their mother and father. One day the kittens went out for a walk and got lost, and their mother and father were worried because they liked their children. The mother went out for a walk to find them and she got lost in the woods. Meanwhile, back to the kittens. They wandered around and they found a cottage where a little girl and her mother lived. The little girl was coming out to go for a walk and she found the kittens on the doorstep. And she took them in the house and asked her mother if she could keep them, and her mother said "Only for a little while." And then a while passed which was a couple of days, and the mother said they would have to let the kittens go because it was too much money to keep them.

But the little girl did not let them go. She kept them in the basement. But soon her mother found them and she told the little girl they were in the basement and that she had to put them out. The little girl asked if she could keep them another day. Then the kitten's mother found her way to the cottage and the girl took her inside and she put the mother with the kittens. And then the father found his way to the cottage and she let him in and put him with the mother and babies. Then the girl's mother said that they could not keep them, but they would have to give them away because it was too much money to feed them, and the mother was allergic to cats. But the little girl put them in the basement again. Then the girl's father came home and said they had to throw them out, but the little girl said to her father—asked him at least to keep the baby. And the father said yes, but the mother said no. So they had to get rid of all of the cats. But there was a dog outside the door. But the little girl said that there was a dog outside the door, and the mother and father said they could keep all the cats. And they lived happily ever after. The end.

232

5. 1/17/74: *Cat's Paws, Dog's Paws, and the Mouse*

Once a cat was walking down a alley on right and a dog was coming down on the left side, and the dog started to chase the cat. And the cat was getting faster because the cat was a mouse. And the mouse saw a kitten. And I am only going to do one more story. The end. [The storytaker queries: "What happened?"] The cat caught the mouse and the dog caught the cat. And the dog died 'cause he ate too much. The end.

6. 1/17/74: *The Lost Kitten*

[handwritten by child]

Once there was a kitten who went for a walk in the woods. She got lost and night came. Luckily cats can see in the dark, or she'd be double lost. Luckily she found a cottage where a little girl lived. The little girl found the kitten and hid her. The little girl's mother found the little kitten and said they could keep her for awhile. But soon it was too much money to feed the little kitten. So the little girl said that she would give the little kitten some of her food. The mother said alright, because she knew she would get tired of feeding the little kitten and forget. But she did not.

7. 9/11/74

[A lot of these are spelling words which were posted in front of Inez.]

Once upon a time there lived a hippopotamus that drove a carriage. The hippo met a dolphin in Manhattan. The dolphin looked in the mirror and thought there was danger. So he played plastic monopoly. Then he read the encyclopedia and the hippo read the dictionary; and they both died of working too hard. The end.

8. 9/11/74

Once upon a time there was a monkey that was dumb. She wore pink pants and a blue, green, yellow and purple and red shirt and her name was Ariadne. The monkey met a lion that was her friend and they played bridge and then they ate a tree. The mountain lion found a cobra and ate it and gave half to the monkey and they died. The end.

9. 9/11/74

[Use of spelling words again.]

Once upon a time there lived a snake, a king cobra snake and it played bridge with a monkey, and the monkey had the highest score after the bridge game. They went on a trip in a rubber rocket to the moon. The monkey ate bananas and so did the snake. They had a mishap and ended in the city New York, in Manhattan.

10. 11/20/74

Once upon a time there was an ordinary family. This ordinary family had an ordinary mother and an ordinary father and an ordinary sister and an ordinary brother. This ordinary family had a dog. But this dog wasn't ordinary. In fact he was extraordinary. He was green and purple with white dots. This dog's name was Tiffany. Next door to this ordinary family lived another ordinary family. This ordinary family had an ordinary father and an ordinary sister and an ordinary brother. This family had a dog also. This dog was extraordinary just like Tiffany. There is only one difference. This dog was green, purple, orange, blue, red, purple, and white with brown polka dots. Tiffany and this dog were friends. The name of this dog is Digby. Digby and Tiffany used to always go to the park. But now they couldn't go anymore because Tiffany died. Digby was very sad. So were both the ordinary fathers and the ordinary mothers and the ordinary sisters and the ordinary brothers. So then the first ordinary family moved away. Then another ordinary family moved in. This ordinary family had an ordinary mother and an ordinary father and an ordinary sister and an ordinary brother and an ordinary dog. This ordinary dog's name was Eve. Eve and Digby weren't good friends at all and Digby used to always chase the other dog and they lived happily ever after. The end.

11. 11/22/74

Once upon a time there was a carrot who was being eaten by a person named Anne F. and she was just getting ready to eat a peanut to kill it and at the time she was wearing her dog tag that said, "Class of '76," a blue sweater and she was wearing purple sneakers and green socks and had yellow teeth, blonde hair, blue eyes, puffy cheeks and a huge fat stomach and is writing down her books. Her best friend is Debbi and her most hated friend is Wendy and Leslie. She isn't in Mark's class. She does not know a girl named Paula P. She did not hear Mark run after Robert with a knife in his hand. She ate the carrot and peanut and there wasn't even a big pocket that said homework and her teacher's last name was not even Johnston.

One day she went out for a walk and met a gorilla eating a piggy and the piggy was not Anne F. She did not even see it and in the desert when she was walking through the forest she saw an alligator. The alligator was trying to catch a fly and the frog was trying to catch a fly too. Anne is a very nice kid, but she is not too.

Then the next day Anne went out for a walk again and she found a cute little puppy playing with a kitty cat. And a bear was coming up to eat it and Anne swat him on the head with a broom. And I forgot to tell you she was carrying a broom. And she was sitting here listening to me telling the story and saying, "Oh boy," like an old boy dummy and then the next day she went out and met a person, after all those animals, and she lived all alone and that person was a pope and he was educated and evil [a spelling word] too. The end.

12. *12/17/74*

Once upon a time there was a girl, she loved animals. She had two cats, five dogs, three horses, a frog, two lizards, a hamster, some fishes, six gerbils, a couple of mice and her name was Nancy. She loved her horses most of all. She loved to read. She adores math and she's always on time for lunch [smiles] and today she made a new friend and that friend's name was Lizzie. Her and that friend took two of her horses and went riding in the woods. They were riding for a long time. Then all of a sudden they couldn't recognize the road. Then they were *lost*. While they were gone, Nancy's gerbils died. Her cats died. Her other horse died of loneliness. Her dogs died. Her hamster died. Her mice died. Her frogs and her lizards died. Her fishes died. All of her animals died. That was very sad. Finally her horses found the way home. But when they got there, the dogs didn't run up and start licking her, the cats didn't run away from the dogs. The frog and the lizards weren't inside. The fish wasn't inside. Her hamster wasn't inside. All of her animals weren't there. Her mother told her about the tragedy. She was very sad. She was down in the droops reading the book. The book was called *Franny and Zooey* [that's what Lizzie in the class is reading]. She felt very sad so she ran away from home. The end.

13. *1/22/75*

Once upon a time there was a little fishy. He was a black little fishy. He lived with all his brothers and sisters who were red little fishies. And all the time all the big fishies tried to eat all the little fishies. Once a big big fat fat huge huge big big fishy came and started and tried to eat them. And this big big fat fat huge huge fishy was a grouper and the big big fat fat huge grouper fishy tried to eat 'em. The black little fishy, who was a tiny little fishy, smaller than his brothers and sisters, and the little black fishy had a good idea, of all the red fishies making a big big huge huge fishy and he would be the eye of the fish and they would scare away all the fishies every day all the time. And then a big huge fat fat big huge huge big fat big huge fat fat jelly fish came along and scared all the fishes so much that they broke up and got really scared and a big whale came along and ate them all up except the black one that swam into a cave (and was never seen again). The end.

14. 1/27/75

Once upon a time there lived a little girl. The little girl had a doggie. But the doggie died. So she got a cat. And the cat died. It's a very sad story. So she got a gerbil. And the gerbil died. So she got a lizard. And the lizard died. So she got a monkey. And the monkey died. So she got some horses. And the horses died. So she got a rabbit. And the rabbit died. So she got a classroom. And the classroom died. There was a gerbil that had babies. Baby gerbils. And there was a rabbit that had baby gerbils also, because they went in there by mistake. And the mother rabbit had baby rabbits too. And so the mother rabbit killed the baby gerbils. And the rabbits died. So the little girl had a classroom. And the classroom crumbled. The end.

15. 2/25/75

Once upon a time there lived a little baby. Now this little baby was a cute little baby. Now this little baby that was a cute little baby had a cute idea. And this cute little baby had the idea of walking up the stairs and sliding down the banister and turning around the pole on the banister and walk up the stairs again. But he fell down all the time and that cute little baby that had the idea of sliding down the banister, saw this thing on the banister and that thing on the banister was a big glob; the glob started crawling closer and closer and closer and finally slid down the banister and the little baby said, "How dare you steal my idea?" So, the little baby thought up another idea, but this time he didn't say it and then the glob came back and started crawling all over his idea and he started crawling closer and closer and closer and finally bahm!, he jumped on the little baby [pause] and then the glob began getting smaller and smaller and smaller and smaller and then the baby went home with just a little glob on his arm, cause the glob stuck to his arm and then his mother said, "You better go to sleep." So he went to sleep, and the glob started going up his arm and finally his mother came in and woke him up and then the glob stopped crawling and growing. So, the mother said that he should not go to sleep for as long as he could but he began getting tired so he finally went to sleep and forgot all about the glob, and then he woke up in the morning and he was all a big glob. So he crawled off the bed and into the hall and his mother saw him and began getting scared. So finally she ran into the big brother's room and woke him up and got him out of bed and told him to run out of the house as fast as he could. He did and he told the police not to shoot him because he was his little brother. So they got out as many squad cars as they could and then the glob ran closer to the mother and closer and closer and finally swallowed her up [pause] and he went out the door and went into the neighbors' house and swallowed up the baby and the grandmother and then he went outside and saw all the squad cars and he turned back into himself and all the people were back again and there was no more glob and they all lived happily ever after.

16. 3/18/75

Introduction

Once there was a classroom and its name was 527 and there was a kid named Alvin. He always pretended to be a girl and he always danced around. And he always pretended to be pregnant and have a baby.

Once there was a class named 527. And they had lots of mice and rats. And one of the rats was Morgan.

Once there was a class in 527 and it had lots of people. One of the peoples was Shana. And then there were the idiots of the classroom. And they were Ronald and Curtis.

The rat and the first idiot were friends and they had other friends in the story, like Shana. And Curtis. There was another person in the story who I did not mention, who is a really nice person. A really nice person. And her name is Melody. And there was another nice person in this story and her name is Alice. She's a really nice person. A really nice person. And they were both friends, good friends. That's the end.

17. 4/29/75

Once there was a little girl and she had a dog named "Pinky." Now this dog was a very nice dog, he always like to run with the little girl and play with her. But soon the doggie started getting old. But he's still only two years. When that dog was a little puppy, he was sick. Now he's not a puppy anymore. He's a dog. The dog was named Pinky because he was pink with brown spots. He was a labrador retriever and he has brown ears and a brown tail. Once this dog came up to a watermelon and said, "Hello." But the watermelon didn't answer. "Hmm-mm," said the doggie, "Why doesn't he answer." And with a sigh he walked away.

Today they were going into the woods to hunt rabbits. But they didn't find any. They were all gone. "Hmmm," said the little girl, "Why aren't there any more rabbits." And with a sigh walked away and Pinky followed. The next day it was Pinky's birthday. Pinky was turning six. And he was getting very old now. He was forty-two in dog years. And he was going to die pretty soon. In two more years he died and everybody was sad. The end.

18. *4/29/75: The Gerbil*

Once upon a time there was a gerbil and it liked to play. He always sticks his nose out the cage and I tickle it. Sometimes he bites me but I don't care. Because it doesn't hurt that much. He has a nice bottle that he sleeps in that's full of colors that's shredded cardboard. He always tries to climb up the water bottle. I love him. The end.

19. *6/2/75*

Once there was a puppy named Hildegard. Her name for short is Heidi. She is my dog. And I love her. She is beautiful. But I had to give her to my uncle. Because she didn't like the city. And I was sad. So I got a new dog named Max. And I love him too. But not as much as Heidi. But I still love him. But then I had to give him to my father but then I got a cat called Paws. I love her too. The end.

Janice

1. *11/14/73: Clarence*

[handwritten by child]

Once there was a lion. She was the biggest lion there and a lot of hunters were after her. One day Clarence met another boy and they liked each other so they stayed together. One day they were walking together when Clarence sensed a hunter near by. All of a sudden Clarence felt a net on her and she ripped it and ran away. She looked everywhere for Leo, but she smelled something else with him. She sensed all the way to him, but he had another girl. So she said to her old boyfriend that he'll be sorry. But he smiled and walked away. So she walked away. The next day Clarence told some of her girlfriends that she wanted to get rid of her boyfriend's girl. So they started looking for her but they couldn't find her. So they looked and looked and looked and finally they found her in the bushes licking her new born babies. The girls looked ferocious at her. She said come in and look. But all of a sudden they all jumped on her and her babies. When they were finished, nothing was left but flesh and blood. But they did not notice that Leo's girlfriend was not there, and they did not kill her. So they went away satisfied. Leo's girlfriend went to him and told him what happened. So they went to Clarence's house. When they got there, she wasn't there. The next day they went out and they saw her and killed her. The next day Leo came and apologized and they started going out again.

2.   11/14/73: *The Glob*

[handwritten by child]

Once there was a man who lived with his family; two boys and a girl and his wife. One day he felt his hand and he saw a little white bubble, like a piece of dough stuck to his hand like a piece of skin and it hurt terribly. So he told his wife. She said he better lie down. So he did. Next morning that stuff had spread up his arm. And it hurt more than ever. So his wife called the doctor. The doctor said he didn't know what it was. All he knew was that it spread overnight, only when he slept. So every night he tried to stay awake. But he kept falling asleep every few minutes, and the stuff kept spreading. One day his wife came down stairs and she screamed. He was a glob! He started rolling towards her. She started running away, but she couldn't out run him. When he tounched her she disappeared, into the glob's stomach and he became fatter. He rolled upstairs. When Susan saw him she screamed. Her two brothers Bob and Michael came running in, but no one was there except the glob. It touched them and they were gone. The glob rolled downstairs, rolled out the door and went to the hospital. He pushed the door down and rolled over everybody, on the first floor screamed and no one was left on the first in ten seconds. He rolled upstairs and went into room 41A. There was a little boy. He started yelling and a doctor came running in with a water hose because he thought there was a fire. But just the glob was left. All of a sudden he turned the hose on and the glob went away. The doctor ran out of the room and outside to the police station. He told the chief police man. He said, "Get in the car and show me where the glob is. So the car started and they raced down the street. All of a sudden the glob rolled right in fron of them. They stopped short because they didn't want to get touched. They started backing up. All of a sudden someone said "run". Then in ten minutes there was a crowd. The police had a telephone, so he called the police station and in ten seconds the police were there. They started shooting, but the bullets bounced right off. So the doctor said to the policeman that he's scared of water. So the police told the other police that he was scared of water and they started spraying. Soon the glob got so scared that he started rolling away. Then a little puppy came running out behind it. All the people started shouting "Stay away!" "Go home!" "Get out of the way!" Then all of a sudden the glob started rolling towards the girl. And all the people could say was "Run little girl, run." But before anyone could say "pickle" she was gone. Her mother came out screaming "You stupid glob for nothing. I hate you. Where's my daughter, where is she? Do you hear, where, where?" And she ran into the house. Then all of a sudden the glob started rolling towards the house, then knocked down the door and tried to catch the little girl's mother. She started screaming. Then the police started running in, but the police were too late. She was already gone. Then the glob started rolling towards a tiny baby. One of the police ran in front of the glob and got the baby and ran out with it. All the people cheered. Then the grandmother came running up the block saying thank you, thank you, thank you. The police said, "You better let us take the baby. She will be more safe." The baby's grandmother said alright. But take good care of it. All of a sudden the police that saved the baby ran towards the chief, gave the baby to him and ran towards the glob. He started squirting the glob. Then all of a sudden the glob turned back into a person and all the people he rolled over were back. Everybody cheered. And he became chief. The end.

3. *2/7/74: Two Dogs*

There were five newborn babies drinking from their mother. She went to the back of the car to pick one up. Then she said, "I have to get food for them but I don't have any money. I forgot about the money. I just robbed, I do have money." So she drove to the store. She got there it was closed. She took a knife and cut the glass window and went in. She got five cans of dog food and then she went out in the car and went away. All of a sudden, she started feeling lazy. She fainted and the car went off the road, but it did not go on fire.

Back at the police station, the police heard the crash and came to it. Then they took Karen out of the car and the dogs and the babies. They looked at the dogs and at Karen's hands and they took and studied the dogs very well and found not Karen's fingerprints on the dogs, but someone else. All of a sudden the mother dog started going crazy. She bit Karen on the leg. They took Karen to the hospital and the dogs to an animal hospital. The next day a scientist, a doctor from the lab came and asked Karen some questions. He asked, "Was anybody with you in the car?" Karen said, "No." Then they brought the dogs and asked if they looked the same to her and she said, "No." Then she said what she had been doing last night. She said she had done it because she had a ticket for $20 and no money. She gave it all back to the police to give back. Then she said she felt better. They said that she could go because they did not have rabies. She asked if anybody had found the real dogs. They said they had been found on the street several hours after the crash and that one of the babies was sick. She said she did not know that they had babies and she'd like to see them.

So they took Karen to see the dogs. One of the police had taken a liking to Karen. He said that he would drive her home. On the way down she said to the nurse downstairs that she'd pick up the dogs next Friday. He drove her home and said his name was Mike. He asked her if she wanted to go to lunch and she said yes. He said he would bring her to The Red Lantern, so they went. That afternoon Mike asked Karen if she would like to go to Coney Island tomorrow. She said yes. The next day he came and picked her up. They drove to Coney Island. At first they went on the big roller coaster. Then they went in the Tunnel of Love and then they went to MacDonald's. He asked her if she would like to go to upstate for a weekend to Rosenblooms. She said yes. That night she said she had a wonderful time and he could pick her up and Friday and they would go up to Rosenblooms and stay there till Sunday. Then she said, "Before you go we must remember to pick up the dogs and get them food." It was Friday and they went to pick up the dogs. They got the dogs, got food and they left. That night when they got into the room he gave her a present. She opened it. It was an engagement ring. She kissed him and then she said, "I will." Then she went into the room and started to write to her friend. Her friend's name was Melissa. She said they were getting married in March, in five months. Five months passed quickly to Karen and then came the big day. She was getting ready in the church and everybody was waiting outside. [She hums the "Wedding March."] Then he came out from the other side of the church and they met and then they walked up to the priest and they were married and he gave her the wedding ring and she gave him the wedding ring.

4. 5/2/74: Witch's Gulumph

A long time ago way back in time lived witches. They always used to have lizards for dinner. But I am going to tell you about the leader of the witches. She was cruel and her eyes were like slits. The part you saw of them were red like fire. She had (instead of lizards) eight frogs, nine lizards and twenty raw fish. Instead of being a scrawny witch whose ribs show, she was fat, very fat. All the other witches called her a big fat pig! After a witch banquet she would burp and say Gulumph. One day when the witch was on her broomstick she happened to see her sister (who she hated) on her own broomstick. Windy, who was the leader of the witch's sister said, "You never deserved to be a leader." The leader said, "I deserve to be it more than you." Then they flew away. When the leader got back to her kingdom she saw a terrible sight. Her castle was, well all the windows were broken. A little boy said he did it. He saved a lot of trouble for himself.

Moral: Tell the truth and save yourself a lot of trouble.

5. 5/2/74: The Witch

Once there was a wicked witch who liked to eat children. All the children were afraid of her. She always went around saying, "I'm going to eat you, ha ha!" Then they would start to cry. One day while the witch was out a girl named Victoria went out. The witch thought to herself, "What a pretty little girl. I will catch her and then children will try to help her and then I will catch them all." So she captured the girl. Then Victoria screamed. The end.

6. 5/23/74

Once upon a time there lived a family of three. There was a little girl named Mary Lynn and her mother and father. The mother, for some reason had trouble with Mary Lynn. In Mary Lynn's mother's childhood she had not many friends and not a very good childhood. So when she grew up she always remembered her childhood and she didn't think it was fair for other children to have good childhoods, so she beat her child a lot. But meanwhile the father didn't know the mother beat her a lot, so whenever the child said to him that the mother beat her up, the father never believed her, and that she should not fight at school and not to play so rough.

One day when Mary Lynn was at school a car drove up and said to her, "Get in the car little girl. Your mother is sick and she wants you at the hospital." So she didn't know what she was doing, so she got in the car and drove away. They drove upstate to an old shack and they asked her what her father's name was. She said she only knew her father's first name, not the last. They asked what it was. And Mary Lynn said it was Michael. Then she said, "Where's my mother?" And they didn't answer. And she repeated her question. And they didn't answer and she started to scream. They gagged her and told her to be quiet. Meanwhile, at home her mother was getting worried. When Mary Lynn's father came home she told him that Mary Lynn wasn't home from school yet and that she hadn't heard anything from her, so they called the police and reported a missing child. The police said they'd do all they could about it, but probably she was at a friend's and not to worry.

Back at the shack the men who held Mary Lynn captive were writing a message saying, "If you want your daughter back you'll have to pay $5 million, and you'd have to have it by next week or else they would kill her." The next day the mother got the letter and it had no return address on it, and the mother said once that she had seen a little shack in upstate New York. That could be where they're keeping her. She said she saw it one day when she had been taking a drive. So that night they drove up to the shack and nobody was there. So they decided to look inside. When they got in they heard a moaning. They checked the whole house and finally they found their daughter. But right at that moment the two men who had kidnapped her jumped in. They gagged up the mother but the father tried to get away. He ran for the door but they got him. They tied him up and they tied the mother up and they gagged the father too. And they left because they had some other business to do. So the father, Mary Lynn and the mother were all tied up. But luckily the father had put his hands in a certain position, so he could get out of the ropes. So he got out and untied his wife and Mary Lynn. He had matches and he went out to gather some wood and he made a fire in the fireplace. And he got on top of the shack and he took his coat and wrote "SOS" with the smoke coming out. He did this because the robbers had taken his car and left theirs without the keys. He kept doing this until he heard the sound of a police car siren. The police car was coming towards the shack. One of the police got out and asked him what happened. They told the story and they said they'd wait there until the two men came back. And from then on the mother never beat her child because she saw that just because she had a bad childhood doesn't mean she had to beat up on everybody else. The end.

7. 6/9/74

[handwritten by child]

Once there was a lion named Pickey. He was very picky, he would only eat rabbit. So one day his mother called him and said you are going to a party and you can't be pickey. But all Pickey said was I'll try I'll try. So that night of the party they were being served by the Mayor of animals who was the hippo. Picky said I must have rabbit stew to the Mayor. That made the Mayor angry, nobody says they must to the Mayor—Nobody he boomed. Pickeys mother who was sitting there tried to calm the Mayor down. The Mayor kept yelling nobody—nobody says they must to me! You must leave, leave at once he said. So Picky and his mother had to.

The next day Picky's mother said to Picky your father is coming home from work and he's bringing home a meal tonight. When Picky's father came home he brought Picky a package. Picky opened it and tasted it he liked it. From then on he ate other food.

8. 9/13/74

[This is partly a manuscript and was partly given orally. The separate parts are marked off with an asterisk.]

Once there was a beautiful girl who lived in this rich lady's house. The lady's name was Mrs. Money. The girl's name was Ella. Mrs. Money made Ella her slave. Ella got one cent every two months. Well one day when Ella was bringing Mrs. Money's breakfast on a tray. She didn't feel so good so she tripped and fell and dropped Mrs. Money's food. Mrs. Money got very angry and hit Ella. "You stupid girl," said Mrs. Money, "don't you know how to carry anything." "But . . ." "But nothing," said Mrs. Money. "I don't feel well," said Ella. "If you don't feel well you sleep. And that's that."

Now Mrs. Money didn't know Ella had a prince visiting.* Ella had a room on the top floor and it was a little room with a sheet on the floor and a sheet for a cover and nothing else. She had lots of mice so the prince, the way he got up to the room was that he disguised himself as a guy who would go in and put rat poison all over the house.

One day, when the prince came in his disguise, Mrs. Money followed him up to Ella's room. When they got up to Ella's room, he knocked five times. Mrs. Money thought to herself, "Hmm, maybe that knock five times is code." She was hiding behind a big arm chair in the hall. When he went in Mrs. Money went to the door to listen. She heard Ella say that she had missed him. So she waited a minute so she could go in and catch

Ella red handed. So she heard them talking and she barged right in. The prince got up and started pretending he was putting mice poison all over, but Mrs. Money got angry and said, to the prince, "Get out!" So the prince got up and left. She went over to Ella and said, "Now you can clean the whole house." So Ella got up and started cleaning.

Mrs. Money stayed with Ella the next day to watch the prince didn't come in, and the next day. After a few days she didn't stay anymore because she was convinced that the prince wouldn't come back. Two days later he came in Ella's room by the window. Right at that Mrs. Money started to come up the stairs. Ella hid the prince behind a black curtain in front of the window. When Mrs. Money came in she said, "You're supposed to be downstairs to get me my breakfast." So Ella went down and gave Mrs. Money her breakfast. Then Ella came back up to her room and the prince took her to his castle and they got married. The end.

9. 11/21/74

[handwritten by child]

One day two men decided that they would take a trip to Africa to explore a place where nobody dares to go. So one day they took off in their little plane. One was named Bob and one was named Danny. It took a week to get there so they stopped a few places. One time they stopped at an old lady's house and she said that they shouldn't go. And she wouldn't let them leave. They had to sneak away at night. One day Danny, who was holding the binoculars said, "Bob, I see it. I see Jungle Danger." So Bob found an open place and he landed. That night in their tent Danny said, "Let's go exploring tomorrow." So they decided and went to sleep. The next day they got dressed and took a rifle and started. Out in the jungle they were walking and they saw a little ship. Danny said, "Let's go inside." They went inside there was everything you could imagine in it. There was a refridgerator and a dining table and food and games. There was a living room and a T.V. "Wow!" said Danny. The next minute there was a rumbling noise and a voice said, "You are now going to planet X, Pluto." Bob said, "Oh no we're not" and he ran to the door but it was locked. There was no escape! They were leaving earth. They passed Mars Jupiter Saturn and all the other planets in twenty minutes. Then they arrived at Pluto. The whirring sound stopped. They tried the door. It opened they stepped out then a loud cheer arose they looked around there looking at them were thousands of big frogs. The biggest one said, "Welcome, oh master."

10. 1/23/75: *The Dizzy Pot*

[handwritten by child]

If I were a pot made on a wheel I would get very dizzy, but it would be fun ti be taken out of a pack of clay and wonder what I'm gonna be. The person would smack me down on the wood and I would start spinning around and then I would feel a hand push down on me and start shaping me. Then I would start sticking to the wheel. I would think should I be easy to make or not. So I would be a real mean pot I would start going off center but after a while I would get tired and just let them shape me. Then it would stop, if I was real I would probably throw up. Then I would be put on a shelf to dry and I would starve. Then when I was dry they would put light blue glaze on me. Then I would start getting cold. Then I would dry again. Then I would be put in a kiln and I would get very very hot! Then the glaze would start blowing up. They would take me out and I would be a nice pot. The end.

11. 2/7/75: *Pal the Dog*

Yesterday I went to my cousins' and they have a dog named Pal. He's a german shepherd. So I'm going in the house and the dog starts barking and the father had to hold him back. I was so scared I thought I'd pee in my pants. They told me, to make matters worse, that he'd bite me if you acted scared. So I walked in like a robot and I didn't even look at the dog. He told me if I just minded my own business and acted natural he wouldn't bother me. So I did and I got along with him very well. After a while I got up enough nerve to pet him. My aunt was playing with him and by mistake he jumped up and put his paw right on my stomach. It hurt a lot but I still like him. The end.

12. 2/18/75: *My Cat*

My cat is black and white. He's really wild, like when I'm asleep. I'll move my feet and he'll attack it. And we have two openings to my kitchen. If I run around one he'll come around the other and attack my feet. If you tickle him on his tummy he'll bite me. Sometimes he'll lie on his stomach and start rolling over. If he sees dogs, he's not scared of them. By the way his name is Toosie. One day when a dog, we were in Vermont, we had a glass door, was looking in. And the cat was just lying on his back looking at him. And he never lets me brush him, he bites me. The end.

13. 4/15/75: *Boulder and Money*

[handwritten by child]

There was a girl named Susan she loved animals. She had two birds one turtle and one dog. She was eight and a half. One morning she woke up. She heard something saying "help help." Then she thought I must be hearing things. Then she heard it again. So she got out of bed and she got dressed, then she went outside. She heard it again! She looked around, then she saw it. There on the ground was a parrot. It had a bullet hole through its wing. She picked it up, and brought it inside herhouse. She asked it "What is your name?" "Inky" said the bird, then it said "go down Blackbird lane, then when you get to a colorful boulder, stamp on it three times." Why this is Blackbird lane thought Susan but "where is that boulder." She said aloud. Then the bird hearing that question flew away. But then about ten feet out the door it fell. She ran out and got it, then she brought it inside again. Then she brought the newspaper in. Then something caught her eyes it said 50,000,000 dollars stole from bank. One robber is caught. He said that the money is hidden but he won't tell where! By Tammy Davis. Then Inky said "Racccck! Boulder and money Boulder and money." Boulder and Money thought Susan. Then she ran upstairs and woke up Katie her big sister who was twelve! She yelled, "Katie Katie wake up!" Then her sister (who Susan thought was a weirdo) woke up and said "I surrender" in a dreamy voice. Then Susan said "come on Katie woke up!" Then Katie said "O.K. O.K. What is it?" Then Susan told her sister about Inky and the missing money and the boulder. Then Katie said "I think Inky knows about the robbers."

So they had breakfast and gave Inky some toast. Then they asked Inky how he got the bullet in his wing. And he said "My owner raack, is a robber and I heard and he tried to kill meeee!" Then he fell down off the table and died! They took him out and buried him, They left their mother a note and it said they were taking a walk. They walked to the dead end of Blackbird lane. Katie and Susan looked for the colorful boulder. Then they found it! Katie said "Wait I have an idea!" Just to play it safe we'll throw three rocks on it. Because who knows if they have big bags of rocks up there. So Katie threw the first rock, nothing happened. Susan threw the second rock, nothing happened.

Then all of a sudden Protector their dog ran over to the rock and started growling. And when Katie was about to throw the third rock he nipped her hand! "OW" said Katie. Then she said to Susan "You pick up the rock like you're going to throw it and I'll throw it, O.K.?"

"O.K." said Susan. So they did it! And when the rock hit the boulder it opened in half! There was suitcase that said Top Secret! And when Katie and Susan ran forward Protector growled and pretended he was going to spring! Just then fire lit up where the boulder was! Protector saved their lives! "Oh Protector you good dog" Susan said.

They all walked over to the rock. They took out the suitcase and opened it! Inside was money money and more money! All of a sudden Katie felt a gun at her back. She turned around and a guy with a shot gun said "get in the car, the dog too!" So they all got in the car (which they hadn't heard drive up) and drove off! Then the guy who had the gun said to the guy driving. "Let's go to the hide out" and Katie watched where they were going. She saw they were going to Long Island! Then finally they got to a little street where they turned off the road and drove into a garage. "Got out of the car kids and follow me and Tom." So they finally got to a camouflaged house. They took Katie, Protector, and Susan inside the house. Then the guy who had the gun and whose name appeared to be Phill said "Now club come to order!" Then he said I'll take attendance. "Jack!" "Here!" yelled the guy who drove the car. "Mark!" "Here!" "Andy!" "Here!" "Jon!" "Here!" "Now I captured these two punks." They found the money and I don't know what to do with them!" "I think we should get ransom money from their mother" Mark said. Then Phill said "Who thinks we should keep them for money?" Chorus of me's! "Hey kid" Phill pointed to Katie (who had been sitting in the corner with Susan and Protector.) "Write a note to your mother asking for 5 thousand dollars!" "O.K." Katie said. They did not know that she was sending a code letter to her friend Janie. And when Janie got the letter it said "Dear Janie, I am kidnapped tell my mother that I'm in Roslyn L.I. and I don't know where tell her I'm o.k. and so is Susan. Love Katie." But the time it got to Janie's, Susan and Katie's mother was a wreck! And shen she got the not from Katie she called the police. She told the police that they were in Roslyn Long Island somewhere. But back in the where they were being held, they were thinging about moving! Susan cried once and they got angry at her! They are going to move to Vermont! So they put Katie in a room with the dog and Susan. Then Katie told Susan she was going to sneak out the back window. And get police. So she snuck out! And when Phill came in she was gone! "Where is she kid come on where is she!" "I-I-I don't know" Susan said. Then Protector started growling! "Shut up dog" Phill said. "Listen kid if you don't tell me I'll kill you!" "All she told me is she is leaving th-that's all!" "O.K. kid but we're leaving!" So he got the club together and told the. "We gotta get out of here! That brat the big one got away. She'll probably get the police!" "So I'll get the other kid and we'll get in the truck and leave!'' So they got Susan and Protector in the truck and they left! Now Katie just got to the police station, and now she could not see the police! When she finnalt got to see thechief he said ''Now kid what do you want!'' ''My sister is kidnapped! And the people who kidnapped her are the ones who stole the money from the bank!'' ''Now you're putting me on little kid.'' ''I'm not'' she cried. ''O.K. kid show me where.'' ''Come on.'' So they got to the house the truck was just leaving so the chief yelled ''Stop this is the police!'' So the robbers gave back the money and Susan and Katie went home! The End.

14. 5/5/75: *Elizabeth*

[handwritten by child]

Once there was a girl named Elizabeth. She thought she was the ugliest girl on her block in New Rochelle (except for the retarded girl on her block.) One day she was walking with her friend Melony and Melony said to Elizabeth, ''You ought to get the job helping Karin the retarded girl on your block.'' ''Oh, I didn't know that they needed a job and anynow why wouly anybody want to have me for a job/'' said Elizabeth. ''You're wonderful with kids'' said Melony. ''Well'' said Elizabeth ''I'll try it.'' ''O.K. but you have to go and try out for the job. You will get two dollars a week.'' said Melony. ''I'm trying out for the job too.'' ''We'll go to the place tomorrow.'' As they walked up to Melony's house, Melony's boyfriend walked up and said ''Come on Melony.'' Elizabeth said, ''Hi Joey and goodbye to Melony and walked away. Wow said Elizabeth two dollars a week! Too bad Dad isn't here. He had died two years ago when she was twelve. She is fourteen now. He had been killed in ahit and run. Her brother almost went into shock. All of a sudden her thoughts were interrupted because Phillip (her secret admirer) bumped into her. ''Hi'' he said. (Elizabeth hated him.) ''Hi'' Elizabeth said. ''Um, Phillip I have to run'' said Elizabeth. And she ran! When she got home her cheeks were red. When her mother saw her she said''What have you been doing?'' ''Nothing'' said Elizabeth and walked into her room. Her brother came running into her room. ''Lizz Lizz I got the job doing a paper route!'' ''Wow that's great'' said Elizabeth. Her brother Andy was 12 and very cute. She walked out into the kitchen. ''How was school today Lizz?'' ''O.K.'' said Elizabeth. ''Oh mom tomorrow I'm trying out for a job with Karin.'' ''That's nice but are you sure it won't upset you?'' ''Oh mom I'm not a baby anymore so please don't act like I am, I'm fourteen now.'' ''Well I'm not gonna be talked to like that now go to your room!'' ''No'' said Elizabeth and grabbed her coat and walked out. She was walking down the street when Buddy a 16 year old kid that every girl had a crush on came over and said "Hi Elizabeth would you like to see a movie with me?" O.K. said Elizabeth. As they were walking Elizabeth's heart felt sky high. Buddy said "We're gonna see Law and Disorder. I was just coming over to ask you if you could come to the movies with me, oh bye the way I always liked you." Elizabeth smiled. Then she noticed that they weren't going towards the movie theatre. Then she said, "We're not going towards the movie theatre!" Then Buddy said, "I know, I'm taking you to the park I reserved a seat." "Oh let's go." said Elizabeth.

When they got there they sat down. Buddy put his arm around her. Then she put her head on his shoulder. Then he kissed her. Elizabeth's head went into a whirl when they stopped kissing. Had Buddy really kissed her, her the ugliest girl on the block be kissed by the cutest boy in town! Elizabeth thought it must be a dream. But then he kissed her again and he kept kissing her until she ashed how late it was, it was 12 o'clock. Then she said I have to go and he walked her home. She saw an ambulance inher front lot. "Oh no!" she cried and Buddy ran in with her there they saw Elizabeth's mother on a stretcher. "What happened" she cried. One man said she had a bad heart attack but she might still be saved. "Oh god" she cried. "Andy!" Then she asked if they had seen a boy about 12. The men said "No." Elizabeth was already running into the woods in back of the house. Buddy ran after her,when he found her she was at a treehouse comforting Andy. At least he didn't go into shock again! They brought him home and put him to bed. Buddy called and told his mother that he would stay with Elizabeth for the night because Andy kept waking up. Then finally Andy fell asleep. Then Buddy kissed her good-bye and left, so in the morning Melony ran over. "I couldn't get over last night my mother wouldn't let me come over." "Oh bye the way are you coming over today for the job?" "Well it depends on if Andy goes to school." "And he's still asleep." "Oh wait here he comes. Hi Andy how are you honey?" "Hi Andy" said Melony,"I'm sorry about what happened." "Yeah I know" said Andy "it's terrible." Melony asked him if he felt like going to school. He said "Yes." So Melony and Elizabeth walked him to school to tell his teacher why he was late. The teacher said "That's terrible should I announce that to the class!" "Well" said Elizabeth "That's up to Andy." "O.K." said Andy. So the teacher told the class. It seemed O.K. then but at recess kids were teasing him. He got so upset he ran out of the schoolyard and kept running until he came to the highway and he still kept running until he almost collapsed. Then he just sat on the highway. Then when school finished back at the school the teacher was collecting names and when she came to his name it wasn't there. The teacher asked, "Where is Andy." Andy's friend Michael said "Kids were teasing him and he ran away towards the highway." Then the teacher asked him who teased, Michael said Sandy Dennys and Tom. The teacher said Michael would you take a note to all their teachers and ask if they could let their kids come to this class? "O.K." said Michael. So when the kids came to the class the teacher said, "Why did you tease Andy about his mother." And they said "Well it's tough and other things like that." So theywere sent to the principal and they were expelled for two days. But at Elizabeth's school all the kids were coming up to her and saying "Oh I'm sorry." But at the end of the day Buddy came over and took her by the hand and said "I just got the message Andy was being teased and he ran to the highway." "Oh no" said Elizabeth. Then she said "We might still be able to find him." "How" said Buddy. "Well we could go to my friend's house she has a car we could go and look on the highway." "Come on." said Buddy. So they ran into the girl's house and told her everything. Then Sue said "O.K. come on." So they went in the car looking for him. They were driving and they saw him. They stopped and Buddy got out and got him in the car. Then he said, "I'm sorry I ran away like that." "That's O.K. Andy I would have done it too." said Elizabeth. "I would have done it too. Also." said Buddy. "Now we'll take you to Acting Class. And me and Melony are gonna try out for the job with Karin. So they brought him to Acting Class and went to Karin's house. When they got there Karin's mother said "Are you here to try out for the job?" And Melony replied "Yes we are Misses Donald." Said Miss Donald, You can come in one at a time girls. Melony went in first. And when she came out Mrs. Donald told Elizabeth to go in. When she came out she said "Ill send the one who made it a letter."

So that night when Andy came home she made a very unfancy dinner and Andy went to bed early. Buddy came over for a little bit and they talked and then he left. Then a very disappointing visitor came! A foster adviser came. Elizabeth was sitting watching T.V. when the doorbell rang she answered it. It was the foster adviser. They told her about her mother and that she probably would not be home for a few months. Then Elizabeth said "If we had some grown up or relative then could we stay here?" "Yes you could" they said. "But do you have any?" "Well" said Elizabeth, "We have my father's mother but she's in Florida." "Well that's a very tough position your in." "I know" Elizabeth said. "But can't we just stay here until my mother comes back?" "You could do that if you were 18 but your not." Then Elizabeth said "Well I'm not leaving this house so you and your partner can leave!" Then the lady said "Well I'm not going to be talked to like that young lady!" Then Elizabeth said "Well I'm not leaving this house so good-bye!" And she shoved them out the door and locked it. The next day she sent Andy to school and waited for Melony to come. It was Friday. Then all of a sudden Melony burst in "Lizz Lizz I got the job working with Karin!" "That's nice" said Elizabeth (she wasn't really so enthusiastic about it.) "I'm going over there now so Mrs. Donald can tell me what I'm going to do!" Well thought Elizabeth I guess I'll go to school without her. But then she called back to Melony and asked her when she would work. Melony said Monday after school and Friday after school. "O.K." said Elizabeth and said good-bye. Just then the telephone rang it was her mother. "Oh Mom how are you?" "I'm sorry I yelled at you last night." "On that's alright honey" she said. "Oh I might not go to school today." "Now honey I don't want you to stop school just because of me." "Well good-bye." Then she hung up. Then she started for school. While she was walking Buddy came and they were walking together then he said"Um-Elizabeth would-would you go out with me?" Elizabeth said "Yes!" "I'm gonna come over tonight." "O.K." said Elizabeth. So that night he came over at 9:30. Andy was asleep. They sat down on the couch. Buddy put his arm around her shoulders. And he hugged her close. Then they kissed. And they talked and had a lot of fun. And then Buddy had to go he said "Good-bye" and left. The next day it was Saturday. Andy wanted to see a movie with Elizabeth. And Elizabeth wanted him to go with a friend so she could go with Buddy. Now I want to tell you what Buddy and Elizabeth and Andy look like. Now Andy looks like a tough kid, he has dark skin, his hair is brown and down his neck. He has a big figure. Elizabeth has blonde hair has well not a great figure, she had a pretty face and a sort of pretty figure and short. Buddy is tall he has a shag hair cut and a husky figure. Blonde hair. Now about the movies. Andy decided to go with his friend. And Buddy and Elizabeth went to the movies. This time they saw Towering Inferno. They really loved each other. That night Andy couldn't sleep so Melony came over they talked a lot. Then Andy came out and said "Can I speak to you Lizzie?" When Elizabeth went in he started crying "I-I want d-dad." Elizabeth said "I know oh don't cry Andy." She took him in her arms and said "It's allright, it's allright." Just then the telephone rang. "I'll get it" cried Elizabeth. "Go back to bed Andy I'll see you in the morning." She ran out to answer the phone, she did answer. It was the foster adviser again. Elizabeth said "Oh you again. Well if it's about leaving forgit it O.K.?" "No it's not O.K. Now listen if your gonna be like that to me forget trying to ignore me about going to a foster home because you are." Elizabeth said "Well I'm going to ignore you whether you like it or not good-bye!" And of course she hung up. Melony who had been listening said "What was that all about?" Then Elizabeth went through the whole story over again. "Oh you could stay with us in my house." Melony said. "Hey that's a good idea" Elizabeth said. Then the phone rang again. "You answer it Melony and if it's them say I'm out" "O.K." Melony said. Then she answered "Hello, oh Buddy wait a minute here she is." Then Elizabeth took the phone. "Hello, Buddy, hi." Then Buddy said hello Elizabeth can I come over. Then Elizabeth said, "Oh sure come on over see you in a while." And she hung up. Then she said to Melony, "Buddy's coming over and I want to be alone. O.K. Good-bye. Five minutes after Melony left Buddy came over. "Hi" he said "let's sit down, so they sat down. This time he brought over a bottle of wine so they had a few drinks and then he had to go he kissed her good-bye and left. But when he left she looked out the window and saw Joey and Melony talking to him about some thing! The next day she looked on the calendar, her birthday was next week she would be 15. "Andy" she called. Today they were going on a picnic with Sue Buddy Joey Melony and Sue's boyfriend Bill they were going to Bear Mountain. "Andy!" She called again. "I'm coming" said Andy. "Well hurry up, Sue and the gang are coming to pick us up in a few minutes." "O.K. O.K. here I come." "Alright we have to wait for them to come now!" Beep! Beep! Beep! "That's them" Andy said he flew out of the house. Then Elizabeth came out and got in the car then they were off! It was a nice sunny day. They were talking alot until they got there. Sue cried "Were here!" Andy was out first he was climbing up a tree. They had a lot of fun then Sue treated them out to dinner and a movie. Then they went home. Elizabeth noticed that they were running out of money. So she said "Andy I'm going across the way to Melony's house to borrow some food." "Alright come back soon" he cried. "O.K." Elizabeth said. So she went across the way to Melony's house. She knocked, no answer. She ran home and got Andy. Then he pushed the door open and all of a sudden the light's went on then, "Happy BIRTHDAY!" She looked around it was Sue, Bill, Buddy, Melony, Joey, and Melony's mother! There was a big pile of presents and the house was decorated. Then Buddy said Elizabeth open the presents. She went over she took the largest one. Guess what it was! It was a big record player! Then she opened thenext one it was a pretty pink shirt with a heart on it. It was from Sue. The record player was from Bill. Then she opened a tiny little package, it was from Melony. They were earings they were little gold flowers with a blue stone in the middle. Then there was the last one. She opened it, it was Buddy's I.D. braclet. They were going steady! She gave him a kiss and they sat down to eat. They talked and played and then everybody started to leave. Buddy came over after the party, Andy was asleep then Buddy left. The next day was Monday. Andy went to school and Melony and

Elizabeth went to school too. Today was exams in Elizabeth's class she was very nervous not only because of exams but because she was going to a party with Buddy. Also she said she would come and she has nobody to stay with Andy because Melony has to work with Karin! Who could stay with him. Oh no my exams so she went to work. There she finished and the bell was going to ring in a few minutes! Ding! Ding! Ding! There goes the bell. Elizabeth was up and running before anybody was even up! She ran out of the school. On the way home she met Buddy, he said, "Are you coming to the party?" "Well" said Elizabeth "I'm not sure; you see Andy has to stay with someone." "Oh that's no problem" Buddy said "My big sister will sit." How old is your sister, oh she's 20 and my little brother is 14. And also my little sister she's 12. And my mother is pregnant again." "Wow" said Elizabeth "that's alot!" "I know". Buddy said. So that night Buddy and Elizabeth went out and Julia his sister came. When theg got to the party they went in and a girl came over she said, "Hi Buddy this must be Elizabeth. Hi I'm Carole come in and make yourself at home." So Elizabeth took her coat off. Then Carole said Now I have a surprise for you, we have the group Chicago here to play for us. So they played a few songs, then they played 7 minutes in heaven. Elizabeth got called by Carole's boyfriend and Buddy. Buddy got called by a girl named Erica and Elizabeth! When Buddy took her home he kissed her good-bye and left, so did his sister. The next day when she was walking with Andy to school, at the house next door there was a moving van, she looked and saw a girl stepping out of a car. Elizabeth thought, Why she's beautiful! She had long brown hair, black eyes, beautiful figure! She was wearing tight jeans and a nice print shirt. And then a lady that looked like she was her mother's age, got out and payed, it was a taxi. Then the lady called "Leah come here and take your suit case!" Then Leah saw Elizabeth "Hi" she said. "Hi" Elizabeth said. Elizabeth asked "Are you moving in?" "Yes" the girl said. Then Elizabeth said "Well good-bye I gotta go now." Then she and Andy walked off. On the way to school Buddy came over. "Hi" he said, I hear that a knew girl is moving in." "Yeah" Elizabethsaid "she moved right next to me!" Then Buddy said "I suppose she'll be coming to school." "Yeah I suppose so." Elizabeth said. When they came to Andy's school he went in then. When they got to Elizabeth's school they both went in. At Elizabeth's math class a teacher said "Elizabeth please do this problem for us" But Elizabeth was too busy thinking about Leah. What if Buddy falls for her and "Elizabeth please do this problem for us" the teacher said. Then Elizabeth got up and started doing the problem. Then at the end of the day she went out of the school, she was walking with Buddy. Andy was doing the paper route. Leah came over and said "Hi" "Hi" Elizabeth said "this is Buddy, Buddy this is Leah." "Hi" Buddy said again. Where are you going?" Then Leah said "Oh I'm just going to register for a class. I think for homeroom I'll get Ms. Barlow." "That's my class" Buddy said. "Well" Leah said "I gotta go now bye." Then she walked off. Buddy said "She is really fancy I don't really like her." Well Elizabeth thought that's a relief. When they got home to Buddy's house, he asked "Can you come over to my house tonight. Everybody is going out and Andy can stay home alone can't he?" "Yeah I guess so" Elizabeth said "See you later." Later, right after dinner, Leah came over when Elizabeth was about to go to Buddy's house. "Hi" Leah said. "Hi" Elizabeth said. "Look I'm going over to my friend's house so can you leave." She said good-bye to Andy and walked to Buddy's. When she got there they had a lot of fun then she left. When she got home she heard someone sobbing, she ran into Andy's room, he ran to her crying "I want Dad." Then the phone rang! The End.

Jill

1. 2/14/74: *The Lost Fox*

Once there was a fox. He was very lonely. One day he went on a walk and he met a tiger. He asked the tiger, "Can you help me find my home?" "Sure, where do you live?" said the tiger. "That's it. I don't know where I live." "Okay. Why don't we go on a walk and if you think you live there, you tell me." So the fox got on the tiger's back and they walked and walked until it got dark. "Oh," said the fox, "It's getting light." "We can sleep and go on in the morning," said the tiger. And so they started off in the morning. And they walked and they walked again. One week later the tiger said, "Well, we can't find your home. What will we do?" "Let's sit down and think," said the fox. "Okay," said the tiger. Then the tiger said, "You can come and live with me." So the fox went to live with the tiger and he was never lonely again.

2. 2/22/74: *A Story About Pussy Willow*

[True story] A few days ago I got a little stuffed cat. I named her Pussy Willow. She smells very nice. I have to hold her very tight and very good, otherwise she'll get hurt. 'Cause to me she is real. So whenever my mother picks her up by her back or ear, I yell, "Don't hold her like that!'' Whenever I put her in my bed and am sleeping over someone's, I put her on top of my nightgown so she does not get hurt. And I love her. The end.

3. 2/28/74: My Best Friend

[True story] My best friend's name is Elisha. She was in my class last year. Elisha always said, ''Can you come to my house?'' But I could never go. She could only come to my house. Whenever she came we had lots of fun with Suzie, my cat. I haven't seen Elisha in a long time, even though she's still in the school. I don't see her because she is on the second floor and eats first lunch. Except one day in a school holiday I want her to come to my house. If I ever went to her house, I think I have lots of fun with her and her dog. But I would not really play with the dog, because Elisha says that it growls a lot if you go near it. She lives right near St. Vincent's Hospital. That is where my mother used to work. The end.

4. 2/28/74: The Great Dane

Once there was a great dane that when he was a puppy, a girl found him. She loved him very much. She kept him for a very long time. Then her mother told her that they had to move and they could not keep the dog. So the girl went to the ASPCA, and the ASPCA said to her, ''You know if we don't find a home for your dog in two weeks, we will have to kill him.'' So the girl took her dog and left. Then she went to the Bide-A-Wee Home and she said, ''Can you keep my dog?'' And they said sure, and the girl asked, ''If you don't find a home for it in awhile, do you kill it?'' ''Of course not.'' ''Then okay, I'll leave him here.'' And then she moved away up in the country. She could not keep it, because up in the country they had a ranch with pigs and hogs and all other farm animals. These farm animals were very scared, so if the dog got near them they'd all run away. But every month she went to visit her dog and they lived happily ever after. The end.

5. 3/21/74: The Rabbit and the Turtle

One day there was a turtle. He was running down the road and he met somebody. He said, ''Have you seen a rabbit go by here?'' The man said, ''Yes, yesterday.'' ''Oh, I'd better catch up with him,'' said the turtle. ''I'm racing him.'' ''Well,'' said the man, ''I have a way you can catch up with him. I'll scare you all the way.'' ''Okay,'' said the turtle. So the man took firecrackers out of his pocket and he popped them all, and scared the turtle all the way to the rabbit. "Now I'll catch up with you, you dumb rabbit." And when they got to the finish line the turtle won. Then the turtle walked back down the road and he saw the man again, and he said, "Can you scare me back to my home?" "I have this heavy medal and can hardly carry it." "Sure," said the man. So he did, and when the turtle got home he felt much better and he said, "I'll never race a rabbit again." The end.

6. 5/2/74: My Sister and Her Dog

There's a girl in my class named Adina. We are going to be blood sisters. I slept over at her house last night and she had a dog who looked very very cute: half collie and half german shepherd. His name is Pepper. He always kisses you. You really get sick and tired of him kissing you. I take that back. Believe it or not, I left my sock at Adina's house. Keep this a secret, but I think she's a nut and her medicine smells horrible. She had a secret bathtub. All night long me and Adina were saying, "Fred's out." [She would not tell me what this means.] Me and her chewed six packs of gum last night. Whenever Adina went to the bathroom, I'd open the door and I'd say something and she'd sing this dumb song. But we had fun and I think she's a monkey, but I love her. The end.

7. 5/8/74: Our Class

We have the craziest kids in our class. Lots of the boys are the craziest. There's one girl in our class who laughs at everything. Her name is Freya, and there's another girl named Deirdre who when we get drunk, we get crazy. And Dara gets drunk with us. We are going to give away the mother and father rabbit so they can make babies and then the other class will give back the father rabbit. But I don't want them to give away any of the rabbits. When we voted this morning to see which rabbits we were going to give away, nobody wanted to give Survivor away. The only thing I don't like about the boys is that they always call me Jill Fuck. Tonight I'm going to sleep over at my aunt's house and then tomorrow Adina is sleeping at my house. The prettiest girl in our class is Debbie, and one of the other girls who is pretty is Rose. And Dan is the best teacher I ever had, and I like M'Lou, too, and Tom and Gigi. The end.

8. 5/20/74: The Lady Who Changed Houses

Once there was a lady who moved to a house. The first night she was sitting down reading a book and she heard some strange noises but she did not pay attention to them. So she just went into her room and went to bed. In the morning she went downstairs into the living room and it was a mess. She thought, "Who could have messed up my house?" Then she remembered the noises of the night and she got a little nervous. It could not be a ghost. There's no such thing. (Of course I'm making this up. Of course there's no such a thing as ghosts.) "But then, who could have messed up my house?" So she cleaned the whole house up and then she went out shopping. And then when she came home, the house was a mess again. She thought and thought. "Could there be such a thing as ghosts?" And then she thought, "Maybe there is such a thing as ghosts." So she called the police and she said, "Whenever I go out or go to bed, when I wake up or I come back, the house is a mess. And I need a guard so my house won't be a mess again! Can you get me a guard?" "Sure," said the policeman. "The guard will be right over." So the guard came and said, "Where do you want me to go?" So the lady went to bed and when she came back the next morning the house was a mess and the guard was sleeping. So finally, the lady decided to move to another house. And so she moved and her new house was never a mess again. The end.

9. *5/30/74: A True Story*

Once there was a girl named Samantha and she taught me how to read and write. And when I came into Dan's class, she was in his class. So was lots of other kids I knew from first and second grade. When I came into the class we had two rabbits. And the father rabbit's name was Sniffles and the mother rabbit's name was Nibblets. And they had a litter and all the babies died except one. We voted and we named him Survivor. Then they had another litter and the mother rabbit didn't have any food, so she had to kill them. So then we had three rabbits and we tried to put the baby rabbit in with the mother, but they tried to make another litter. Then we put it in with the father, but the father tried to kill it. Se we had to put it in its own tiny cage. But since the cage was so small we had to give the mother rabbit away. We now just have Sniffles and Survivor.

10. *10/16/74*

Once there was a little pig named Piglet. One day Piglet went for a walk and he met a little bird, named Sarah. Piglet said, "Do you want to come into my pigpen?" And the bird said, "Okay but only if I can make a nest there." "Okay," said Piglet. "Do you like left over corn and other

vegetables?'' No way,'' said the bird. ''My favorite food is worms.''
''Well then you can fly off in the morning and find worms and I'll just
eat what I get,'' said Piglet. ''Okay,'' said the bird. And so they were
friends for a long time after that. The end.

11. 10/16/74: Dream, Saturday

I dreamed that I was at my grandmother's house and I went out in the
garden and I saw a rabbit lying there. I took him inside and gave him
some food and then he started hopping around the house. So then I had
my cat with me, Suzie. And the rabbit and Suzie made friends. And
when we had to go home, Suzie would not go without the rabbit so I had
to take the rabbit home with me. And when I got home, we taught the
rabbit how to go in the kitty litter and so when I went to school and my
mother went to work they were always together and when I came home
and I fed them and play with them and I went to sleep. The end.

12. 11/13/74: The Black Stallion

Once there was a black stallion that lived far away in the country. One
day a girl brown stallion came into the country and the black stallion and
the brown stallion had a little colt. There were three colts in all. When
the colts were big, two of them ran away and the one that stayed, they
called the black stallion.

And then a man came on a boat and he took the little black stallion
away. And a long time after the colts were gone, a few years, the big black
stallion and the brown stallion died. The end.

13. 11/13/74

[only part]

I turned into a cartoon person and me and Snoopy went to the beach and
on a picnic and then one day with Charlie Brown and Violet and Snoopy
we went to an amusement park.

14. 1/23/75

[handwritten by child]

I'm the classes girbel. I'm always getting hurt. Everyone is always playing
with me! I can't stand it. Some kids are nice to me but some kids are

always changing my cage and they always have to hold me and then put me back and then take me out again and I do not like it! But otherwise I like it. The food is great! The water is ok. I have fun watching the kids. I get sort of lonely on weekends. The class is going on lots of trips this year.

15.   1/29/75

Once there was a little kid who wanted to go to elementary school but she was too small. So one day she sneaked out of the house and there was a school across the street. So she decided to go there. When she got in the classroom she sat down at an empty desk and the teacher asked who she was. And then the teacher said, "You're too young to go to elementary school." And so then the teacher asked her how to spell walk. And she said, "Waa" and the teacher said, "No, that's wrong. You spell it walk!" Then she asked her to spell go, and she said, "Gu." The teacher said, "No, that's wrong. You spell it, "Go." And then the teacher asked her to spell kitten and she said, "Carton." The teacher said, "No, that's absolutely wrong. You spell it kitten." So then the day was over and the kid had not spelled one word right. So then she went home and her mother said, "Where were you?" And she said, "I was at school and I got every single word the teacher asked me right." So the mother said, "I'll have to talk with your teacher then." So she went to the school and she asked the teacher if it was true. And the teacher said, "Absolutely not. She got every word wrong." So the mother went home and told her daughter that she told a lie. So the mother said you can't go to school until you're bigger. The end.

16.   2/18/75

Once there was a little mouse who lived in a studio and people used to rehearse there for shows. And so one day when the people weren't rehearsing he went out to the studio and all these lights were shining on him. So then the producer comes out of this show and sees him standing there in the middle of the studio. So he goes into another room and gets some fabric, so he makes a little suit for the mouse. And he says to the mouse he can be in the show. So they find a real top hat and a little room for the mouse, and they put furniture in it.

It's the night of the show and the mouse gets all ready and the show begins. And when it's finished, everyone's checking for the little mouse and then he went into his room and fell asleep. The end.

17. 3/19/75

Once there was a little girl who had a goldfish. It was a girl goldfish. And so one day she went out and bought a boy girlfish. One day and one morning she saw all the baby goldfish in the fish tank. And so she decided to get another fish tank just for the babies. And so she kept on feeding them and feeding them and they got bigger and bigger. And then the baby goldfish had babies. And so she put the new babies in another tank. And one day she had so many goldfish that she decided to sell them. She sold the mother and father of the first litter and mother and father of the second litter. And then one day she saw the goldfish weren't having any more babies so she decided to keep all her little babies since they weren't going to have any more babies. And they lived happily ever after. The end.

18. 4/15/75

My cat's name is Suzie. She's a Burmese cat. She is very dark brown. And everyone thinks she's black. She's three years old and her birthday is December 20th. She usually sleeps and when she's awake she's always hungry. And then you give her something to eat and she bites you. And then she keeps on crying because she's hungry. When you give her something to eat she bites you. And then she keeps crying for more. But then she never eats what you give her. She scratches me a lot and bites me a lot. And my mother always wants to give her away. But I won't let her 'cause I like her too much.

19. 4/29/75

Once there was a little girl who had a dog named Rover. One day the little girl took her dog out for a walk. Then she hears like a mumbling sound. And she looks down at the dog and he's almost talking. So she starts talking to the dog and the dog starts to talk back. The little girl said dogs don't talk. And the dog said, "But I do. I'm Superdog. And I can fly, and I can drive a car, and almost anything a person can do." So when they get home she had this toy car she could ride in and she said to the dog, "Can you ride this car?" "Sure," says the dog. And so he started riding around in it. And riding all over the house and knocking things all over. Then the little girl's mother came into the room, and saw the dog riding all over the house. And so she started screaming at him. And the little girl said, "He didn't mean any harm. He's Superdog." Then the mother found out he was a good dog and so she never screamed at him again.

20. *6/2/75*

He was so adorable and so nice. He pushed me right down on the floor and played with me. I was rolling all over. I wish I had a dog just like that. The end.

Nine Years

Jerome

1. 2/7/74

Once upon a time there was a boy named Jerome and he was walking down the street and he saw his friend that wasn't in school for a week and his name was Miles, and he was playing with my brother. When I was coming back from school, 'cause my brother didn't go to school that day. So I started playing with them. We were playing tag. It was fun and then Miles had to go home. We walked Miles home and the next day we were going on a camping trip and I went and it was for four days. We had a good time and they served us in bed. Then the next day we went home and there was no school that day 'cause it was Lincoln's birthday. And the Saturday and Sunday passed by and I rode my bike in Central Park and me and my brother and my father came back home on our bikes and that was the best time of that year. That I had in 1974. And it was fun and on Sunday we rode our bikes again and we came home and that's the end.

2. 2/28/74

Once upon a time I was walking in the woods and I saw this thing and it had sharp fingernails, eyeballs made out of blubber, bony fingers, skinny legs and fat body. And I was running and it was chasing me and I saw another one and I was surrounded by a whole bunch of them and I ran through one and it looked ugly inside. And I kept on running and all of them had clubs and spikes and they were throwing spikes at me and one hit me on the head. And I almost forgot about all those monsters in back of me. And then I started running faster and faster and then I saw my brother and I told him to run and then I woke up. It was all a dream.

[Storytaker asked him if this was a story or a dream, and he answered that it was really a story and not a real dream.]

3. 6/14/74

Once upon a time there was a cow and a dog and a lamb and a sheep and horses. And there was a farmer and that's a farm. And there was a boy walking down the street to the farm and the boy, he went on the horse. The farmer said he could go on the horse and he go a ride and he had fun and that's the end. No. And he went all the way to the barn and he got another ride to the World Trade Center. And then the horse got to eat and the horse liked his food. And the next day the boy got a ride again. And he liked the horse and the man gave it to him for one hundred twenty-five dollars. And so when him and his horse they ride, sometimes they went to far places. They went all the way out to New Jersey because they lived in the country and stuff and the horse ate all his hay and they lived happily ever after. The end.

4. 9/3/74: The Monster

Once upon a time there was a boy. He lived in the country. And one day he went out in the woods and saw a big monster. And he started running as fast as he could. And the monster only came out every six years. A lot of people got killed from that monster. Then the boy went over and told the police and the police went out to try and find the monster. They couldn't find the monster and they thought the boy was only kidding about the monster because the police were from the city. They didn't know the monster came down every six years. And then the monster came in the village in the country and was killing everybody. And someone got the police again and the monster went back in the woods. The police didn't believe there was a monster and they planted a bomb in the woods and the monster died and the village went on fire and everybody died. Some people lived, but that's the end of the story.

Jonathan

1. 1/16/74

Once upon a time there was a dog named Heather. He was a street dog. There was a meat man who would always give him bones and he got water from a fire hydrant that was always running. And he lived in a friendly little junk yard and he lived in a big school bus that was wrecked. And he had a friend named Spot and Spot always spended the night at his school bus. Spot lived in an old truck. But the man who have his meat didn't like Spot and he only gave meat to Heather, but Heather shared with Spot all the time. Spot drunk from the same fire hydrant. Once Spot found a friend who owned a department store and he shared his lunch with Spot. And Spot came home and shared the man who owned the department store's lunch with Heather. And the man who owned the department store said for Spot to come to his department store anytime he was hungry and he would share his lunch with Spot. So one day later Spot came to the department store, hoping the man would give him some lunch but the man didn't. So he went back to Heather's house and Heather had a big steak from the meat man. And they had a nice lunch and they had enough steak for supper and breakfast the next day. So they were both happy because the man always gave Heather a big steak and Heather would share it with Spot.

2. 2/21/74

Once upon a time there was a little fish named Josh and he was going to a fish fair and there were fishers over the fish fair and the fishermen caught everyone including Josh. Then they put all the fish in the fishers' hole and there were sharks and sting rays and a sting ray was going after Josh and then a shark chased the sting ray because he wanted to eat the sting ray. So the sting ray stopped chasing Josh and ran away from the shark. So the shark and the sting ray got into a big fight. But then another shark was going after Josh, but then instead the shark gobbled up his mother (Josh's mother), and Josh's dad, and Josh's sister. And then he left. And then Josh was left alone with the other fish. Well the boat was sailing and sailing and sailing. And then there was a big storm that night. And it hit against the rocks and made a big hole in the fishes hole and Josh escaped and went back to his house and he stayed there until he was big. And he met a friend who was a blue whale named Alfalfa. And they were good friends and once a shark tried to get Josh and Alfalfa came and killed the shark. And they were good friends and got an apartment together and were roommates and lived happily ever after.

3. 3/28/74: *Wonderman*

Wonderman came from a different planet. It was exploding. He was twenty years old and he could fly but bullets could still hurt him. But he wasn't as strong as Superman, in fact he wasn't half as strong as Superman. But he was pretty strong. Well, when he came down from the planet he pretended he was an Earthling and he found out everything about Earth that you would know. And he wanted to be a superhero. And his ex-enemy was The Dog-Faced Burglar who was quite happy until Wonderman came along. He isn't a dog but he dresses in a dog costume.

Once Wonderman decided to spend a nice quiet evening at home but the Dog-Faced Burglar broke through the window and shot him in the heart. But he had bullet proof on and it did not hurt him, but he pretended like he was dead. Then the Dog-Faced Burglar went out the window and went to his hideout. Then Wonderman got up and changed and brushed his teeth and washed his face and took a bath. You can see he's a very clean person. Then he jumped out the window and flew away to the Dog-Faced Burglar's hideout, which wasn't really a hideout because he knew where it was. And he broke through the door and there was a lady and she screamed, "What are you doing in my apartment?" And so he said, "Excuse me Ma'am," and flew away.

Then the Dog-Faced Burglar got out of his lady costume and said, "Wonderman is a schmuck to fall for such a bad trick." Then Wonderman busted through the door and said, "I did not fall for that bad trick and I'm not a schmuck." And he kicked him in the pants. Then the Dog-Faced Burglar pulled out a gun and said, "I know you have bullet proof on but I'll shoot you in the head." Then Wonderman kicked the gun out of his hand and gave him a Kung Fu, Judo, Ju-Jitsu flip and that hurts. Then the Dog-Faced Burglar got up and ran out the door, but Wonderman ran after him and got him and took him up and flew with him; flew to jail, put him in jail. But the Dog-Faced Burglar had a file and when Wonderman flew away he cut the jail open and ran away. And was not seen again until my next Wonderman comic book. The end.

4. *5/8/74: The Secret Wonderman Gun*

Wonderman's ex-enemy is the Dog-Faced Burglar. One night Wonderman was flying around the city patrolling the area and he saw the Dog-Faced Burglar shoot a man with the Dog-Faced Burglar's very good friend Vulture Man. So he flew down and tried to get him, but they ran away and Wonderman started flying after them. Then they got to their hideout. Wonderman knew where it was, but couldn't break in the door because it was made out of gold and it's underground in the country. And they go in and Wonderman did not know what to do because Wonderman is very strong but not strong enough to bust through gold. So he decided to leave and come back tomorrow.

Meanwhile, the Dog-Faced Burglar was planning to kill Wonderman with a gun; planning to shoot him in the head because Wonderman has bullet proof, so if he shot him in the head it would kill him. The reason he never got shot is because he moves real fast and it's very hard to aim at him. So the Dog-Faced Burglar made a new gun, sort of like a robot computer to aim wherever V.C. (a chemical that is in Wonderman's blood because he came from another planet) is. So the gun would aim wherever Wonderman went. But right now Wonderman was in his hideout and the Dog-Faced Burglar would have to wait until he came out of his hideout. Wonderman did not know that the Dog-Faced Burglar had a gun that could do that. So all the Dog-Faced Burglar had to do is go in the Dog-Faced Burglar car and wait until Wonderman came out of his hideout and shoot him.

So he drived over in his car to Wonderman's hideout and waited. So he did wait and wait and waited and waited. But what he did not know, Wonderman was looking at him with his secret Wonderman spyscope that's cleverly disguised as a tree because Wonderman's hideout is in the country underground. And he did not like the looks of the gun. And he saw with his super-super vision in little letters on the gun, "The Dog-Faced Burglar's V.C. Chemical Detector." So he did not come out and he decided to make a plan. He'd come out of his secret surprise attack hole which the Dog-Faced Burglar did not know about. He made it for people who were trying to wait for him, and when he came out try to kill him. So he came out of his secret surprise attack entrance, flew over the Dog-Faced Burglar's secret V.C. detector and busted it. And then he got the Dog-Faced Burglar and put him in jail. But the Dog-Faced Burglar soon escaped. Join in for our next exciting adventure of Wonderman. The end.

5. 5/23/74

So far the Dog-Faced Burglar made a big robot that looked like himself. It took him three years to make it. It's as big as the Empire State Building. So far the robot bust all New York City, stepped on a little boy, a little dog, a pregnant woman and wrecked the whole city, breaking buildings and took Wonderman's Wondermobile and busted it and took Wonderman's Wondermoplane and busted it and went to Wonderman's hideout and busted in the door. And Wonderman thought nothing could bust in his door. And Wonderman built another Wondermobile that was very good. The Dog-Faced Burglar robot was trying to wreck the Wondermobile but he couldn't do it. The Dog-Faced Burglar wanted to take over the world with his robot. The Dog-Faced Burglar also had a friend, the Rat, who also made a robot and together they were going to take over the world. Wonderman had a friend named the Shadow and together they were going to try and stop the robots. And here's my story.

The Dog-Faced Burglar's robot was trying to wreck Wonderman's new Wondermobile by shooting beans at it, but Wonderman was trying to break the robot by shooting bombs at it. Nobody's winning at this point. Then Wonderman's friend The Shadow comes in and helps. And then the Rat's robot comes and helps the Dog-Faced Burglar's robot. The Dog-Faced Burglar and the Rat are inside their robots. Then a big war goes on, beans go all over the place, fire goes all over the place, bombs go all over the place, smoke is all over the place. Then the Dog-Faced Burglar's and the Rat's robots go away. And so Wonderman and The Shadow are happy, but then they find out they're going to another city and they have to save the city, so they follow the robots. Then the robots are wrecking the city. The robots are destroying everything, and Wonderman and Shadow can't do anything about it. And they try but they can't, and they try and they try and they try, but they can't. Then the robots stop wrecking the city and go to their hideouts to make plans. What will the robots do? Join in in the next adventure of the two robots.

6. 6/13/74: A Dog

Once upon a time there was a boy named Steven. He wanted a dog but his parents were very poor and could not afford it. His father was a garbage man and did not make much money, so they could not afford a dog.

His father said if Steve saved up one hundred dollars of his allowance, which was thirty-five cents a week, he could get a dog. He saved up a lot of money. He had fifty dollars. One day he had an accident. He broke a window in the accident and had to pay for it with his money. And it costed a lot of money, so he did not have a chance of getting a dog. Then he saved up ninety-nine dollars. Then his father broke his arm and so his ma did not have enough money to pay the hospital bills. She would, if she had ninety-nine dollars. So he paid it and then he had no money. And then his father was all better again, and he started giving him an allowance again. And he saved and he saved and he saved and he saved. And then he did not want a dog anymore.

7. *9/25/74*

[handwritten by child]

Once upon a time there was a man namead Mr. Cookaracha and he was very hungry and he was avery poor but he was nice. And he did not know how to spell or write. or read and he didnot know math. One day he deacided to go to school, he felt embarrassed because he was a 55 the oldest person in the class and he learned and he learned and he learned and he learned. Then he finished school and he got a job and he got married. And he was a 60 and then he had a child. And the child and the child was a little brat and he was a slob and hiscusting little thing and Mr. Cookaracha was very unproud of his little basteread and he wanted to kill him but he thought he would chages as he got older but he did not he was ten and he still was a little basteread and he did not know what to do he whanted to kill him but he did not kinly he did and told his wife. His wife wantead to kill him to so she was not that mad at him. That night his wife got scared that he was foing to kill her to butthat was not true at all. He loved her well she did inl way and she letf a not that sigded Dear x husband I got frtand you were going to kill me but if you did not want to kill me I am sorry love you X wife when the man woke up the neaxt day he was hart broken and cimited suewasied and the wife lived happily ever after The End

8. *1/15/75*

One day I woke up and found that I was Dan, my teacher. It was very embarrassing waking up. I had bacon, eggs, toast, milk, pancakes, waffles and cereal. I don't eat breakfast normally so after I ate the bacon and eggs I was full. And then Dan's wife came in and then she said, "You did not eat your breakfast. Don't you like my cooking?" Then unfortunately something came out of my mouth that I did not want to. I said, "Listen lady, I don't usually eat a good breakfast." I think that made her mad because she said, "Oh, so you don't think I'm a good cook, do you? Well, you can cook your own lousy breakfast." Then she screamed and went into her room. Then with a lot of force I ate the breakfast. Then the lady came out again and said she was sorry and kissed me. That embarrassed me so much. Then she said, "Time for you to go to work." I guess she meant school. Well, I knew I couldn't drive the car so I got ten dollars out of Dan's wallet and took a taxi to school. On the taxi I wondered, "When does Dan's wife go to work? Oh well, that's the least thing to worry about now." Well the taxi cost ten dollars so I could not tip him. And then the taxi driver said, "Where's my tip?" Then I said, "In my pocket." Well the day was hell and six hours seemed like six days. Well the day was over. Then outside of the school I saw my Mom. I felt like crying when I saw her kiss a kid like me. Then she came over to me and said, "How is John doing in school?" Well then I said, "He is the best in the class," and the whole teacher routine. Then I came with a bad problem. I had no money to take a taxi back. Then it happened. I went crazy. My mind went upside down and I fell on the sidewalk. Then I found myself in my bed and I was me again. And my Mom kissed me goodnight and left and I was me again and then I wondered where Dan was.

Ken

1.   1/11/75

There's a swastika to trick the Germans. He's shooting at the Americans. He shot the anti-aircraft guns. He's trying to hit another plane. This is the water and this the land. This is the Nazis. The German ship found out it wasn't really a Nazi so they're firing at him. [Storytaker: What happened to the pilot?] He got shot and he's going to parachute. Now he had to parachute. He's parachuting. [Storytaker: What's going to happen to him?] They can't shoot him when he's in the air. [Storytaker: What happens when he lands?] They'll fire at him. The Nazis cheated and fired at the pilot when he's in the air. Torpedoes are coming at the hill. [Storytaker: But what happens to the pilot?] Well, he parachuted and the Germans shot at him and hit the parachute and hit him again, and the air rushes out real fast. But he's going to fall in the river and swim to land—it's Nazi land. They cut the strings. The pilot is going to land on or swim to a battleship. [Storytaker: American?] Yeah, and be saved.

2. 4/5/74: *Galopalus*

My monster attacks an ocean liner; a submarine above the water. Here's the submarine and there's the torpedo. There's the monster. His head is above the water and he blows force at the sub. A plane comes along and shoots a bomb at the monster but misses. Shoots again and hits the monster in the face. The plane gets a hot back with a beam and is destroyed. The beam of electricity comes out of the horn in-between his eyes. The monsters are attacking the bad submarine. The people get off the sub onto life boats. Another monster comes along and shot a beam to the boat but missed. It went all the way down to the bottom of the ocean, hit the bottom, churned all the water and giant rocks and they hit the boat and blew it up.

Monster two blows air at the sub's stacks and breaks the biggest one. There's a snake monster too. He eats the human leftovers when the sub gets sunk. He shoots radioactive fire at the spot light. He puts out a beam and eats your skin and leaves the skeleton. He eats machine gun bullets. His ears send out sonic waves and the bombs return to whatever shot them, and blow it up. And an airplane comes along and starts the doors open to drop bombs on the snake. Before it reaches him, he sends out the sonic beam, which sends the bomb back to the plane. The doors open and the bomb returns and blows up the plane.

3. 4/5/74: *World War II*

This picture is about war. The Nazis are fighting the Americans. The tanks are shooting at each other. We're the only ones with torpedoes. The Germans do not have enough ammunition. There are explosions. They are killing each other to take each other's land. Barbed wire is stretched along the land so the Nazis can't get through to the American side. They (the Nazis) are dropping aluminum foil in the radar so they (the Americans) can't pick up what's coming.

4. 4/18/74

The earth people put all explosives bombs on the moon and blew it to pieces. Then the moon people glued the moon all back together and the man in the moon died. The moon people challenged the earth people. The earth people are making more bombs but they will use sonic things.

We're dumb, we use hydrogen bombs. The whole world against the moon. The Pakistan people get in the plane and shoot at the moon people who came to earth. They knew the moon people would come back and saved more bombs. The moon people landed on Pakistan. The Pakistans called to the world for help; even to Gamra. Gamra comes and the moon people shot Gamra's feet from their funny kind of flying saucer, but did not hurt him. Now he's mad. He fires electricity at the moon flying saucer. Then Gamra's cousin comes. Her name is Monster X. She shoots electricity from her eye at the moon people. The three heads don't decide on each other. They all want to go in different directions and the legs too. The middle head is the most powerful. The Pakistan plane helps the monster. The eye beams are lighter than the mouth beams. She shoots beams of electricity from the mouths of two heads and the eye of the third at the moon ships and is bringing down their whole army. A special tank comes along. It's a special moon tank; it has radar to tell what's coming. The tank shot one of our planes. So that's what you want, and Monster X shoots another of their ships. We are winning. A Pakistan plane with two big cannons are coming and shoot the moon tank and destroy it. Some tanks are equipped with sonic something to return bombs and blow up the other plane, but this one does not have it. Now comes an American plane. Then torpedo hatch opens. The moon ship is about to shoot a Pakistan plane, but the American plane hits it first. In the end the earth people and moon people make up and become friends. The moon machine hits the middle head and then the end head, so there is only one head. An earth plane and Monster X destroy the moon large machine. A flying saucer comes in and crashes on Monster X's tail. Our plane crashed—it was going too fast. The moon people are winning. Monster X got blown up. Then they all became friends.

5. *5/2/74: Getting a Yoyo*

It was hard. I said in the morning to my mother, "Could you get me a yoyo?" And she went to the store and they were all out. And when she came home I ran downstairs and I said, "Did you get me a yoyo?" And she said, "They were all out." And I cried and she said, "All right, we'll go to the store." And we snuck out of the house so my brother would not come. And then she said, "Where should we go first?" And the first store we went to was Andy's. The second was the Gingerbread House. The third shop we went to was a Japanese shop and then we went to another Japanese shop around there, and the Japanese had big ones. But I did not want a big one. Then I saw a store that looked like it had yoyos, and I asked the man and they did. He said, "I just ordered a half dozen and they came in today."

6. 9/11/74

It's about a murderer. They use swords, daggers, knives, spears, loon-chuks, different kinds of stars. He pokes peoples eyes out with files and daggers. He pokes peoples eyes out with chick-blocks. He beats people up in the stomach with loon-chuks with three sticks. Certain kinds of knives for certain murders. Hatchets and what he used most of the time was a stick with a throwing star at the end. He'd dip it in poison. He'd use a jack knife. He also knew kung-fu, karate, jujitsu, judo, aikido, tai quan do, kun jitsui, tai chi and other certain methods unknown plus thai boxing. And last night he murdered a little kid who knew kung-fu and his father knew it too and he's after him now with the police. And he killed the father too and he murdered every weekend until by an unknown man that knew a martial art that nobody ever knew and he was after him for a long time and they had a fight and the unknown man won. They went to prison and afterwards, when they got out, the unknown man killed him. When he killed him, he kept going after bad guys until another murderer came into town and the new man was killed by him. He kept going killing people until he was arrested for life. He broke out of prison by melting the bars. He never murdered again. The end.

7. 9/11/74

[handwritten by child]

I turned into my brother for one day. My brother had to bring me to school and all he did was beat me up all morning long. He took me up to Roz and ran. Then he was in the bathroom and he was climbing and I came into the bathroom and watched.

Laurie

1. 2/22/74: *Three Girls*

[handwritten by child]

There were three girls playing one day. Their names were Suw, Jenny and Sara. When they were playing Jenny and Sara decided to gag-up on Suw.

273

They made Suw cry and then Suw went up in her bed and cried. Then Jenny and Sara side they were sorry and they made-up and went on playing. The end.

2.   2/22/74:   *The Princess And The Rose*

[handwritten by child]

Once upon a time there lived a princess and her name was Belinda. One morning her father King Arak of Zicin side that she must marry soon. So that day he sent out a messinger to each part of the country. And the proclamation read: Whoever Can Give The Princess A Gift That She Likes May Marry Her. And the next morning as she was eating breakfast her messenger came in saying, "A box for the princess! A box for the princess!" He gave the box to the princess and she opened it up. Inside was a glass rose, the most beautiful glass rose she had ever seen in her life. She said that she would marry the man who had made the glass rose.

That night there was a knock at the door. She opened the door. There was a man there. She invited him in for tea. She learned that he was the man that made the glass rose. They made plans to be married the next day. The next day they were married and they lived happily ever after. The end.

3.   2/22/74:   *Harry The Hipo In Find A Wife*

[handwritten by child]

Harry woke up early that morning and looked all around and saw in the pond that every hipo had a wife and he falt loanly that he had no wife. So he went out to find a wife and it seemed that every girl hipo was already a wife or they were so yoky that he wouldn't marry them if they were the last hipos in the world.

As he was looking he saw a hipo cering [crying] and he went over and said why are you cering, and she said no one wants to marry me, and then he said I'm sad too. No one wants to marry me either. So I will marry you horry! Oh you will side lou lou the hipo. And they got married the next day. Their wedding was the best in all of afraca. The end.

4.   3/28/74

Jimmy is a mushroom. Issac is a bull, a very stupid bully. Curtis is very smart. Van is jive. Josh is unpredictable. Darius is delirious. Josh is skinny and stupid. Milo is a monkey. Kichi is a retard. Vinnie is intelligent. Dara is cute. Rose is nice. Pam is dumb. Samantha is a good friend. Melissa is stingy. Deirdre is nice. Kate is a corny cornflake. Ian is obnoxious. Tarek is tall. Raul is very quiet. Lisa F. is chubby. Lisa B. is strange. Freya is overweight but very nice. Dana is the biggest girl in the class.

5. 4/25/74: Helen and Her New Friends

[handwritten by child]

One morning Helen woke up. She was very lonely. All her friends had gone away for summer vacation and her mother said that they could not go this summer. That evening she saw a van drive up into the empty house down the street where the Browns used to live. Then a car drove up to the house too. Kids got out of the car and two grown-ups got out. Then they went in the house. Suddenly her mother called her to dinner. After dinner she went upstairs and looked out of her window and saw the lights going out in the house down the street. Then her father came upstairs to her room and said that he was sorry that they were not going on a trip that summer but that he didn't have any time to go. Helen said that it was all right. The next day she went out to play and saw the two kids playing in their backyard and then she felt even more lonely because they were having fun and she wasn't. Then they called Helen over. Helen ran down the street and when she got there, they wanted her to play with them and she did and they were good friends from that day on. The end.

6. 4/25/74: Rabbit Staff

[handwritten by child]

Once there was a rabbit. Its name was Niblets. Then there was another rabbit. Its name was Niblets Jr. Then we got another rabbit a little later. At the end of the year of school we went away for summer vacation. I don't remember how took home then. The next day I went to P.S. 41 and Mrs. M. I didn't like her. All she did was yell at me. So I went back to P.S. 3 and saw Niblets and a new rabbit who doesn't have a name. But now Niblets had a litter and only one lived. Its name is Survivor because it was the last one alive. Then Niblets had another litter and they all died of starvation in a night but Niblets and Survivor are happy and that's all that counts. The end.

7. 4/25/74: My Dog

[handwritten by child]

I have a dog whose name is Hony. She's a Springer Spaniel about 11 ½ months old. I got Hony for Christmas. She slept under the tree all night.

I love her very much. So does my mother. We loay alot together. Hony likes to walk on her back paws and jump a little sometime. The end.

8. *4/25/74: A Poem Called Lonely*

[handwritten by child]

When I'm away from you my heart is sad. It's not the kind of sad that you feel just any time. It's the kind that's real. This poem was for my mother when I was at my friend's house.

9. *5/8/74: A Big Breakfast*

Once upon a time there lived two girls named Dara and Lisa who fought all day. Dara is a pussycat and Lisa is a lion. Dara is quite small and Lisa is about a foot bigger than her. Dara is very sweet sometimes. Then there's a girl named Samantha. Samantha is a dog. Debbie is a mouse. Adina is a kangophant. They all lived in a big house and one morning when they all got up at the same time, which was quite a mistake. The dog came running out of his room. The cat came running out of his. The mouse and the kangophant came running out of their rooms, and so did Lisa the lion. They all met in the middle and had a terrifying fight. They fought all the way down the stairs. Then the kitty cat ate the mouse. The dog ate the cat. The kangophant ate the dog and the lion ate the kangophant whole. And all at once he got heart burn and stomache ache at the same time, because they were still fighting inside of him. The lion was quite satisfied with his breakfast, but the kangophant, the dog, the cat, and the mouse were still quite unhappy. Soon the kangophant jumped out of the lion, the dog jumped out of the kangophant, the cat jumped out of the dog, the mouse jumped out of the cat, and they were all quite happy and ate breakfast and lunch and dinner, and breakfast and lunch and dinner and all lived together happily ever after in a big house. The end.

10. *5/14/74*

Once upon a time a little girl named Freya had a dream. She dreamt that her mother gave her a guinea pig. Now one morning when her mother gave the guinea pig to her, she said it was magic. She said that the only way they could ship cows to different states was to turn them into guinea pigs. So her mother bought her a guinea pig at the store and when she got it home she decided to give shots to it so if it bit somebody it wouldn't hurt them. The vet said that the guinea pig was the kind that turned into cows. So my mother still wanted Freya to have the guinea pig. So she gave it to her and she went all over the place with her guinea pig. One night she brought it to a friend's house and it got lost and Freya started to cry and when her mother took her home again Freya went all over the place in a strange sort of subway where the wind was so strong that when the train came in, it started to pull you off the track. Then Freya got on the subway and she couldn't find the guinea pig anywhere. Then when she got home her mother said she had a surprise for her and showed a little calf. Freya asked where it came from and her mother said that since it was lost at the house that one night when her friends were asleep, the little guinea pig turned into a calf and popped its head out of a garbage can. The little girl's mother gave it to Freya's mother and then Freya fed the calf some warm milk out of a baby bottle. The little calf grew up a tannish color. And Freya named the calf Lovable. And they all lived happily ever after.

11. 5/15/74: One Little Black Sheep

[handwritten by child]

Once upon a time there were six little sheep and one was black, a very bad color to be when you're a sheep. So for many years she was called names and no one would play with her, so her mother used to say she would play with her. But when the little sheep really wanted to play, she was too busy or she just plain said no. Then one afternoon the mother called five of the little sheep so that she could talk to them all at once and then she told them they were the most stupid sheep she had ever seen in her life, because they did not like the little sheep for its color and they all felt dumb and they played with her and had the best time ever. And the moral of the story is: No matter what the color, a friend is a friend.

12. 6/18/74: The Princess and Cardone

Once in the deep woods there was a castle made out of pure glass. It had no doors or windows and inside lived the beautiful princess Belanda. She lived with her father and mother, the King and Queen of Nezra. One morning on the princess's twentieth birthday the King told her that she must go on away and get married. But first she must find a secret door out of the castle. Belanda had seen many towns far off through the glass walls of her room. She had longed to journey far and wide across these lands but she must find first the secret door hidden within any of the walls.

There was a great staircase circling around the outside of the castle made of pure diamonds. The secret door had never been found, but once by the king and since the great staircase the door could be on any floor. Belanda searched the walls for an opening but to her disappointment she couldn't find it.

One day while eating supper she saw two hinges on one side of the room. She got up and ran toward the great glass wall. She had found the doorway. There was one flight of stairs to go down on the outside of the castle. She packed her things in a large trunk. A servant helped her down the stairs. A stable boy put the trunk on a beautiful white horse and she rode away.

She rode for many hours towards a far off land where there was a castle three times as big as hers. It had twelve hundred rooms and was made of solid rubies. In the castle lived Queen Nedia and her son Cardone. Princess Belanda knocked on the great doors of the castle, when a man opened the door and said, "This is the castle of the great King Nedro and his son Cardone." Soon the King came to the door and she entered into a great hallway. The King brought her to a room with a huge table in the middle with fifty chairs around it. Soon the King pulled a great chain hanging from the ceiling. A man entered and said, "The great King, have you called your Highness?" "Yes, get my son Cardone." He told Belanda to sit down.

He asked her why she journeyed so far from her home. She said her father had told her to journey to find the man she would marry. He said it was unusual for the princess to journey and not the prince. She told him that she lived so far in the woods that no prince would ever find her. He said that she would be welcome to marry his son.

When Cardone walked down the stairs he was just about to tell her that if his prince loved her, but only then would he be allowed to marry her. When Cardone saw the beauty of Belanda he fell in love with her on first sight. Cardone was just as handsome as Belanda was beautiful, and she fell in love with him on first sight. They fell in love and asked King Nedro if they may get married. He said yes. They rode off to Nezra's castle. He asked him for her hand in marriage. He said yes.

They got married in the largest church between Cardone's father's castle and Belanda's father's castle. All the Kings and Queens and ladies of the court were there to see the great wedding of the beautiful princess Belanda and the prince Cardone. They were given a castle made of rubies, diamonds, and glass with fifteen hundred rooms and with the best furniture. Soon they had children and their names were Cardia, Norvdon, Rosalita, and Landia. They grew up, had children and they all lived happily ever after.

13. *9/19/74: The Day I Turned into my Dog*

[handwritten by child]

One morning I woke up in my dogs bed, (and I had to go to the bathroom). But I could only sniff the toilet. Of course when I looked around I found that a tail that looked exactly like my dog's, Oh! no I knew it. It seemed unbelievable. Once I heard a story about a girl who changed into her mother. That was pretty unbelievable. But a dog, oh no! that means dog food for dinner and. . . . oh! god, a flee (ech ech, scratch, scratch) Hony! Hony! Come here girl, Oh that must be Michael. Then I walked into the living room and saw my mother. I wagged my tail, my mother gave me a pat on the head and I walked to my bed and went to sleep. I had a bad nightmare and when I woke up it was 1:00 in the afternoon. I walked into the bathroom to see if I had grown and found out I hadn't and boy did I have to go to the bathroom. But I had to wait until 3:30. Oh well I guess I can wait. But boy I'm thirsty. Well I guess I can start waiting for Sally. I'll go look out of the window. Oh good, it's snowing. I hope that Sally takes me out for a long time today and to the park even though somehow I don't really feel like playing with other dogs, oh look, it's already 2:00. Now I only have an hour. Good here comes a bus. Oh wait, I remember that we get out of school early. But she isn't on that bus. I waited five minutes and another bus came and came Sally. I ran to the door and Sally came up the stairs, in the house and put the leash on me and said the magic words, By By Out. I wagged my tail and we went out to the park and had alot of fun. When we came back I had some awful dog food with crunchys in it and went to bed and when I woke up I was myself again. The End.

Leslie

1. *11/15/73: Superstitions*

The mother's calling the children. "Lucy, Tommy, Amy, Terry," called Mrs. White, who was the children's mother. (Did I say Susan? Put in Susan.) "Go get Sally. Come here, I have something to tell you." "Okay mom, we'll go get her." "Don't forget Sally now." "We won't, Susan already went to get her. Here they come now." "Does she have Sally?" said Mrs. White. "Yes," said Tom. Slam! In came Sally and Susan.

"Good, now we may talk," said Mrs. White. "I think this is going to come as a shock to you, but you have to go to your aunt 'cause I have to go out on a job." "Why can't our father take care of us?" You see Sally had never known that her father had died in the war before she was born. She thinks her father is working.

"We must tell you that your father had died. What we said before, we were lying," said Mrs. White carefully. Sally ran upstairs and slammed her bedroom door behind her, crying. The children ran up after her. They opened her bedroom door and said, "Come on, cheer up." But Tom interrupted, "Why should she cheer up because we all are going to Aunt Sissy." Then Sally said, "Nobody can be that bad," said Sally in a low voice. "Yes, they can," said all the children at once. (This was the end of the chapter. What will happen next?)

They will go to the aunt's house. They will go in and there will be no one there. Then Tom breaks a mirror. Susan says, "Don't, you'll have seven years bad luck." The other children say that's a silly superstition. Then Tom walked under a ladder and Susan said, "Don't do that." They all said, "Silly superstition again, huh, Sally." Sally said she heard a creak and a noise. "Starting up with the superstition again Sally," said Tom. "Wait," said Tom, "I hear something too." "I see it," said Terry. "Let's scat."

They all ran as fast as they could. The one problem was Sally couldn't run fast and she was too heavy for even Tom, who was eleven, to carry her. So Susan takes her by the arm and drags her away. There came a knock on the door of the old house and in came their mother. Seeing them lying on the floor panting, she asked, "What's wrong?"

They tell her the whole story and finally they find out that their Aunt Sissy was just trying to scare them because they had a rich fortune with them which their mother gave them when they left the house. The Aunt Sissy got put in jail and they all went home and had a good life from there on.

2. 1/10/74: *Pets for Pam*

[handwritten by child]

Chapter 1: *The Turtle*

One day a girl named Pam was walking home from school. As she was walking she looked in a pet shop window and saw a tank of turtles. One looked at her. She looked back at him. He smiled at her. She smiled back at him. She ran home as fast as she could. She ran up the stairs as fast as she could. When she got to her house she rung the bell. Her mother opened the door. The first thing Pam said was "Can I have a turtle mom?" Her mother said no. But Pam said "No buts." "We have no money to spend on a good for nothing turtle," said her mother. Pam ran to her room.

Chapter 2: A Job
The next day Pam woke up with an idea. She would get a job. But what kind of a job? She did not know. As she was thinking she heard a voice. The voice came from her mother. It was saying, "Come on Pam, you will be late for school." "I am coming," said Pam. After she ate breakfast and got her clothes on she was on her way to school. At least that was what her mother thought. Actually she went around town looking for a job. West? No, east? No, south? Yes! A little job, but a job. "10¢ an hour, mother's helper," said the sign of the door. She went in. "May I come?" she said. "I have come to fill in the job." "Why you look less than 5 years of age." "I am 10," said Pam. "What do you know about babies?" "A lot. How many children were you planning to have me take care of?" "Oh, only one. Her name is Trouble." "Why do you call her Trouble?" "You will find out tomorrow at five o'clock, A.M."

Chapter 3: The Meeting
Five o'clock the next day Pam ran out of the house. Her mother heard her and said, "Pam is it eight o'clock already?" By the time her mother got up Pam was two blocks away. By the time Pam got there it was 5:30. She knocked on the door. A little girl about 4 years old answered the door and said "Come in. I've been waiting for you. Sit down please." "Are you Trouble," said Pam. "Of course not, my name is Small. I'm Trouble's sister. She will be down soon." "How old are you?" asked Pam. "Seven," the girl answered. "Here comes Trouble." Trouble came down the stairs. "Throing [?] father's troup [tore up] your pillow again," said Small. Trouble did not say anything. All she did was walk down.

Chapter 4: The Day Begins
Small said "This is your new baby sitter." Then Pam said, "Hi, my name is Pam." But Trouble did not answer. All she did was walk down. "Well, I'll have to be going," said Small. So Small went and slammed the door behind her. "Would you like to go up to your room and show me some of your things?" She did not answer. All she did was walk up the stairs. A couple of minutes later Trouble came down the stairs and went into the kitchen. Pam said, "I don't know why her name is Trouble. She's really nice."

The next minute Pam ran into the kitchen. You should have seen that mess! Eggs on the floor, sugar on the table, chocolate syrup on the plates, broken cups and saucers. Pam almost fainted when she saw the mess. How could a little girl make such a mess by herself? Well Pam found out. She did not quite. Out of one of the hunks of dough came a little black and white skunk. Then Pam sent Trouble up to her room and told her to get rid of the skunk. Pam cleaned up. It had been five hours already, 50¢. She wished the parents would come soon. She had enough money to buy the turtle.

Around six hours later the parents came home. "I hope she did not give you any trouble," said the parents. "No," said Pam. "Not a bit," hiding the skunk under her skirt. It was nine o'clock already. Wouldn't her mother be worried! She didn't have time to buy the turtle. When she got home her mother asked "What took you so long?" "I helped the teacher clean-up the class," said Pam.

Chapter 5: The Next Pet
The next day Pam woke up and went to school. After school she went to the turtle shop. She had $1.10 and the turtle was only 20¢. Well as she went into the pet shop she noticed a kitty in a little cage. It did not look very happy either. She went over to it and it started meowing. Then the cat grabbed her arm softly. This was a problem. It was $1.20 and she wanted the turtle too. Maybe I'll work again, not with Trouble. So she went over and bought the turtle. She brought it home and sneaked it in her room and fed it and it seemed very happy.

Chapter 6 [resumed on 2/7/74]
The next day she did the same thing she had done the other day. She went out looking for a job. On her way guess who she met! Trouble and her parents. Trouble instantly said "Hi Pam, nice to see you again." "Yes Pam, our child told us what fun you two had. We'll raise the price to one dollar per hour." "Well I'm sure". . . . . "We knew you'd be glad to start at five o'clock tomorrow morning."

Later Pam's parents follow her to Trouble's house and find out what she was doing. Then they decided to take her to the country, since she wants to see animals. And they go to the country to her aunt's house. And she falls in love with the animals, especially the horse. And the aunt dies and in the will her aunt left, gave the farm and animals to Pam. And her family moves to the farm.

3. *5/15/74: Alicia*

Chapter 1
In a poor part of New York lived a girl named Alicia. She spent most of her time working in the pizza parlor her father could just afford to rent out. When she was not working in the pizza parlor, she was sleeping on the stoop and dreaming about being very rich; living in a big house, wearing minks and jewels. But her best dream of all was to have a cat; a white cat with a brown nose and a brown dot on the tip of its tail. The certain day she was sleeping on the door step but on the sidewalk near the

pizza parlor, but it did not matter because no one walked there. As she was sleeping and dreaming she felt a slight pitter patter on her stomach. When she looked up, there were two big green eyes staring right at her. Scared by it at first, she jumped up. Seeing that it was only a little kitten with brown nose and brown dot at the end of its tail. Smiling with joy Alicia picked up the cat and went running into the pizza parlor screaming, "Mama, Mama, look what I got." Her mother was not there but her father was there standing behind the counter. He was very surprised at his child screaming like that. He fell flat on his face, tumbling right over the counter. "My child, what are you screaming about. You'll wake up Mama." "Look what I found on the street Papa. It's a kitten." "I think you ought to be quiet for another reason. You know Mama's allergic." "But Papa . . ." "No, but you know how Mama is with her temper." [Part missing here where she puts the cat out and leaves it.] She walked back into the pizza parlor sadly.

Chapter 2: The Cat Returns
That night as she was lying in bed she felt something at her foot. Then she jumped up with a little shriek, and there was that little kitten again. The wonderful kitten with the brown spot on his nose and one on the top of his tail. By the way, this kitten had just bitten her toe and that is why she gave a shriek. And picking up the kitten and scolding it badly, she walked into her mother's room. Waking up her mother she said, "Can I keep the cat?" Sneezing, "I don't know." She got up and said, "A cat, what do you mean a cat?" Then the cat immediately jumped out of Alicia's arms and into her mother's and licked her face. "Well, okay," said the mother with a sneeze. "Only if she doesn't jump on furniture, break things." Then she walked into her room with a sigh. "What shall I name this mischief-maker? I don't know what to name it because I don't know if it is a girl or a boy. I'll go to Tom's pet store tomorrow. Surely he'll know if it's a boy or girl." So she brought the kitten into bed and went to sleep. The kitten was jumping around in bed trying to find a position to sleep, finally settling down on Alicia's stomach with a purr.

Chapter 3: The Naming of the Kitten
The next day she got up and brought the kitten to Tom's pet shop and found out that the kitten was a boy. But there was still one more problem, what to name it! Looking up at a store called the Champee, she decided that would be the beginning of a name. Then remembering her last name Ezio, she decided to name it Champeezio, saying to him, "Do you like your new name?" Not being able to talk the kitten licked her face in approval. Then the kitten jumped out of her arms onto the sidewalk. She thought that was silly, but started to walk home thinking

that the kitten would sit in the middle of the street meowing. But surprisingly it followed her all the way home.

Chapter 4: A Little Trouble with the Chinese Lamp and Out Goes Champeezio
When she got home she went into her room. This time the kitten did not follow her but sat in the middle of the floor meowing. She thought it would happen in the street and not in the room. She she picked up the kitten, went into her room and decided to take a little nap. Champeezio did not like this idea because he wanted to play. He decided to go and explore the pizza parlor because it was the only place he'd ever lived except the street. As he walked out of the room the first thing that caught his eye was a beautiful Chinese lamp with decorations of Siamese cats on it. Loving cats as he did, since he was a cat, he climbed up on the Chinese lamp and it fell onto the floor into one hundred tiny pieces. Champeezio, being a little scared jumped back. Then Alicia woke up and went into the room. "Well I'm really going to get into trouble this time." She scolded Champeezio. Champeezio feeling sorry for himself let out a long slow meow, and jumped out of her arms and lay on the ground. At that moment Mama walked in. "Did you do that Alicia?" Alicia, not a lying kid, said "Not really. Champeezio did it." "Out goes that cat," she said with a sneeze. So it ended up that Champeezio did go out, sadly.

Chapter 5: Champeezio Returns With A Friend [5/31/74]
That night Alicia woke up hearing a scratch and proud meow at the door. She went to the door and saw it was Champeezio with a bird on its head. She thought it was queer since cats kill birds, but this did not seem to be true with Champeezio. So she picked up the bird from Champeezio's head and let Champeezio in, thinking that her mother would love a bird. This proved to be true, since that morning she gave the beautiful bird to her mother. The bird had a green and yellow and purple tail with spots of blue on the ends and a blue body. She had orange on both sides of her head with a blue stripe in the middle and a bluish-greenish neck and an orange beak with a little point of green on the end.

Her mother loved it. When her mother asked how it got there Alicia explained about Champeezio and the bird. Her mother screamed, "Get that cat out of here!" While putting the bird in a beautiful cage over her bed, Alicia knew not to since Champeezio would just keep returning with more pets. So after she had lunch and dinner, she went to sleep to think about this problem.

In the middle of the night Champeezio thought, "My friend locked up in a cage just does not seem right." So he ran into Alicia's mother's bedroom, jumped on the bed and quick as lightning, unhooked the cage and ran out. Alicia's mother being startled, thinking it was just another alley cat going after her beautiful bird. She jumped up to see how the bird was and fainted when she saw it was not there. Alicia ran in the room to see what had happened. The cage was empty with the door wide open hanging over the bed. And there was her mother fainted and Champeezio sitting right next to her at the scene of the crime. She grabbed Champeezio and ran into her room. And in her room there was Chowuz waiting for Champeezio. Then she thought "I've got to find a hiding place for you both. It's both your fault Champeezio, but I love you, so don't worry." And she laid down on her bed and went to sleep.

Chapter 6: The Hiding of Champeezio and Chowuz
The next morning when she woke up the first thing she did was to look for a hiding place. Under the bed? No, a cat and a bird need room. The house was no good since there was no room. She'd have to check the alleys. So she ran outside and searched up and down the alleys until she found an alley that she thought was just perfect, with an old chicken cage in it almost as big as the alley itself. She said, "This will be perfect. No one will find them. There will be room for the bird to fly around and put some grass and tiny trees and plants for the kitten. There will be plenty of room to run around in and I don't think Mama's goldfish would mind if I gave them to the cat. And I'll get a couple of worms for the bird. She'll just love it. I'd better go get them quickly and bring them here." So she did. She ran home, picked up the cat and the bird and she could not help picking up the bird since it was on Champeezio's head. And then she ran as fast as she could to the cage and put them in and closed the door quickly.

Chapter 7: The Naming of the Bird and Champeezio and Chowuz a Hero
The next morning Alicia woke up and thought. "I haven't named the bird yet. It must be something like Champeezio," she said. "Chowow," but she said, "That's a boy's name. It must be something more like a girl. Chowez, no that just didn't sound right. How about Chowuz? [pronounced Choweyes]. That sounded right. That will be her name." Then she decided to forget about the animals right then and just go out and sleep on the door step as usual. Mama decided to go out on a walk right then and buy something with her life's savings; two hundred dollars, the most that anybody in the family had ever had. Then two men came up to her and tried to steal her money. But she was in the alley with Champeezio and Chowuz. Champeezio sensed danger and struggled to get out of the cage, and bit a hole just large enough for Chowuz to get through. Once out she went right to the latch and opened it so Champeezio could get out. Champeezio jumped on the robber and

Chowuz pecked at the other. The robbers were astonished and ran away as fast as they could, thinking policemen were poking guns or something. Then Alicia's mother not knowing what had happened looked down and there was Champeezio and Chowuz sitting on the sidewalk. She picked them up and took them home and lived a happy life for ever and ever and ever. But with one slight problem—two dead goldfish and some grass and trees and an old chicken house. The end.

4. 4/14/75

One day in a small lion tribe, in the den the head lion wife was born some cubs. Two girls and three boys. The lions grew quickly and surely. Soon it came the time to christen the cubs. The head of the tribe called all the lions together to vote on the name. The first little boy lion was put out so all could see him. He looked bold and strong. Soon it came out the name would be Killer. Killer walked out of the ring of lions proud of his name. Then next came a meek little girl, she walked into the circle slowly. Her name would be Alice. Next came the other boy, he would be named Sam. He also came out very proud of his name. The other girl came out, her name would be Samantha. The next cub resisted to go out. He was meek and shy and all the lions scared him so. He hid his head and tried to walk. The result of this was he went head off and did a tumble. His name shall be Lucifer. Lucifer was still and would not move. He was just too scared. His mother picked him up in her mouth and carried him back to the den. All the other cubs followed. The days went by and the cubs grew bigger. Killer bolder, Sam handsomer, Alice more beautiful, and Samantha more graceful. And Lucifer . . . and Lucifer much more shy. It came time that they would have to learn to hunt. Their father brought them. When they got to the plain there were a herd of zebras. The father said, "You first Lucifer." But where's Lucifer. Lucifer was not to be found. They trotted back to the den and lo and behold there's Lucifer, snuggling against his mother, quite happy. "You're a disgrace," said the father, "Out of my den." The mother tried to calm him but it did not work. Lucifer went out sadly. This life is hard for Lucifer, out in the wild for he was a bad hunter and didn't like leaves and berries. Lucifer always tried to make friends but he never did. Years came to pass. Lucifer became a fairly good hunter. One day Lucifer saw a beautiful girl lion. He went up to her and asked, "What is your name?" "My name is Ellie, the daughter of the head of this tribe." Lucifer and Ellie became good friends and soon were married and had cubs. And now Lucifer was head of his own tribe and lived happily forever with his wife Ellie.

5. 5/27/75: *Turley and his Friends*

Once upon a time, in a house on a mountain, lived a little turtle and his name was Turley. He had two friends, Batty and Froggy. They all lived together in a house. They weren't brothers or sisters but they were best friends. Every Saturday they went on a picnic. One fine sunny Saturday they decided to go out and have a big feast instead of just a picnic. And so they did. All you heard from Batty was, I don't want to do this, I don't want to do that. They started on their way to find a nice place to eat. Meanwhile, Batty is flying behind keeping a look out for a good spot. As they were walking Turley tripped and stubbed his toe. Froggy and Batty helped him up and they started on their way. Finally Batty saw a big, big area. So they settled down and started to eat. They didn't seem to notice a rustle behind the bushes, but next thing they knew they were being attacked by a big, big snake. Turley dashes for cover in a hollow log. Froggy jumped in the water and Batty flew to the trees. The snake tried to get them but he didn't succeed. So he decided to go find something else. They all slowly came out of hiding and decided to eat again. But when they went to it, it was all covered with ants. So they decided to go home and eat instead. And it turned out to be just another day for Turley and his friends. The end.

Lolla

1. 12/12/73: *Herbert and Henrietta*

[handwritten by child]

Chapter 1: Herbert And Henrietta Get Caught

One fresh morning when Herbert woke up in his mouse hole and got up to get some breakfast in the hotel, he saw Miss Burger. Miss Burger is the owner of the hotel. Herbert ran back to his hole and woke up Henrietta and they went to get some breakfast. They had cheese for breakfast. Miss Burger is very rich. Miss Burger has a boy. His name is Georgy and he is very spoiled. After Herbert and Henrietta got finished with breakfast, Georgy knew that the two mice were in the house. Georgy hid and when the two mice went walking, Georgy grabbed them and put them in a cage! The two mice were stuck and they felt awful. Henrietta started to cry, but Herbert said "Stop crying, that won't help." Miss Burger had a little girl too and her name is Judy. Judy is not spoiled and she is at camp.

"Judy will come back soon," Herbert said. Georgy fed the two mice but they still felt awful. A week went passed and Judy came back and asked what happened. So the two mice told Judy and she let them free.

Chapter 2: The Mice Go Home
As soon as they were set free they went back to the hole and stayed there. The next morning Judy knew what happened and brought them breakfast in the hole. When they finished with breakfast they went out for a walk. A dog saw them and chased them half a mile. They were exhausted, so they decided that they would sleep on the street and go home in the morning. The next morning they went home.

Chapter 3: The Mice Move
One night Henrietta and Herbert decided that they would move because it was too dangerous. They would move to a nearby stable. They picked that place because it was near Judy. They had been there and there was corn and other things to eat. They talked to Judy and she said it would be all right as long as she could visit them. She would call them up when Georgy was not there. So that morning they moved out and Judy helped. They are now living in the Garden Gay Stables. If you go there and find a mouse hole, knock and say "Henrietta and Herbert, are you there?" They will answer "yes". The end.

2. *6/24/74*

Once there was this girl who would always write on her pants and then go home and get screamed at for writing on her pants. And then she'd tell her mother she did not like her pants because there was writing on them. And her mother would not buy her new pants because all she would do is write on them. And so then she would be very mad at her mother and go to her father, and her father would buy her a new pair of pants because she would cry and throw tantrums.

She had a friend and her friend was spoiled like she was. So they did not make a very good pair because they would always get into fights. The girl thought she had a lot of friends but the friends she had were not really her friends. They first did not want to hurt her feelings and say they weren't, because then she'd cry and throw tantrums and they would get in trouble for saying it. So the next year she could not stay in the school she was in and so she went to another school her mother told her to go to and she wanted to go to which was for spoiled kids, but the kids that went there did not know that. So she got there and it was an overnight school and they would teach her not to be so spoiled. And she went to another school and she was a nice kid. The end.

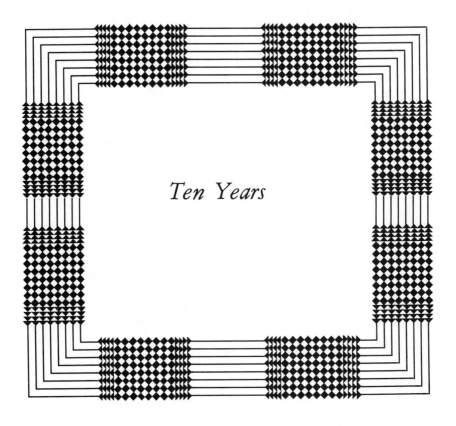

Ten Years

Martin

1. 12/6/73

Once there was a man who was very poor and he was fishing out by the sea. And he caught a fish that could talk. And the fish said, "I'm a magic fish and I'll grant you any wish you want if you let me go." So the man went back up to his house and asked his wife for what she wanted. She said she wanted a cottage. So the man went back to the fish and asked him for a cottage and the fish said, "Go back to your house and there will be a cottage." So the man went back and he found the cottage with his wife in it. But his wife was greedy and she wanted a mansion. So the man went back down to the fish and asked the fish if he could have a mansion. And the fish said, "Go back to your house and there will be a mansion." But his wife wanted a palace. So the man had to go back to the fish and asked for a palace. But the man told his wife that the fish might be angry that they were so greedy, but the wife made him go. So he asked the fish

PLOT STORIES

if he could have a palace. And the fish said, "Go back to your house and there you will find your wife in a palace." But the man's wife wanted more. She wanted the moon and the sun and she also wanted all the servants she could have and be the richest person in the world. So the man went back to the fish and asked the fish for the palace, the servants, and all the riches in the world. But the fish said, "No! I've given you enough chances to have enough things you wanted. Go back to your home and do not come back again." And there he found his wife in the old cabin they had in the first place.

2. 12/6/73

Once there was an alligator who lived in New York City and all the children were his friends and he wouldn't hurt anybody. And one day he got a note saying, "Mr. Alligator, I hate you." And Mr. Alligator always kept feeling bad because everybody liked him. But while he was walking through the grocery store he saw a little girl writing a note. The note said, "Mr. Alligator, I hate you." And he asked the little girl why he hated him. The girl said, "Because you're taking my friends away from me. They always want to play with you." Mr. Alligator said, "Why don't you play with me too?" And she said, "My mother doesn't like alligators and won't let me. She thinks they'll bite." So Mr. Alligator went to the little girl's house and said to her mother, "I'm not going to bite anybody." And the little girl's mother said, "All right, I can see that." The alligator said, "Good, so everybody else can play with me."

3. 2/14/74: The Living Sour Cream Monster

One day a person named Josh was making some roast potatoes with sour cream. All of a sudden the sour cream jumped out at Josh and said, "Take me to your peanut butter." So Josh said, "No, I won't take you to my peanut butter." And the sour cream said, "Either you take me to your peanut butter or you'll get sour cream in your face." And Josh said, "All right, all right. I'll take you to my peanut butter."

So Josh took him to the peanut butter and the sour cream said, "Reporting for duty, sir." And the peanut butter said, "See if you can find jelly. I have a message for him." And the peanut butter said, "Okay, I'll see if I can find him. You come with me too, Josh." Josh said, "But, but, but, I'm hungry." "You can have a taste of me," said peanut butter.

After that sour cream went to find jelly. He found jelly, but jelly was in the middle of talking to Mr. Tabasco Sauce. Mr. Tabasco Sauce said, "That human being, Gil, has been shaking too much of me on his food.

290

I'm getting sick." And Miss Jelly said, "I've got to go now. I'll see you later." And sour cream said, "Come with me. Mr. Peanut Butter wants to see you. He has a message for you." So they went to Mr. Peanut Butter. Mr. Peanut Butter said, "See here, you've got to find out where Mr. Bread is hiding. Josh is hungry." And Jelly said, "Maybe we should get out the mustard force." So they called up the mustard force on the phone.

The mustard force came over and asked what was wrong. And they said, "Go out and search for Bread." So they went out and searched for Bread, but couldn't find him after two hours. Then after half an hour later they found a few crumbs lying down on the floor. They said, "We're on the trail." They caught up with Bread. Three and a half hours later they were back with the bread. Mr. Peanut Butter and Miss Jelly made a sandwich out of the bread and they gave it to Josh. And Josh said, "Thank you," and walked home. And his mother said, "Where have you been?" And Josh said, "You wouldn't believe me, mom." The end.

4. 2/28/74: *The Strawberry Monster*

Once upon a time there was an old man who loved strawberries and usually went to the field to pick strawberries. One day he went out to the field and it was a little different. He found that there was absolutely no strawberries left, but there were a lot yesterday. And he thought who would take all those strawberries. So he went back to his house and took a nap for about an hour. He woke up and thought, "I forgot my basket." So he went back to the field.

When he got back to the field he found about seventeen thousand strawberries, so he started picking strawberries. All of a sudden there was a rustle in the strawberries. He went to see what the rustle was about. So he went over to the rustle and he found this one strawberry shaking and he looked at the strawberry and said, "This particular strawberry is the only strawberry I ever saw that shakes and it's very big." And the strawberry slowly was getting to two feet big in his hand, so he had to carry it very strongly back to his house.

So when he got back to the house he put it on the table and was about to start eating it when the strawberry yelled, "Stop!" So he looked around to see if there was anyone around who yelled "stop," but there was no one. And then he went back to the strawberry and was about to put his knife in it when he heard, "Stop!" again. He looked around, but there was nobody there. Then he noticed something on the strawberry head, the green part, the top. He found a little hand scratching. And he checked where the hand came from and the hand actually came from the strawberry.

In the meantime the strawberry had grown three feet long by now. And he came and he checked to see what was the matter; checked over the strawberry and found a mouth, and inside the mouth he checked and he found a bunco os [?] strawberry and inside was an ant controlling the thing with strings and saying, "Man, what I could have done without you around." Then the man said, "What are you doing in there and what are those strings for?" And the ant said, "Oh, nothing. I'm just controlling this big strawberry to get people to leave all the other strawberries, 'cause I want them for myself." The man said, "There are so many strawberries that why can't you share them with everybody." " 'Cause I want it all for myself." "Well, ah," the man said, "Why don't you take that silly costume off and anyway, what are you doing there?" And he said, "I'm scaring people with it so they won't eat my strawberry." "Well," the man said, "I'll let you go if you share the strawberry." And the ant said, "All right, I'll do it on one condition. You build me an anthill with air conditioning and wall-to-wall carpeting and ten strawberries a day." The end.

5. 5/28/74: Happy Birthday

Once upon a time there was a record player who lived in a classroom of P.S.3. The teacher's name was Dan. At first this record player was always hearing Elvis Presley. He didn't like that very much. Then they started playing the Jackson 5. Finally they started playing the Beach Boys. The record player didn't mind Elvis Presley, didn't mind the Jackson 5 either, but he hated the Beach Boys. Then one day when somebody turned him on before putting the needle on the record, he heard something from the radio. He had gotten a radio transmitter tube. So whenever they put on the Beach Boys, which was almost always, he'd listen to the radio. Then they started to play the Beach Boys on the radio. He hated that. Then they started playing just a little bit of Elvis and a little bit of the Jackson 5. They still had a lot of Beach Boys. Then the little record player was very frustrated and I guess it's going to stay that way. He listens to the Beach Boys. And he lived miserably ever after listening to the Beach Boys.

Maynard

1. 9/24/73: My Classmates
[handwritten by child]

I have many classmates, but some of them are very special. Such as Jimmy. He is crazy about girls. Or Donald, he is the only one in the class who can do funny things with his eyes. I personally like Doris. She is just like me. She writes sloppy, but she writes very good. Ian and Frank are both very famous for interrupting the class during a meeting or discussion. Alice's so kooky that I can't describe her. Coleen is the only one in the class who gets upset about the littlest thing so quickly. The brave young teacher that is in charge of all these kids and many more is . . . Dave.

2. 9/24/73: *How I Act In Class And How Dave Reacts To Me*

[handwritten by child]

I act not so good myself but nobody's perfect. For instance sometimes I talk with Jimmy and Dave says go sit by the gerbil cage. I think Dave does this for his sake to teach us whats right and whats wrong. Sometimes I wonder why I do things that are not right. I guess people do things that are not right because they have a feeling that they have to do it. I hope Dave understands why we like to do it. I guess when your'e young you can't help it.

3. 9/24/73: *How My Teacher Reacts*

[handwritten by child]

My teacher reacts differently to different kids. When Dave sees Jimmy chasing girls he tells him to stop running around. When Ian and Frank are interrupting the class Dave gets so mad he picks them up and drags them away. Coleen gets mad that he curses in the middle of the meeting and Dave washes his mouth out with soap. When Alice gets kooky (like always) Dave just ignores her. I don't ever think Dave notices when Donald does with his eyes. When Debbie writes sloppy but very good Dave doesn't care. I think Dave is doing the right thing.

4. 11/29/73

Once upon a time there was a little boy whose name was Anthony. Whenever Anthony played baseball he always broke windows. Whenever he broke a window his parents had to pay and they always got very mad at Anthony. One day, while Anthony was playing baseball he heard a crash. After he finished the game he went home and *he* got blamed for the broken window.

That night as he was sleeping, he woke up and ran away from home. That morning his mother screamed when she saw the empty bed. Immediately they called the police, and in about ten minutes they were on the go. Two hours later they found him sitting under a tree two miles from home. They asked him why he ran away and he said because he got blamed for breaking the window and he didn't. From then on, whenever Anthony broke a window his parents just paid for the window and forgot about it.

5. 11/30/73: *A Trip To The Aquarium*

[handwritten by child]

On Wednesday we went to the Aquarium and saw a pregnant whale. My class and I saw all kinds of weird fish. For instance we saw sharks, shark suckers, huge turtles. We saw little fish that looked like bubbles and best of all I saw a blowfish. A blowfish is a kind of fish that blows itself up when it is very scared or excited. After we saw all these weird fish we went to the beach. At the beach we climbed the rocks but eventually Dave told us it was too dangerous. Jimmy and I make a football field about fifty yards. Ken, Jimmy, and I played football. Soon after we started the game Dave told us it was time to leave. Naturally Dave didn't leave for half an hour. As soon as we got back to school I was so glad that we were back because there weren't any bus like there were in Coney Island.

6. 1/31/74

Every Thursday a man comes in and takes stories from children. This man's name is ?????. This man is a very weird man. One day he was skipping rope and he was counting. When I came over this is what I heard, "32, 60-12, 12 teen, 70-50." And I came over and said, "Hi." And he said, "You made me lose my count." And that's the story of Mr. ?????.

7. 2/7/74

Chapter 1
Once upon a time a boy named Jimmy was walking around 110 Bedford Street and talking to Ken and then James came up and said, "Let's go to Ken's house at 23B." And Jimmy said, "No, let's go to my house at 80 Bleecker Street and invite the girls over for lunch." And then Ken said, "Who shall we invite?" "Alice and Debbie." And then Jimmy said, "We going to have lots of fun." And Ken said, "Tsk, tsk."

Chapter 2
The girls came over and when they walked in, out of nowhere came Ken and jumped and leaped on top of the girls. And all of a sudden Jimmy

came out and took off the girls' clothes. And Ken said, "I have a bones." And finally Jimmy finished them off with his lips.

Chapter 3
When the girl's mother found out about the sexual assault to their daughters, they steamed over to Jimmy and Ken and James and said, "Good work!" And Jimmy, Ken and James lived happily ever after with the girl's parents. The end.

8. *2/7/74*

Once upon a time there was a boy named Ken and a boy named Ian. One day when Ken was walking in the park Ian came along and said, "Let's invite the girls over for lunch." Ken said, "Who'll we invite?" "Sally and Alice." When the girls arrived Ken took their coats and hung them up for the girls. When Ken saw the girls without their coats on he said, "Wowee! and Whoopee!" When Ian came into the room he said to Ken, "Naughty, naughty." Then Ken saw Jimmy walking on the street. When Jimmy saw the girls he leaped into the house and Ken asked through the door and landed plop right on the girls and said, "May I cut in?" And I said, "Tsk, tsk." The end.

9. *2/14/74*

Once upon a time there was a boy named Jimmy and he lived in a broken-down brownstone and had a sister named Jill. One day while they were both sleeping Jimmy got up and walked over to Jill and woke her up because it was time for breakfast. Not to mention they also had a brother named Ken. The next night when all three of them were sleeping Ken got up in the middle of the night, walked over to Jill's bed and he stared at Jill for a while. He walked into the bathroom and took off his clothes and took a shower. The next night when all were asleep Jimmy and Ken both got up, walked over to Jill's bed and gave her something. In the morning Jill said, "That felt good." The next night Jimmy and Ken said, "We always give good massages." The next night Ken was sleepwalking. He got out of bed, walked over to Jill and kissed her on the lips. And Jill said, "Woooo! Wooooo!" The next night Jimmy got out of bed and walked over to Jill and said, "I have a bones." The next night Ken, and Jimmy and Jill, all three of them, got out of bed and said, "Good night." The end.
[Added a little later] The next day Jimmy got out of bed and said to Jill, "That wasn't me that said that last night. That was a recording of Ken."

10. 3/28/74: A Dog For Joshua

Once upon a time there was a boy named Joshua. He always wanted a pet but not just any pet. He wanted a pet he could cuddle up with and pet. Finally one day he asked his father if he could have a pet and his father screamed at him and said, "No chance!" Joshua was very sad and for the next year he was very sad. One day he came home from school and walked into the house. He took off his coat and walked into his room. When he got there he was very surprised because on his bed was a great big Alaskan sled dog, a Huskie. That night Josh was very happy. For the rest of his life he will probably be very happy.

11. 4/4/74

It was a long time ago when this incident took place. I was getting vaccinations and they were fitting on my uniform. When I was in my uniform they took me to a model spacecraft to practice in. This spacecraft was a high speed jet. I got into the jet, pulled down the lid and tested the communication system. I started the jet and took off. Everything was A-OK. I was in flight and the communication system worked perfectly. But then, all of a sudden, I started to lose altitude and I had to blow out. The ship was losing control. I finally crashed. I was barely alive.

They took me to a special hospital called Testing in Bionics. They had the technology to make me stronger, better, faster, twice as good as I was before. I could run sixty mph. I could lift one hundred pounds in one hand and I could leap over fences without the use of my hands. When I came out of the hospital I had a bionic leg, bionic arm, and a bionic eye. The man that put me together so well was Dr. Wells. When I came out I started a new TV series called "The Five Million Dollar Boy." Of course I forgot to mention in this story that I was a boy testing a toy rocket. From here on in I show fantastic feats of strength; rescue cats from trees, leap over baseball fences, kick footballs hundreds of yards, run faster than any child in the world. I could lift hundreds of pounds without any problem, except the one element that could weaken my parts. That element is called radiation.

12. 5/23/74: The Love Story

Once upon a time there was a boy named Ken and he had a sister named Kim. They were very much in love. Ken used to be Ken B. Ken and Kim were so in love with each other that they slept in the same bunk. Ken was madly in love with her, but so was Ken's brother Jimmy. Ken and Jimmy fought all night about who won the love of Kim. Ken won the fight. Kim gave him a big kiss. Then they both lied down on the couch and watched TV. That night when they went to bed Ken rolled in his sleep right on top of Kim. That morning, for some strange reason she was so fat she had a big breakfast. Ken and Kim lived happily married ever after.

13. 5/28/74

Once upon a time there was a boy named Ken. Ken had a sister named Freya. Ken and Freya were in love. They slept in the same bed together. They had a lot of babies. But Ken didn't like Freya, so he found a new girlfriend. His girlfriend's name was Rose. Rose was just right. Ken and Rose were madly in love with each other. So they finally got married. They had ten thousand babies. Ken was not satisfied, so they had ten thousand more. Well Rose wasn't right, so he gave up Rose. Ken married a new girl named Pamela. Well Ken knew Pam wasn't right, so he gave her up right away. Then he met a new girl. This girl's name was Lexa. Lexa was perfect, even better than Rose. Well, Ken and Lexa had a couple of thousand babies, but Ken wasn't satisfied, so they had a couple thousand more. Ken and Lexa were *madly* in love. Ken didn't like her, so he gave her up and met a new girl. The new girl was named Ruthie. Ruthie and Ken were so happy together so they got married and had ten million babies. But that wasn't enough for Ken, so they had ten million more.

. . . My name is Ken. Let me explain how you have babies. You lie in bed with all your clothes off with another person of the opposite sex. You come close to each other and whoops, my mother's coming, we have to continue the story.

Anyway, to get back to the story, Ken and Ruthie were madly in love. This reminded Ken of his school days when he and another girl were kissing in the bathroom, the boy's bathroom of course, and while they were kissing their braces got caught together. While their lips were touching each other, the principal walked in. Ken didn't mind but he got out of the braces mess and started kissing the principal who was female. That girl got so mad at Ken that she slapped him in the ponderosa [rear end] and walked out. Well back to the story. Ken and Ruthie were having a good time together, a real good time and they both lived happily ever after. The end. P.S. *Very* happily ever after.

14. 5/30/74

Once upon a time there was a boy named Ken. He had a brother named Jimmy. Jimmy and Ken were enemies, but Ken wanted to be Jimmy's friend so much that he made up. Ken and Jimmy had a lot of fun at the fair, they went to the next day. Ken and Jimmy went on the ferris wheel right after they had hot dogs and soda. Boy, did they feel sick. While they were walking home, Ken tripped and got amnesia. While they were continuing their walk home a boy came up to Ken and said, "You're a girl." Ken didn't know what was going on, so he assumed he was a girl. Ken was in a sexy mood and so was Jimmy. Since Ken was a girl and Jimmy was a boy, they figured it to be about right. While Ken was climbing into bed he knocked his head on the edge. Then he realized he was Ken again. From then on Ken will be very careful when he bumped his head.

15.   6/14/74

Once upon a time there were three kids. Their names were Robert Wagner, Laurence Olivier, and James Cagney. These three people wanted to start a rock group. They had a lot of trouble thinking of a name for their new group. They finally thought of a name. The name of the group was "The Pepper Shakers." This is not a real group. What they did was they would put on the record, they would make sure the record player wasn't visible, they would turn on a record player and pretend they were singing the words and playing the music.

One day they played for a graduation party. Everybody thought they were really great except one boy who had a steady A average and who was considered the smartest kid in the school. The boy whispered into one of the kids ears who was watching the band play and said, "They're dubbing it." The girls said, "What does dubbing mean?" So the boy expalined. Slowly the word passed through the whole crowd and people started leaving. All of a sudden the band stopped playing because they realized they didn't have an audience. The end.

The moral of the story is: If you want to start your own group, you better play your own music.

Mischa

1.   12/20/73:   *The Case of the Missing Mummy*

There was once a haunted house. A mummy lived in it. One night a man came into the house and stole the mummy's charm that was on the table. And so the mummy came out of his coffin. He started following the man. When the man got in his car, the mummy was in the back seat waiting for him. Just when the man started choking the man to death. The next day they hired Mr. Cucaracha the detective. He said, "How much is that charm?" to his assistant. His assistant said, "Duh, I dunno." The detective said, "Oh dear, I think we'll have to investigate the house."

When they went in a dagger fell from the ceiling and killed the assistant. The doors locked when the dagger fell from the ceiling. The detective was all alone in the haunted house. When he went upstairs he found this bedroom. There was a secret panel on the wall. He pressed a little button in the wall and the secret panel opened. When he went in he found a wax museum. When he scratched off some of the wax he found there were real people inside. He went over to the guillotine. He saw a dead head staring at him. It belonged to Jimmy, another detective who was there years ago. Mr. C. said to himself, "He must have got angry and lost his head."

Then suddenly out of the wall came the mummy. The detective said, "Here's my chance to find out who killed all these people." So he ran and took a giant leap right on the mummy's back. He pulled off the mummy's disguise and discovered Darius and Vinnie on top of each other. The detective said, "Oh dear, I think we'll have to go down to headquarters." So they ran through the house and busted open the front door. When they got back to headquarters, he was awarded an official medal for courage. As for Darius and Vinnie, well . . . shall we say that they got kicked in jail.

2. 1/16/74: *The Night Frankenstein Walked*

There once was an old mad scientist named Frankie and he had this old laboratory and underground hideout. And one night he invented Frankenstein. And just in one minute Frankenstein rose up and tried to strangle the doctor. But the mad scientist, he took a flame of fire (Frankenstein is scared of fire), and scared him back.

And then he ordered him to go bring a beautiful girl to his castle. Then when they got her to the castle they holded her for a hostage. The girl was Mr. Cucaracha's daughter, the detective. Mr. C. was rich and the mad scientist needed to make Frankenstein more powerful. And then the next day Mr. C. he found out his daughter was missing from the bedroom and a note was on the table that said, "They're holding me hostage. Frankenstein is holding me hostage." And then Mr. C. was furious. They took a gun and ran over the big, giant castle and he busted open the castle door and found the girl locked up in chains with alligators on her feet—dead alligators. And he jumped Frankenstein and took off his head—mask—and found out that he was two little Santa Claus dwarfs. And he jumped the fat mad scientist and found out that it was Santa

Claus and his reindeer. And Mr. C. took off his mask and that he was his daughter, and they captured Mr. C. instead of his daughter.

[The end of the story was almost lost in a frenzy of laughter over all the transformations that he was making at the last minute.]

3. 1/16/74

Once there was two boys named Jack and Jim. They went up the hill to play golf. Jim hit the ball. It went right in. Then it was Jack's turn. Then Jack hit the ball and he missed and he said, "Aw, shucks, I missed." And then Jim said, "Don't ever use that language." Jim hit it and it went right in. Then Jack hit it and he said, "Aw shucks, I missed." Jim said, "Don't ever use that language. Next time you use that language, I hope a bolt of lightning hits you." So Jim went and got it right in. Then Jack went and he missed. And he said, "Aw shucks, I missed." And a bolt of lightning hit Jim, not Jack. And a little voice from heaven said, "Aw shucks, I missed." You see, he was aiming for Jack and said, "Aw shucks, I missed."

4. 2/6/74: *The Dangerous Mummy*

Once upon a time there was a mummy Cunto and then this man came to the house and then the man wanted to find out what was in the mummy and he unwrapped it and it was a big ass. So he threw it out and it kept growing and growing and got so big it ate him up and spit him out and he stinks. And the reason why he was getting so big is that he had to shit and it stinked up the house.

5. 2/6/74

There was a lady. She has three fat tits. And went out into the street naked and a man fucked her and squeezed her ass until her cocky came out. And then she had a baby and then the boy ate the shit. And when the baby came out she was a girl, so the father fucked her too. And then the baby had another baby and so on and so on and the last little baby was tiny. Just big enough to fit in the mother's cunt. And he ate the fuzzy stuff and grew bigger and bigger and then he stuck his head in his mother's ass and his head grew so big and she grew so big and he ate her cocky and he was sick and they called the doctor. And the doctor examined her pussy. Some piss came out in her eye. And then the doctor said she's not sick. She's just going to have a dick. The end.

TEN YEARS

Natalie

1. 10/73: *Halloween*

[handwritten by child]

On Halloween night, everything is a fright. Witch in the attic, ghosts drinking brew, spiders flying in the air, bats in lais bair.

2. 1/10/74: *A Month at the Movies*

One night Pat and Ann were in bed. They overheard their parents saying that they were going to put Pat and Ann up for adoption. When they heard that they decided to run away, but they could not decide where. Pat suggested, "What about the movies?" So they got all of their money and went to see "Snoopy Come Home." After the movie was over they stayed in the movie theater. They walked around looking for a place to sleep. They found a storage room where they stored all the candy for the candy machine and everything. Since they were hungry they both took some candy. Then they heard footsteps. Pat said, "It must be the night watchman." About an hour later lights went on in the theater. They came out of the storage room and found seats. They both fell asleep in the middle of it. In the morning they found a piece of the evening paper. It said that there would be a search of the main movie theaters. This is the one they were in. After the second movie of the day when everybody left, they left too. As they were walking down the corners they saw their mother and father. Ann said, "What are we going to do now?" Just then their mother saw them and came running up to them and said, "Where have you been?" "Hiding in the movie theater," said Pat. "We're glad to have you back," said the father. "Well, we're glad to be back," said Ann.

3. 2/25/74: *The Seasons*

[handwritten by child]

Winter beginning the new year and cold and [soun ?] but you don't fear because Spring come next with warmth and rain and pretty flower the about all game. Then comes Summer as hot as can be. Hope we don't run out of energy. Then comes Fall the end of the year.

4. 4/18/74

[handwritten by child]

It was April 15 the year 2074. Sargent Mel Solen called in [illegible] Mark

301

Asboad and Ben Miler into his office and said, "Mark and Ben prepare to fly the 308 flight mission on April 30 to all nine planets." The days went before they knew it. It was April 30th. Mark and Ben were in the glazer 11. Just then they heard, "10-9-8-7-6-5-4-3-2-1-blast off." And later Ben said, "Do we have to stay cooped up in this suit all 30 days?" "No silly, only till we get past the moon." They past the moon in [illegible] time. When they past the moon they saw what looked like a red, white and blue comet, but it was an American flag. It looked like a comet because they were going so fast. Ben asked, "Where are we going first?" "To Mercury," said Mark. That night Ben said, "It's impossible to sleep with all these straps on us." They woke up and they saw what looked to be the moon. Ben said, "Let's go back to sleep, it's the middle of the night." "You can go back to sleep if you want, but that was only Venus," said Mark.

The day went quickly preparing for the landing on Mercury the next day. The next day when they landed on Mercury the hills were in the shape of stars, but elevated. The hills were white and the ditches were like impressions of stars with purple water in them. They spent the day collecting specimens. As they were walking they saw a sign saying, "Pluto, 8,000,000 miles." While testing the water they noticed it was all mercury. They spent the night on Mercury. [Natalie did not want to finish it. She said it would be too long, thirty days. So far three had gone by. They were going to visit all the planets beyond Mercury.]

5. 5/20/74

In Connecticut, in the woods there was a family of ants. There was a mother and a father and a girl and boy. The boy's name was 17. The girl's name was 24904. Their ant hill was four leaves away from the big oak tree. One night 24904 was doing her homework and 17 was using the ant hill as a sliding pond when their parents were away. As 17 was sliding down their home caved in on top of them. 24904 started to scream. Finally she made her way out of the house. A few minutes later she found 17. 17 said "We'd better runaway." "Why should we runaway? You're the one who caused the house to fall down." "If we stay here what will we do? Mother and dad will kill us," said 17.

Just then their friend 8 walked by and said, "What's the matter?" 24904 said, "17 was just sliding down the house and he caused the house to cave in!" They all sat down and thought for awhile. Then 8 said, "Why don't we dig out the house from the mound of dirt." They tried that but it did not work, just caved back in again. A short while later their parents came home and said, "What's going on here?" 24904 said, "17 was sliding and the house fell on my homework." "We'll have to find a new house," said the mother. So they got on top of their salamander, except for 17. He had to ride inside the mouth of the salamander because of what he did. The end.

6. *5/24/74: The Adventures Of Squirm The Worm*

[handwritten by child]

Squirm the Worm lived by Small Pond. His home consisted of a beech leaf over some moss, a stick to sit on, and a pebble to use as a table. His best friend was Tad the Tadpole, who lived over by Long Pond. One day Squirm and Tad were fishing for minnows for Squirm because his girlfriend, Minny the Minnow was coming over for dinner. That night when Minnie came over she said, "Mm, this is good! What is it?" "Fried minnows," replied Squirm. "Goodbye," said Minnie in disgust.

The next day while Squirm was brushing his teeth his house came down around him. Luckily he got out in time. As he got out he saw Nat the Cat getting off what used to be his house. Squirm said to himself, 'Maybe I'll go over to Tad's house." When he was half way there he met Tad. Tad said, "Where are you going?" "Over to your place," said Squirm. "Why don't you sleep at your own house?" asked Tad. "Because Nat squashed it," answered Squirm. "Oh well, you could live with me," said Tad. "Thank you very much," said Squirm.

Tad's house was the rotted tiller of the boat "Queen Alphabet Soup." It was about 18 leaps from Long Pond. It was perfect for Squirm because it had a good supply of insects which were his favorite food. The only thing that was wrong, was that it was too far away from the water. Squirm and Tad decided that they should move the tiller down to the water. They pushed and pulled for about half an hour. Then they decided that it was not going to work. Squirm said sadly, "It's no use. I can't live here if there isn't any water."

Just then Big Talk the Hawk flew down and said, "Need some help, Tad?" "Would you?" asked Tad. "Very well," said Hawk. "Thank you very much," said Squirm and Tad. "By the way, why do you want to move it?" asked Hawk. "Because Nat squashed Squirm's house, so he came to live with me. But he needs to be closer to water. My house is far from water, so we tried to move it and did not succeed. You know what happened from there," replied Tad. After Hawk had left, Squirm asked Tad how come Hawk's name was Big Talk. Tad's reply was, "Because he asks about everything."

That night their house rolled all over the place. Tad said, "I will see

303

what is going on outside." When Tad came back in he said, "It is Chuck and Huck Muffin." "Who are they?" asked Squirm. "They are two boys who live by Hoot's tree," replied Tad.

In the morning Squirm said, "Do you know what today is?" "Yes," said Tad, "It is the 30th of April." "No, I mean a special day." "I give up," said Tad. "It's your birthday," said Squirm. "It is!" said Tad in shock. "You go catch some fish and I will cook them any way you want," said Squirm. "You mean it?" asked Tad. "Sure," said Squirm "But you'd better not bring home any minnows." About two hours and four minutes later Tad returned with four flounder, three trout and fifteen killies. When he walked in there was not a bit of noise. Then suddenly Tad heard, HAPPY BIRTHDAY! All of Tad's friends were there, even Minny, Squirm, Hawk, Willie the Woodpecker and Tammy the Tarantula were all there. Hawk asked, "What kind of fish did you catch?" "Four flounder, three trout and fifteen killies," answered Tad.

After the fish were gone the house began to roll again. Tammy said, "We must stop this or my legs get tied in knots." Willie thought for awhile. There was complete silence. Willie said in a wise voice, "I think I've got it." "What is your plan?" asked Squirm. "My idea is that I will peck a hole in the wood and Squirm and Tad will dig a hole in the ground and we can all crawl into the hole and stay out of the rain." Hawk asked, "I am supposed to crawl too?" "No," they answered, "You can fly out in the rain and tell us when it stops. You can also tell us why the house keeps on rolling."

About one hour later the hole was done, but there was not much room in it at all. Tammy kept complaining that everyone was sitting on her legs. Other than that everything was O.K. An hour later Hawk called in to say that everything was O.K. When everybody climbed back into the house Minny said, "Who was rolling the house?" Hawk answered, "Chuck and Huck Muffin. They were just fooling around." "Oh," said Minny, "some fooling around!"

The next morning Minny came over to help clean up. After the house was clean Squirm asked Minny, "Can I walk you home?" "Sure," said Minny. As they were walking Minny said, "Squirm, I'm sorry about what happened last week. It was silly of me not to tell you that I can't stand eating minnows." "It's OK, I should have known better," said Squirm. They walked a bit more till they reached Minny's house. Then they said goodbye to each other. On the way home Squirm saw a big yellow monster. He ran the rest of the way home. When he got there he said to Tad, "There's a big yellow monster out there . . . Come see for yourself." "OK," said Tad. "Gee, your'e right!" "Let's call Willie and see what he thinks of it." When Tad got off the phone Squirm asked,

"What did he say? Should we call the police?" Tad said, "He said that our monster is a tractor!"

A week later when Squirm and Tad were going to school they saw some big rock-hard grey blocks. In school they had to write a five word sentence describing something they had seen on the way to school. The papers that they wrote looked like this. After school was out Mrs. Centipede said, "Squirm and Tad, I want to see you." So Squirm and Tad went to her desk. Mrs. Centipede said, "Squirm, Tad, I'm surprised at you two because you wrote the exact same thing and I told you not to copy." "Excuse me," said Squirm, "But we walk to school together. That was the only thing that was new to us." Just then as they were leaving Tad asked Mrs. Centipede, "What were those things we saw?" "Concrete," she answered.

That night Squirm said, "I feel sick." "So do I," said Tad. "Let's go for a walk." As they started to leave they felt the house move. "Darn, it must be Huck and Chuck fooling around again." It wasn't! When they got out Squirm shouted, "We're in the air! What's going on?" The construction company had started to build right where they lived and the tractor had lifted their house high in the air. Just in time Hawk and Willie the Woodpecker flew by and Hawk lifted up their house, and Tad and Squirm climbed on to Willie's back. First they flew to Minny's, and she climbed up on Hawk's back. Next they went to Tammy's and she sat on Hawk also. They flew for three hours looking for a new home. Finally they found a quiet place. It was perfect for everybody except for Tammy, because the only kind of spiders were Daddy Long Legs. Hawk said he'd find some tarantulas for her to play with. Other than that, things were good. There was a pond that was full of fish and water bugs. There was an oak tree for Hawk and Willie.

About a month later people started to come to the pond. As time went on, the pond started to become polluted. But why now and not before was the question that everyone asked. One day a tall man in a tan shirt and brown pants came and gave the people tickets for polluting. The next day Tammy found a piece of paper. She gave it to Tad and Squirm because they could read. They read it and it said: "The person to whom this is given has to pay $200.00." "How much is $200.00 in our money?" asked Minny. "Four hundred stones," replied Squirm.

As the days went on they kept finding these papers. Then they decided to bring the notes to the tall man. They did, and he thanked them and gave them each a gold star and some of their favorite foods. He said that the people would be leaving soon because the summer was coming to an end. The next day Squirm, Tad and Minny were swimming. Tad asked, "Has anybody seen Tammy?" "No, why do you want to know?'' asked Minny. ''Because I think today is her birthday.'' ''Then I know where she is,'' said Minny. ''Where?'' asked Squirm. ''She probably locked herself in her house,'' said Minny. ''But why?'' asked Tad. ''Because last year Willie pushed a pie in her face on her birthday,'' said Minny.

A week later a man came with a curved rod with string attached to both ends and a bunch of short pointed rods. Hawk asked, ''Who is he?'' ''I do not know,'' said Tad. ''Let's go ask the tall man with the brown pants and tan shirt.'' When they got there they asked him what his name was. He told them that he was Ranger Dave but said that they could call him Dave. ''Dave, I have a question for you,'' said Hawk. ''What is it,'' asked Dave. ''A little while ago I saw a man with a big curved stick and some short sharp sticks. Would he hurt any of us?'' ''You bet!'' said Dave. ''Show me where you saw him.'' It was a long walk. When they got there they saw the same man. Dave pointed to a sign that said NO HUNTING. Dave gave the man a ticket and took away his sticks.

The next day while Squirm and Tad were playing cards, water began to leak through the house. ''Tad, hand me your bubble gum,'' said Squirm. Squirm stuck the gum in the leaking crack and then they finished the card game. Tad got up and walked right under the bubble gum. His head stuck in it. When they got his head out of the bubble gum, Squirm went out in the rain to get a leaf to put over the gum. ''Minny,'' screamed Squirm. ''What about her?'' asked Tad. ''She lives in a puddle,'' said Squirm. ''But in this rain it will become a lake and she will drown.'' ''Your right,'' said Tad. ''Let's go see her.'' ''OK,'' said Squirm.

So they put on their raincoats and boots and went to see how she was doing. When they were half there they saw Dave's car. He stopped and asked, ''Where are you going?'' ''We're going to see how Minny is.'' ''That's the same place that I'm going. Hop in,'' said Dave. They were there in no time. When they got there Dave took a fish bowl from behind the seat and put some water in it, and then Minny. ''Why don't you get the rest of the gang and meet us at the station,'' said Dave. ''Will do,'' said Squirm.

About ten minutes later they found Tammy, Hawk and Willie. Squirm and Tad got on Hawk's back and Tammy on Willie's. There was only one light on when they got there. Squirm opened the door and turned on the other light. When he did he read a big sign, HAPPY BIRTHDAY SQUIRM. There were streamers and presents from everyone. There was everybody's favorite food. They ate and ate until they were full. The rain kept falling. It looked like it would never stop. When it finally stopped Willie and Hawk went home, but Dave asked Tammy,

Tad, Squirm and Minny to spend the night with him. They did and when they woke up the next morning they found a frog in the bed that Tad had slept in. The frog woke up and said, "What's everybody staring at?" In a giggle Squirm said, "Tad . . . you're a frog!"

The weather got cold and Willie and Hawk flew South. Tammy asked, "Where can I get a bus for Arizona?" Squirm and Tad got ready to hibernate. Minny decided to spend the winter with Dave. And that was the end of the best summer of their lives.

7. 6/17/74

One night while an astronomer named Henry Windo was looking out at Jupiter through a telescope he saw what looked to be a comet. It had all the colors in the rainbow. He rushed to the telephone and called up the Mount Palomar Observatory. Just as he picked up the telephone everything began to shake. He thought it must be an earthquake. He thought to himself, "What a queer thing to happen. Just when I discover this comet thing an earthquake happens practically. I know that people used to think that a comet was bad luck and everything, but it's been proven not true."

He went outside, He looked around and then he saw a big round ball in his back yard. He called his wife Kate over and told her to call the police department. Then as he was looking at it he saw on the big ball a sign saying "Happy New Year, 1854." Then there was really funny writing underneath. Then he heard the police coming. Two detectives came up to him. One detective said, "Another thing exactly like that was found in Paris, but it had a code. The thing in Paris was first seen being launched from Jupiter. It also had some writing which looked like Chinese, but it isn't Chinese at all. It's a whole other . . . " Just then they heard on the detective walkie-talkie that a piece of paper was falling out of the sky; a code with all the letters and these funny letters. "Come with me back to the station and we can get a copy of the code and we can decode what they said."

They got back from the station and decoded it. After they finished decoding it, it said, "How come you Earthlings say there is not life on the other planets? We will be friendly if you will. We are also interested in finding out if there is life on any other planets. If it's okay with you, we will send down a couple of people so we can talk. You can tell if you're willing to have some people of ours come down to your planet, light a hundred firecrackers all at once. Then we will be coming down in the same spot as where you light the fire crackers."

Immediately they flew to Mount Palomar Observatory and lit the firecrackers. They waited. Three hours later they saw a bright light coming towards them. Finally it lands. It's a rocket ship similar to an Apollo rocket. Out come four people about five feet tall. The one who appeared to be the leader said, "My name is 646. I am the leader of our planet's space program. This is 249. He is my assistant. This is 228 who is my wife. And this is 717, who is my assistant wife." "Glad to meet you," said the head person at Mount Palomar Observatory. "My name is Ross Punch and this is Henry Windo, who first discovered the comet-like ball you launched." "Oh yes, that. It's our new year on Jupiter now. Is it 1854? Because that's what it is on Jupiter." "No, it isn't," said Henry. "It's 1974 on Earth." "Why don't we go inside and talk about what we found out about life on other planets," said Ross.

They went inside and Ross said, "We have been seeing a lot of UFO's. Do you know what they are?" "Yes," said 646. "They're unidentified flying objects." "Can you explain that?" "I can explain that," said 646. "Well, what are they?" "Well, we've been sending space-like ships to see if the atmosphere and the temperature and that stuff is all right for us." "A lot of people are scared that there are Martians and Boogies and all that junk." "646, I've got a question for you. How come there is a red spot on Jupiter?" "Well, that's our guard station, a floating guard station." "How interesting," said Ross.

All of a sudden they heard these weird radio waves. 646 said, "We've got to go now. Something's gone wrong on Jupiter. Oh well, we had a nice meeting. Maybe we can get together and talk again. Bye." The end.

Natasha

1. *12/20/73: The Night It Came*

[handwritten by child]

One dark cold night Mr. Fox went out for a bit of air. And as he was smoking his pipe he heard something in the trees and went to investigate. He saw nothing. But just then he felt some cold slimy hands, no they felt more like claws. On his neck he screamed a terrible scream then died. The end. That was a mysterious story wasn't it?

[The story had a picture at the bottom of a creature standing with a wolfish head and oversized claws; claws with long pointed nails dripping with blood on a man lying down at its feet.]

308

2.   1/31/74:   *The Howl of the Wolf*

It takes place at the North Pole. Once there was a man named Josh Star and he wanted to go to the North Pole to see wolves. So he got tickets for a plane to the North Pole and the next day he went there. He went to the airport. In a couple of hours he got to the North Pole. He had all his equipment with him. He saw a big white wolf and he named it Snowy. It was only a cub, a big cub. He took it back to America with him and he raised it.

After one year the wolf turned on him because he wanted his freedom. The wolf bit the man and the man died. Everybody in the town was after the wolf 'cause he killed the man. The wolf snuck aboard an airplane going to the North Pole and the North Pole was the only stop. So he got off the airplane and saw this nice big black wolf and it was a boy and they had babies. Snowy and the black wolf had babies. That's the end of my story.

3.   5/2/74:   *The Asylum*

One night a girl named Lisa went to an asylum to see her father and mother. When she got there all these crazy people would not let her in. Of course they were crazy, that's why they were in an asylum. Finally they let her in and she saw her mother and father. And her mother was being a little baby and her father was being her mother. She started cracking up 'cause everybody was being so funny. Then the guards were coming to take her out of the asylum and she did not want to leave, so she got into nutty clothes and pretended she was a person from the asylum. When the guards came in they could not find her. They looked all over but they still could not find her, so they left. So Lisa finally got to stay with her father and mother and the guards could not tell her that she was not one of them.

4.   5/29/74:   *Animals of the Grave*

Well it's about this girl who never took care of her animals. So as you know they all died. Just in case you're wondering how many animals she had and what kinds, I'll start from the very beginning. That's when she moved to the country and got a farm. And on the farm she had horses, cows, chickens and dogs, and cats. And she had a lion and rabbits and gerbils and rats and mice and three parrots and two pigeons and she had lots of others which I can't remember.

Now I'll start the story. The girl's name was Lisa. One day she went to feed her horses and they were dead. So she went crying to her mother and her mother said, "Lisa, it's all your fault because you never take care of your animals." So she ran into her room, threw herself on her bed and started crying. "It's all my fault, it's all my fault."

Finally every day another animal died until she did not have any animals. They had a big grassy area, so she decided to bury all the animals there. So she buried all the animals and went to bed. In the middle of the night she woke up and she heard all these animals outside, and she looked out the window and they disappeared. So she ran out into her father's room and he was lying on the bed, dead. He was lying on the bed with his head hanging over. Lisa screamed. Her mother came running into the room. Then her mother screamed and they both ran out crying and sat under the weeping willow tree, which they always thought they should cry under if anything tragic happened. By this time you're probably wondering how old Lisa is. Well, she's around thirteen.

5. 5/31/74: *The Death Of The Father*

Her mother was trying to figure out how her father died. So they went back in the room and they were staring at the father and they saw a hoof mark on her father's chest. They were wondering how it got there, since all the animals were dead. Then she told her mother about what she heard. Her mother said, "There's no such thing as ghosts." But she did not believe her. Her mother said, "Go back to bed now Lisa. We'll bury your father in the morning."

So Lisa went back to bed and fell asleep, and then she woke up again. This time she not only heard the animals, but saw them and ran to get her mother. She got her mother out of bed and took her to the window, and her mother saw the anmials roaming about all out of their cages. Her mother could not believe that they were ghosts. She went running out of the house and all the animals disappeared again.

She went running to the church in town and called the priest to tell him about the strange happenings at the house. So the priest went with them back to the house. And when they got there they saw Lisa's father riding on Lisa's favorite pony Nightmare. They went inside the house and started a ceremony to make the ghosts go away. The priest said it would most likely work, but that sometimes it doesn't work, so don't count on it. They had finished the ceremony by this time and they looked out the window, but the ghosts were still there. So they tried the ceremony again. This time it mostly worked, except her father and Nightmare were still there. The priest said that it was not worth trying again and they have to pay him one hundred twenty-five dollars. They were looking all over the house for the one hundred twenty-five dollars. Then Lisa found it in a cookie jar, and that was the last of the money.

Olive

1. 12/73: Henry Tick

Chapter 1

A few years ago Henry Tick lived in a hippie's hair, but he got a crew cut so Henry had to move. He went to the dog pound but it was closed. He went to the pet shop but it was closed too. Finally he found a nice basset hound. So he moved in. He got a good job at the circus jumping two inches in mid-air into a glass of water. One day he jumped but there was no water. He was rushed to the hospital. They put twelve stitches in his leg. Well, he never went there again. The end.

Chapter 2

One day Henry Tick was walking down the street when he was almost stepped on. He was so startled he jumped in the shoe! He was in the shoe for about fifteen minutes when the person took off the shoes and put them in the closet. Henry jumped out and ran into the next room, which happened to be the bathroom. He jumped into the toilet, by mistake of course. He was trying to get out when some nut flushed the toilet. Henry almost went down the drain.

Chapter 3

Henry got out of the toilet. The first thing he did was wash. He found a damp washcloth in the sink. He wiped himself thoroughly and then dried off. He went into the next room and watched the football game. The end.

Publications of the American Folklore Society
New Series
General Editor, Marta Weigle

1   Stanley Brandes, *Metaphors of Masculinity: Sex and Status in Andalusian Folklore*

2   Roger deV. Renwick, *English Folk Poetry: Structure and Meaning*

3   Brian Sutton-Smith, *The Folkstories of Children*